99 Jumpstarts for Kids:

Getting Started in Research

Peggy J. Whitley

Susan Williams Goodwin

LIBRARIES UNLIMITED

U N L I M I T E D

A Member of the Greenwood Publishing Group

Westport, Connecticut • London

Library of Congress Cataloging-in-Publication Data

Whitley, Peggy.
    99 jumpstarts for kids : getting started in research / Peggy J. Whitley and Susan Williams Goodwin.
       p. cm.
    Includes bibliographical references and index.
    ISBN: 1–56308–956–4 (alk. paper)
    1. Research—Methodology—Study and teaching (Elementary) 2. Information
retrieval—Study and teaching (Elementary) 3. Report writing—Study and teaching
(Elementary) 4. Information resources—United States. I. Title: Ninety-nine jumpstarts for
kids. II. Goodwin, Susan Williams. III. Title.
    ZA3075.W475 2003
    372.13'028'1—dc21   2003053873

British Library Cataloguing in Publication Data is available.

Library of Congress Catalog Card Number: 2003053873
ISBN: 1-56308-956-4

First published in 2003

Libraries Unlimited, Inc., 88 Post Road West, Westport, CT 06881
A Member of the Greenwood Publishing Group, Inc.
www.lu.com

Printed in the United States of America

The paper used in this book complies with the
Permanent Paper Standard issued by the National
Information Standards Organization (Z39.48–1984).

10 9 8 7 6 5 4 3 2 1

Contents

Preface

In our previous book, *99 Jumpstarts to Research: Topic Guides for Finding Information on Current Issues*, we focused on showing high school and beginning college students how to research current topics. In *99 Jumpstarts for Kids*, we have chosen 99 topics we believe students from grades three through eight will enjoy. Each jumpstart provides several sections to help beginning researchers get a handle on the process.

Previous generations of researchers had to deal with a scarcity of information. Today, especially with the advent of the Internet and journal databases, students have access to such an abundance of information that evaluating and selecting the best resources can be overwhelming. Fortunately these skills can be taught.

A successful report process is all in the preparation—for the teacher and the student. We believe a little planning and organization will help even the youngest students avoid that sinking feeling that often accompanies a research assignment. We think research should be satisfying and enjoyable—and we want others to feel that way, too. It goes without saying that the most important ingredient in a good research project is the guiding hand of the librarian and teacher, throughout the process. Helping students get a handle on the research maze is very rewarding. We know. We do it all the time!

We hope you find our book useful as a jumpstart for finding and evaluating the best information available. We have found that the attitude teachers take toward research deeply affects the way young students feel about it. So, have fun. Help develop the natural curiosity kids have. Use the "Beginning the Process" section in this book, which offers guidelines to research, or jump right in. There are several very good report processes available today, including the Big Six.

As college librarians now and elementary and high school librarians in our past lives, we especially want to thank school librarians everywhere for introducing students to the research process. It is never too early to begin the process of critically analyzing information. Every day we see college students who are clueless about gathering information and writing a short report. So, believe us, when you have taught it, we know. And we appreciate it. If you have comments or suggestions, let us hear from you.

Peggy Whitley
Dean of Educational Services, Kingwood College
peggy.whitley@nhmccd.edu

Susan Goodwin
Reference Librarian, Kingwood College
sue.goodwin@nhmccd.edu

How This Book Is Organized

Each jumpstart is divided into the following sections:

- **Thinking About the Topic** introduces ideas to whet the appetite. It helps the students consider different aspects of the topic and begin to refine or narrow it to a manageable size.

- **Directions** include suggestions for refining the topic and questions to help organize the research. Our sample questions are there so students can begin to see the variety of information, even within a fairly narrowed topic. But we see no reason why students can't be taught early to write their own open-ended questions.

- **Books** suggests subject keywords for the library catalog and books that are generally available.

- **Internet** sites are kid-friendly and have staying power.

- **Other Resources** include video clips, films, audio recordings, and additional ideas for research.

- **For the Teacher** has links to online lesson plans, enrichment activities, and more complex Web sites.

- **Something Extra, a Joke, a Limerick, or Check It Out** are added for extra amusement and fun.

The only things that we have NOT added in our book, but hope teachers and students will, are newspaper and journal full-text databases. If available, articles in newspapers and magazines can be very useful.

Beginning the Process

Students should learn that gathering information and writing a report can be deeply satisfying. In fact, approached positively, young students hardly realize they are learning a process that will help them throughout their lives. They look forward to "research." They think it is *supposed* to be fun! What a payoff! Be warned! This will be the result of careful planning and teamwork between librarian and teachers.

Celebrate the completion of your big research project. One of the rewarding phases of the reporting process can be culminating activities. When reports are written, students love to get together for a special time to share their new knowledge. You might call it the icing on the cake. Consider having a special reports day for the class or grade level. Gather together in the library. A beginning ballerina can report on the life of Maria Tallchief, then dance an excerpt from *The Nutcracker*. A budding musician can talk about Yo-Yo Ma, then perform a short selection of his own. An artist may share her own Picasso-style artwork. A science reporter can explain his invention. It would definitely be fun to serve spaghetti in a large iron caldron if a student has written a report on Strega Nona or Tomie dePaola. Invite the parents, if you dare. They will think you are wonderful.

Not all students will want to perform. Allow those students to set up poster sessions on tables around the library. They can stand nearby and quietly share their newly discovered information with classmates. You get the idea. We hope you will find some interesting way to celebrate both new knowledge and student talent. Students will remember it for a long time.

As every instructor knows, there are many methods of teaching report writing. The Big Six has proven successful. The important thing is to guide the process. We found it helpful to precede research with an activity that introduces using different types of resources, books, journals, the Internet, interviews, etc. The students become more comfortable with using the different resources. Their information literacy rating skyrockets as they begin to think critically about different formats for information, deciding where they will be found. The samples below are accompanied by readiness activities. You probably have some of your own. If not, ours have been tried and enjoyed.

Younger Grades

Activity: Treasure Hunt

This activity is fun and offers early researchers practice in locating information in books. If you choose a topic from a science or social studies unit you are studying, students will benefit even more. This activity also provides practice working with a partner. Use the classroom or the library. You will want to have prizes or library "Treasure Hunt Winner" certificates for all who complete the project.

Objective: To teach students how to find information in a book, using the index and table of contents, and to look for sentence keywords.

Example: What does the brontosaurus eat? (Keywords: *eat, food*)

Preparations: Select half as many books on one subject as you have students (e.g., 30 students, 15 books). Try to find books with tables of contents and indexes. They should at least have subject headings inside the text. Prepare a 3-by-5-inch index card, or use cover stock, which runs through the printer and can be cut, for each book. Number each card and include the book title and a question that can be found in the book by using the index or table of contents. Do not make this too hard. It is supposed to be fun. Arrange the books on tables with their question cards.

> **3 x 5 card**
>
> Question 1.
> BOOK TITLE
> QUESTION

Method: Before they begin, have the students number their answer sheets. There should be one answer sheet for each partnership. Divide the students so that you have help for the ones who will need it most. Students do not have to go in any particular order. They can step up to a book after the couple before them has stepped away. Be sure each couple understands that they should match the answer on their paper to the number of the question with the book. Encourage students to keep their voices down so they will not give away answers to the next couple. It will be worth the time if you have the students answer in complete sentences, since you are going to ask them to take notes in complete sentences when they actually write their reports.

Middle Grades

Activity: Using the Encyclopedia

The World Book Encyclopedia offers free or inexpensive reprints of entries (e.g., "Insects"). Order a classroom set and use them for a variety of activities, including class reports. An alternative is to print an encyclopedia topic off the Internet. Schedule a library period to learn about reading and understanding encyclopedia articles, covering the following features:

• Encyclopedia format (Every article is laid out in much the same way.)

• Outlines (headings and subheadings)

• Related articles (What other articles does the *World Book* have on this topic?)

- Questions (Divide the students into small groups and let each group find the answer to one of the questions you have prepared and report back to the class. Have them explain how they found the answer.)

Report Sample

Students can handle two or three resources by the time they get to the fourth and fifth grades. Our suggestion is that third grade is a perfect time to have all students use the same books and questions, if possible. Students will find more information, and they should draw a conclusion about their findings for each question. The conclusion will become their topic sentence for the paragraph. Other details from notes will be added to the paragraphs. We encourage teachers to order encyclopedia reprints and a classroom set of easy to read books on the topic. The New True Book Series is one of several series that is perfect for this report. It has an index, table of contents, and enough information without overwhelming the student. If students have access to the Internet, the teacher can decide if this is an appropriate resource. If one single Web site is selected, it will add spice and the students will enjoy their research more. Teachers might even provide a film students can watch to take notes that will answer their questions. Remember, more is not often better, and too many resources will result in confusion. They will certainly make teaching the process more difficult.

Step One

The students research answers in the resources you have selected. Encourage the use of contents and indexes. When they complete the note-taking phase, students will draw conclusions about their answers. Be sure the questions are open-ended and lead to good information. Following is an example of one question from a report written by a third grader.

Book Titles	Who are the snake's enemies, and how does he protect himself?
Reptiles (True Book) by Melissa Stewart Children's Press, 2001	Snakes protect themselves in different ways. A scarlet king snake is protected because it has a poisonous twin.
"Reptiles." *The World Book Encyclopedia*, 1999.	The snake's enemies are other animals like the pig or other snakes. The snake protects himself by doing many things. He disguises himself, hides, makes scary noises, rubs his side scales together, inflates his lung, he poisons, makes a noise by vibrating his tail on dry leaves.
	CONCLUSION Snakes have many enemies and they protect themselves by doing all sorts of things.

Step Two

The teacher can work with each student to write a conclusion from the information he or she has written down. Often the librarian will help with this. The teacher or librarian should then assist the student in numbering the note-taking information so it will be easy to copy into paragraphs. (See our example below.) The goal is to show the student how to combine information from different sources. Anything repeated is marked out. Believe it or not, even using the same resources, reports will be different.

Book Titles	Who are the snake's enemies, and how does he protect himself?
Reptiles (True Book) by Melissa Stewart Children's Press, 2001	② The snake's enemies are a little mongoose, and a hawk, ④Snakes protect themselves in different ways. ⑥A scarlet king snake is protected because it has a poisonous twin.
"Reptiles." *The World Book Encyclopedia,* 1998.	The snake's enemies are ③and other animals like the pig and other snakes. ⑤The snake protects himself by doing many things. He disguises himself, hides, makes scary noises, rubs his side scales together, inflates his lung, he poisons, or makes a noise by vibrating his tail on dry leaves.
	CONCLUSION ① Snakes have many enemies. They are pretty smart and it can protects themselves by doing all sorts of things.

Step Three

The student will now copy the report, putting his or her conclusion at the beginning of the paragraph and using the numbered order. Remember, there will be three questions and three paragraphs. An illustration can be drawn by the student or scanned from a book, if the students are using the computer.

SNAKES

Snakes have many enemies. They are pretty smart and can protect themselves by doing all sorts of things. The snake's enemies are a little mongoose, a hawk, and other animals, like the pig and other snakes. Snakes protect themselves in different ways. The snake protects himself by doing many things. He disguises himself, hides, makes scary noises, rubs his side scales together, inflates his lung, poisons, or makes a noise by vibrating his tail on dry leaves. A scarlet king snake is protected because it has a poisonous twin.

Reptiles (True Book) by Melissa Stewart. Children's Press, 2001
"Reptiles." *The World Book Encyclopedia,* 1998. Report by Shawn

Upper Grade Reports

Activity: Evaluating the Internet

The greatest problem facing researchers today is too much information. With help, young students can begin evaluating the information they find on the Internet. Here is an activity that will help students decide whether a site is appropriate for the research they are doing.

Objective: To evaluate the information on a Web page. Does this Web page have what I need?

Preparation: It is a good idea to have the class work on at least one Web page with the librarian or teacher before they evaluate on their own. Select a good page and a poor one. Have the students evaluate the pages with you. Discuss the following concepts with students. It is important that they know who created the page, what their credentials are (sometimes a second-grade class creates a beautiful Web site, but we do not think it is appropriate in a report), whether the information is current (if currency is important), whether the information is appropriate for their age and reading ability, whether the content gives them the information they want, whether it is biased or objective, and whether the Web page is easy to navigate: Can they find the information they need?

Method: The teacher or librarian will select Web pages for small group evaluation. Students can work in groups of three or four to analyze Web sites. (Make sure everyone contributes.) **Note:** You may use the authors' *American Cultural History Web Site*, http://kclibrary.nhmccd.edu/decades. html. Have each group choose and examine a different decade. You can discuss the information together later. Each decade has the same format, and students will be able to answer all of the questions on the form. There is a sample Web page evaluation form on page xvi.

Reports

By fifth grade, the librarian and teacher will provide students with a variety of resources. We have not included magazine or newspaper articles, but they should definitely be considered if a Reader's Guide index or databases are available. Students should begin to consider where the best information for their topic can be found. For example, books may be the best place to find historical information, and the Internet or a magazine or newspaper may have the most current information about what is happening in the world. Help students by giving them an opportunity to practice. Name several topics and allow time for students to discuss where information on those topics most likely will be found.

Encourage students to use a variety of resources. However, having more than four sources will probably confuse students when they try to organize the information. They probably will not find additional information by using more resources. It will also be more difficult for you to guide the process.

As before, students will find information in each of their sources and draw a conclusion about their findings. The conclusion will be the topic sentence. The paragraph details will come from the notes.

We hope you will enjoy using our topic and question suggestions. By sixth or seventh grade, you can encourage students to write their own questions or at least half of them Asking good open-ended questions is an art and is the heart of a good research paper. Save yourself time and aggravation by approving all questions before the students begin their research.

Consider having a session on semantic mapping—and create questions from the maps. Students can refine a broad topic and hone in on one aspect of it. As students mature, they should grasp a large topic enough to pull it apart. For example, a student doing a report on country music may write about the history of country music, country music in the fifties, why country music is so popular in the South, a biography of a country music singer, or the country fiddle.

We believe it is easier to guide the research process if all students continue to write and arrange questions one per sheet of paper—stapled together—and store them in a folder with any articles or Web pages they might use. Good luck! Research is something to celebrate, especially if it is a job well done. Let us hear from you!

Web Page Evaluation

NAMES _____ DECADE _____

http://kclibrary.nhmccd.edu/decades.html (Link to your decade)

Link to the decade you have been assigned. Pretend you have to find information about the decade and decide whether this page is one you could use in your report. With your partners, answer the following questions about the page.

1. CONTENT:

Does this Web page contain information that will help you research the 19_0s? _____

Why or why not? _____

2. AUTHORITY:

Who wrote this page? _____

What makes them an expert on this subject? _____

3. ACCURACY:

Is the information on this page accurate? _____

Why do you think so (or not)? _____

4. TIMELINESS OR CURRENCY:

When was this page last revised? _____

(Sometimes currency is very important. Sometimes it is not. Currency can suggest how recently the links were checked.)

5. APPROPRIATENESS:

Does this page have the information I need for my report? _____

Is it easy enough for me to understand? Or is it too easy? _____

6. DESIGN

Can I find the information easily? _____

What makes this page easy (or not easy) to navigate?_____

ASSIGN THIS WEB PAGE A GRADE

A ___ B____ C_____ D____ F____

AIDS IN CHILDREN

Something Extra
Visit an animated interactive house of kids who have HIV/AIDS: http://www.kidsconnect.org/kids/

Thinking About the Topic

AIDS is a particularly frightening disease for children. Children worry that they might die. Some children may not even be sick, but if their parent had AIDS, they know that the virus could be inside them and one day may become active. They worry that others may be afraid of them, afraid they will get sick, too. But they also hope. Many scientists are working on cures for AIDS.

Directions

Use three sources to find information on the AIDS virus. This is an excellent topic to find out about. You might think of other questions to ask after you have read a little about the topic. Be sure to define AIDS for your readers. Include statistics in your report.

1.   What is AIDS? How many people in the United States have AIDS?

2.   What is HIV? How are HIV and AIDS related?

3.   How can children get AIDS? What does AIDS do to the body?

4.   What are two ways doctors are treating AIDS patients?

5.   What research is being done to find a cure? How successful has it been?

Books

Keywords: *AIDS, Auto Immune Deficiency Syndrome; HIV.*

New Book of Popular Science. Danbury, CT: Grolier, 2000.

Newton, David E., Rob Nagel, and Bridget Travers, eds. *UXL Encyclopedia of Science.* Detroit: UXL, 1998.

Olendorf, Donna, Christine Jeryan, and Karen Boyden, eds. *Gale Encyclopedia of Medicine.* Farmington Hills, MI: Gale, 1999.

Travers, Bridget, and Fran Locher Freidman, eds. *Medical Discoveries and the People Who Developed Them.* Detroit: WXL, 1997.

Weiner, Lori, Aprille Best, and Philip A. Pizzo. *Be a Friend: Children Who Have HIV Speak.* Morton Grove, IL: Albert Whitman, 1994.

World Book Encyclopedia of People and Places. Chicago: World Book. 2000. Available at http://www2.worldbook.com.

Internet

Kids Health	http://kidshealth.org/kid/talk/qa/aids.html	What is AIDS? How do you get it? How is it treated?
Centers for Disease Control	http://www.cdc.gov/hiv/pubs/faqs.htm	Get the real facts from the U.S. government.
Thinkquest, Jr.	http://library.thinkquest.org/J003087F/	Kids, all you need to know about AIDS. Includes activities.

Other Resources

Animated progression of AIDS cases in the United States, 1983–1997: http://www.cdc.gov/hiv/graphics/images/dotmaps/dotmapan.htm

Friends for Life: Living with AIDS (video). Burbank, CA: Walt Disney Home Studios, 2002.

Aids. Teen Health video series. Wynnewood, PA: Schlessinger Media, 2002.

For the Teacher

Talking with Kids About HIV/Aids: http://www.talkingwithkids.org/aids.html

Information about a CD-ROM program for ages six through twelve from the University of Texas: http://www2.uta.edu/cussn/kidshiv/kidsaids.html. The information is helpful even without the CD-ROM.

Have a speaker talk to the students about AIDS.

Show You Care

Find out about what is happening in your community to help the families of kids with AIDS. It may be a Fun Run or another activity. Join in.

AIRPLANES

Something Extra
Make the best paper airplane in the world: http://www.zurqui.com/crinfocus/paper/airplane.html

Thinking About the Topic

Up, up in the air, soaring around like a bird! People have always wished they could fly. Long ago, people made wings and jumped off cliffs. Children flew kites and dreamed they were up on the end of the string. Early flying machines were always heavier than air, so down they came. Learn how the airplane was finally invented and what makes it work.

Directions

Read about airplanes. You may want to write about a special plane. Ask your teacher for help with your questions. Definitely answer question 1, then choose any other two questions below. Write each question at the top of a sheet of paper. Answer the question from the research you have done. This will form a paragraph for your report. Then write a conclusion for each question. This conclusion will be your topic sentence for each paragraph.

1.   How does an airplane work?

2.   Tell about the ways that people tried to fly before airplanes. What made them successful? What made them fail?

3.   Compare two types of airplanes. How are they different?

4.   Pick a famous pilot, such as Charles Lindbergh or Amelia Earhardt, and tell about his or her famous flight.

Books

Keywords: *Airplanes; Aircraft.*

Loves, June. *Airplanes*. Brookmall, PA: Chelsea House, 2001.

Macaulay, David. *The Way Things Work*. London: Dorling Kindersley, 1988.

Richards, Jon. *Fantastic Cutaway Book of Flight*. Brookfield, CT: Cooper Beech Books, 1998.

Schmittroth, Linda, Mary R. McCall, and Bridget Travers. *Eureka*. New York: UXL, 1999.

Witman, Kathleen L. *CDs, Super Glue & Salsa: How Everyday Products Are Made.* Farmington Hills, MI: UXL, 1996.

World Book Encyclopedia. Chicago: World Book, 2002.

Zumerchik, John, ed. *Macmillan Encyclopedia of Energy.* New York: Macmillan Reference, 2001.

Internet

Gary Bradshaw	http://www.wam.umd.edu/~stwright/WrBr/taleplane.html	The invention of the airplane.
Federal Aviation Administration	http://www.faa.gov/education/resource/kidcornr.htm	All sorts of fun activities from the FAA. Be sure to look all the way down the page.
How Stuff Works	http://www.howstuffworks.com/airplane.htm	How airplanes work.

Other Resources

Downloadable films on the invention of the airplane: http://invention.psychology.msstate.edu/gallery/airphotos.html

The Wright Brothers. Inventors of the World video series. Wynnewood, PA: Schlessinger Media, 2001.

For the Teacher

Science lesson plans for elementary students from Rutgers University: http://www.physics.rutgers.edu/hex/visit/lesson/lesson_links1.html. Many are relevant to this topic.

Lesson plans and experiments in aviation from ProTeacher: http://www.proteacher.com/110069.shtml

---

Joke

Q: Where do rabbits learn to fly?

A: In the Hare Force!

ALLERGIES

> **Something Extra**
>
> Puzzles and games from AAAAI:
> http://www.aaaai.org/patients/just4kids/puzzles/default.stm

Thinking About the Topic

Wheee! Let's roll down the hill! It's so much fun! But then Sarah rolls over a bee. Ouch! It stings. Soon she has a big bump on her arm. Later, Jason has a bumpy rash on his face. Oh, no! Poison ivy grows on that hill. Megan's nose is running. It must be the flowers she rolled in! What do they have in common? Allergies!

Directions

Read all about allergies. If you decide if you are going to write about an allergy you have, change the questions a little. Ask your teacher for help. Following are several questions about allergies. Answer question 1 and any other two questions below. Write each question at the top of a sheet of paper. Answer the question from the research you have done. This will form a paragraph for your report. Then write a conclusion for each question. This conclusion will be your topic sentence for each paragraph.

1. Describe two or three types of allergies and the problems they cause.

2. How do you know when you have an allergy instead of a common cold?

3. Can allergies be cured?

4. If you have allergies, what can you do to keep from having a reaction?

5. What makes one person be allergic when another person is not?

Books

Keywords: *Allergy; Food allergy; Asthma; Allergy in children.*

Deane, Peter M. *Coping with Allergies.* New York: Rosen Publishing Group, 1999.

Edelson, Edward. *Allergies.* Brookmall, PA: Chelsea House, 1999.

Encyclopedia of Family Health. New York: Marshall Cavendish, 1998.

Human Diseases and Conditions. New York: Charles Scribner's Sons, 2000.

Silverstein, Alvin, Virginia Silverstein, and Laura Silverstein Nunn. *Allergies*. New York: Franklin Watts, 1999.

Internet

Allergy ABCs	http://allergyabcs.com/allergies.htm	What is an allergy? How are allergies treated?
Kid's Health	http://kidshealth.org/kid/health_problems/allergy/allergies.html	How do you know if you have allergies? A site just for kids.
American Association of Allergy, Asthma and Immunology	http://aaaai.org/patients.stm	How to cope with asthma. This site is also available in Spanish.

Other Resources

Interview someone who has allergies. Take good notes. You might want to tape record the session. Have your questions ready. Here are a few examples:

- How did you find out about your allergies?
- What happens to you when you are exposed to strawberries [or whatever the person is allergic to]?
- How long does it last?
- Is there anything you can do to make yourself feel better?
- Do you take medicine or shots? How do they help?

Video clip, *What's Asthma All About*, from Neomedicus: http://www.whatsasthma.org/

Tim and Moby Explain Asthma: http://www.aaaai.org/patients/just4kids/brainpop/default.stm

For the Teacher

Facts to help you spot or avoid allergies in the classroom: http://www.allergyabcs.com/teachers.htm

---

Joke

Q: How can you make a fire-breathing dragon burn his fingers?

A: Tickle the dragon's nose and watch him sneeze. He'll try to cover his mouth with his hand!

ALTERNATIVE ENERGY

Something Extra

Puzzles, mazes, and crossword puzzles:
http://www.hawaii.gov/dbedt/ert/activitybook/

Thinking About the Topic

When you turn on a light, when your folks drive a car, or when you microwave popcorn, you are using energy. Most of our energy comes from *fossil fuels* like gasoline and coal. Those take millions of years to develop and some day will run out. What can we do? Explore other sources of energy, *renewable energy*. It comes from things that will not come to an end, like the sun, wind, rivers, and even garbage. If you learn new words, be sure to define them in your report.

Directions

Read about alternative fuels in an encyclopedia. This is a hard topic—do not try to tackle too much. Ask your teacher for help in narrowing your topic. Answer question 1 and any other two questions below. Write each question at the top of a sheet of paper. Answer the question from the research you have done. This will form a paragraph for your report. Write a conclusion for each question. The conclusion will be your topic sentence for each paragraph.

1. Discuss the way electricity is produced in your town.

2. Choose a type of alternative energy. Discuss its advantages and disadvantages.

3. What alternatives exist for fueling cars and trucks?

4. If you were running the electric plant, what method would you choose for producing power? Why is it better than the others?

Books

Keywords: *Electricity; Renewable energy; Biomass energy; Alternative energy; Solar; Wind energy; Geothermal; Nuclear; Water power.*

Chandler, Gery, and Kevin Graham. *Alternative Energy Sources.* New York: Twenty-First Century Books, 1996.

Engelbert, Phyllis. *Technology in Action: Science Applied to Everyday Life.* Detroit: UXL, 1998.

Featherstone, Jane. *Energy.* Austin, TX: Raintree Steck-Vaughn, 1999.

Graham, Ian. *Energy Forever: Geothermal and Bioenergy.* Austin, TX: Raintree Steck-Vaughn, 1999.

McLeish, Ewan. *Energy Resources: Our Impact on the Planet.* Austin, TX: Raintree Steck-Vaughn, 2002.

Zumerchik, John, ed. *Macmillan Encyclopedia of Energy.* New York: Macmillan Reference, 2001.

Internet

California Department of Energy	http://www.energy.ca.gov/education/AFVs/index.html	Information about seven different types of alternative fuel.
How Stuff Works	http://www.howstuffworks.com/	Learn how energy and electricity work. Use keywords for searching.
Energy Information Administration	http://www.eia.doe.gov/kids/	How energy works, including renewable and nonrenewable energy.

Other Resources

Film clip on fuel cells: http://www.brainpop.com/tech/engines/fuelcell/index.weml

For the Teacher

Energy-smart schools and a free lesson planner CD, from the U.S. Department of Energy: http://www.eren.doe.gov/energysmartschools/

Students design their own racecars from recycled materials: http://www.thirteen.org/edonline/lessons/racecar/index.html

Classroom resource for energy-related lessons, from the Energy Information Administration: http://www.eia.doe.gov/kids/cc/index.html

---

Joke

Visitor: What became of the other windmill you used to have?

Farmer: Oh, there was only enough wind for one, so we took the other one down.

AMERICAN HEROES

Something Extra

Martin Luther King Jr. is an American hero. Listen to his "I have a dream" speech at http://www.webcorp.com/civilrights/mlkfr.htm

What do you dream about for your own future and the future of America?

Thinking About the Topic

Everyone needs a role model or hero, and the United States has many. You may want to write about what it takes to be a hero. If so, be sure you give examples. Or choose a hero. It could be someone from your own ethnic group or a person out of American history. Recent heroes were the firefighters and others who went into the World Trade Center looking for survivors.

Directions

Consider current heroes or heroes from America's past. Choose someone you admire and enjoy your research. Think about the person as a hero rather than just writing a biography of his or her life. Answer question 1 and two other questions below about your person. Each question should be answered in a paragraph with at least three sentences.

1. What is a hero? What makes a person a hero?

2. Who is your hero? Why?

3. Tell a little about the life of the person you admire.

4. What impact has this person's achievements had on others?

5. What is the difference between a hero and a role model? Give examples.

Books

Keywords: *American heroes; Hispanic heroes; African American heroes; Women heroes; American war heroes;* specific names like *Martin Luther King Jr.*

Boys Who Rocked the World: From King Tut to Tiger Woods. Hillsboro, OR: Beyond Words Publishing, 2001.

Brody, Seymour. *Jewish Heroes & Heroines of America: 150 True Stories of American Jewish Heroism.* Hollywood, FL: Lifetime Books, 1996.

Hacker, Carlotta. *Great African Americans in History.* New York: Crabtree, 1997.

Louis, Nancy. *Heroes of the Day: The War on Terrorism.* Edina, MN: Abdo, 2002.

Roehm, Michelle. *Girls Who Rocked the World 2: Heroines from Harriet Tubman to Mia Hamm.* Hillsboro, OR: Beyond Words Publishing, 2000.

Internet

Time Remembers	http://www.time.com/time/covers/ 1101020909/index.html?cnn=yes	*Time* magazine follows the lives of eleven people altered forever by 9/11.
Our Young Heroes	http://www.lodinews.com/heroes2001/	Five children who performed selfless deeds. Read their stories.
Real African American Heroes	http://www.raaheroes.com/	Biographies from World War I to astronauts. (Look for ethnic groups as well.)
John Glenn, American Hero	http://www.pbs.org/kcet/johnglenn/	About Astronaut John Glenn.
Women of the Century	http://school.discovery.com/ schooladventures/womenofthecentury/	Choose a hero from this Web site.

Other Resources

Video clips of Jackie Robinson, Martin Luther King Jr., and more, from CNN: http://www. cnn.com/EVENTS/black_history/movies/

Animated Hero Classics Library: http://www.familyfun101.com/audio.shtml. Nineteen American heroes on video.

For the Teacher

American Heroes Lesson Plans: http://members.aol.com/MrDonnLessons/3LessonPlans.html. Scroll down for several lessons.

African American Heroes: http://www.teachervision.com/lesson-plans/lesson-4123.html

---

Joke

Q: What could you do if an angry dragon breathing smoke and fire was chasing your friend?

A: Throw water at him and he will let off steam.

SUSAN B. ANTHONY

Something Extra
Find out what life was like during Susan B. Anthony's lifetime: www.pbs.org/stantonanthony/sa_kids/index.html

Thinking About the Topic

Girls can't do math! Sissy! You act like a girl! Do girls hear things like this from other kids? Does it make you mad when people say girls cannot do something boys can do? It made Susan B. Anthony mad when people said, "Women can't vote! Women can't own property! Women aren't smart enough to speak in public." So she did something about it!

Directions

Using several resources, answer question 1 and two other questions below. Write each question at the top of a separate page. Take notes on the pages you create. Your notes should be written in complete sentences. Each question will become a paragraph in your report. After you have found the answers, draw a conclusion about your information. Your conclusion will be the topic sentence for the paragraph.

1. Susan B. Anthony cared about many things. Describe several of her causes.

2. Why did Susan B. Anthony believe it was so important for women to vote?

3. What did she do to try to get women the right to vote? How well did her attempts work?

4. How did women finally get the right to vote?

5. What has been done to help us remember Susan B. Anthony?

Books

Keywords: *Anthony, Susan B.; Suffragists.*

Bohannon, Lisa Frederkisen. *Failure Is Impossible: The Story of Susan B. Anthony.* Greensboro, NC: Morgan Reynolds, 2001.

Grolier Library of North American Biographies. Danbury, CT: Grolier Educational Corporation, 1994.

Monroe, Judy. *Susan B. Anthony Women's Voting Rights Trial: A Headline Court Case.* Berkeley Heights, NH: Enslow, 2002.

Moss, Joyce, and George Wilson. *Profiles in American History*. Farmington Hills, MI: Gale, 1995.

Raatma, Lucia. *Susan B. Anthony*. Minneapolis, MN: Compass Point Books, 2001.

Rustad, Martha E. H. *Susan B. Anthony*. Mankato, MN: Capstone Press, 2002.

Internet

Huntington Library Online Votes for Women Exhibit	http://www.huntington.org/vfw/imp/anthony.html	Biography.
Liz Library	http://www.gate.net/~liz/suffrage/index.html	Women's suffrage timeline.
Susan B. Anthony House	http://www.susanbanthonyhouse.org	Biography and timeline.

Other Resources

The Susan B. Anthony Story (video). Richardson, TX: Grace Products Corporation, 1994. Information on classroom use at http://www.graceproducts.com/anthony/

Click on the picture for video clips: http://www.pbs.org/stantonanthony/

Susan B. Anthony. Great Americans for Children video series. Wynnewood, PA: Schlessinger Media, 2003.

For the Teacher

Teaching activities from the National Archives: http://www.nara.gov/education/teaching/woman/teach.html

---

Look It Up

What year did women get the right to vote in America, and what amendment gave them the right?

ANTS AND OTHER SOCIAL INSECTS

> ## Something Extra
>
> Make ants your research project. Get an ant farm and observe the ants as they build their colony. For helpful tips on ant farms, go to http://www.infowest.com/life/anttips.htm
>
> **NOTE:** If you decide to have an ant farm, be prepared to care for it.

Thinking About the Topic

Have you ever watched an ant at work? The ant travels from its nest to find food, carrying back a bread crumb even bigger than itself. Ants are always hard at work. Put a twig in an ant's way and see what he does. Watch ants as they pass each other and see how they touch. Why do they do this?

Directions

Using several sources, answer question 1 and two other questions below. Write each question at the top of a separate page. Take notes on the pages you create. Your notes should be written in complete sentences. Each question will become a paragraph in your report. After you have found the answers, draw a conclusion about your information. Your conclusion will be the topic sentence for the paragraph.

1. Describe an ant's lifestyle.

2. The queen ant is an important part of each ant colony. What does she do for the colony? What do the other ants do for her?

3. How does a new ant colony form?

4. Choose a particular type of ant, such as a fire ant, army ant, or carpenter ant, and compare it to other types of ants.

5. What are ants good for? What harm do they cause?

Books

Keywords: *Ants—Juvenile Literature; Insects.*

Furgang, Kathy. *Let's Take a Field Trip to an Ant Colony.* New York: PowerKids Press, 1999.

Hartley, Karen, and Chris Macro. *Ant.* Des Plaines, IL: Heinemann, 1998.

Parker, Steve. *Ants.* Pleasantville, NY: Readers' Digest Children's Books, 1999.

Raintree Steck-Vaughn Illustrated Science Encyclopedia. Austin, TX: Raintree Steck-Vaughn, 1997.

Stidworthy, John. *Macmillan Encyclopedia of Science.* New York: Macmillan Reference, 1997.

Internet

Thornton Jr. High School	http://www.insecta-inspecta.com/	All about fire ants, army ants, and more.
Myremecology Organization	http://www.myrmecology.org/	The scientific study of ants. Includes sections on habitat, biology, and recommended reading.
Texas A&M University	http://fireant.tamu.edu/antfacts/	History and identification.

Other Resources

Stevenson, Joycelynn. *The Magic School Bus Gets Ants in its Pants* (video). New York: Kid Vision, 1997.

Ants. Bug City Video Series. Wyneewood, PA: Schlessinger Media, 1998.

For the Teacher

Activities based on the movies *Antz* and *A Bug's Life*, with questions at various grade levels: http://www.education-world.com/a_lesson/lesson087.shtml

Activities by the University of Kentucky, including observations, discussion ideas, and ant traps: http://www.uky.edu/Agriculture/Entomology/ythfacts/allyr/ants.htm

Insect Lesson Plans from the University of Arizona: http://insected.arizona.edu/lessons.htm

---

Joke

Q: What is the biggest ant in the world?

A: A Gi-ant!

ARTHUR

> **Something Extra**
>
> How to draw Arthur:
> http://www.pbs.org/wgbh/arthur/dw/draw_arthur/index.html
> Practice drawing Arthur. It is fun and easy.

Thinking About the Topic

Children all over the world love Arthur. Arthur knows how to have fun. He has lots of friends, and he is smart. Marc Brown is the famous children's book author who wrote the Arthur books. If you enjoy Marc Brown's books, you might write about Arthur. You might even write about his teacher, Mr. Ratburn, or his friends, Buster, DW, or Francine. Many children's book characters are loved generation after generation. You may have a different character in a series of books that you would like to write about. How about Ramona and Beezus? How about Encyclopedia Brown or Nancy Drew? You can follow this same format for any book character.

Directions

For your book character report, read several Marc Brown Arthur books. When you think you know Arthur (or another character) pretty well, it will be time to answer the questions. Write your information in complete sentences. Write one question at the top of each page. Answer question 1 and choose two other questions below. After you have answered your questions, using several resources, draw conclusions for each question. Each conclusion will be the title sentence for its paragraph.

1. Who is Arthur? Describe him.

2. What does Arthur like? What is Arthur afraid of?

3. Is Arthur a good friend? Why or why not?

4. What did Arthur do that makes you laugh?

5. What do you like best about Arthur? Why do you think he is so popular with children?

6. Do you think Arthur acts like you or someone you know? Why?

Books

Keywords: *Brown, Mark; Arthur; Aardvarks in literature.*

"Marc Brown." In *Biography for Beginners*. Pleasant Ridge, MI: Favorable Impressions, 1998.

"Marc Brown." In *Something About the Author, Volume 80*. Detroit: Gale, 1995.

Woods, Mae. *Marc Brown*. New York: Abdo & Daughters, 2001.

Internet

Arthur's Own Page	http://www.pbs.org/wgbh/ arthur/arthur/index.html	PBS page for Marc Brown and Arthur.
In the Spotlight with Marc Brown	http://teacher.scholastic.com/ authorsandbooks/events/brown/	Author information and interview.
Telling Stories with Pictures	http://www.decordova.org/ decordova/exhibit/stories/ brown.html	About Marc Brown's illustrations.

Other Resources

It is a good idea to ask the author questions. Be very polite and use your best handwriting. Marc Brown, c/o Little, Brown, and Company, 3 Center Plaza, Boston, MA 02108.

Or e-mail your questions online at http://www.pbs.org/wgbh/arthur/feedback/index.html

Watch Arthur shows on PBS or rent the videos from a video store. Many libraries lend these videos for free.

For the Teacher

Marc Brown Lesson Plans: http://etrc33.louisiana.edu/edres/lessons/elementary/lesson3.html

Marc Brown: Teacher's Resources: http://falcon.jmu.edu/~ramseyil/mbrown.html

Teacher's Corner: http://www.pbs.org/wgbh/arthur/teachers/resources/guides.htm

A Book Character Day is one of those memorable occasions in elementary school. Plan such a day with your colleagues. Have the students wear costumes, write or draw about their favorite characters, and generally celebrate reading. Invite parents for readings. Be sure to include the librarian!

Look It Up

Arthur is the world's most famous aardvark. What awards has Marc Brown won for his Arthur books?

AUTOMOBILE

> **Something Extra**
>
> Playing games in the car makes a trip go faster. Find travel games at http://www.activitiesforkids.com/travel/travel_games.htm

Thinking About the Topic

It's really an engine on wheels! The rest of an automobile is just for comfort. The first automobiles had great big bicycle wheels and a seat big enough for one. You can almost imagine peddling it down the street like a go-cart. Write about early automobiles. Find out how your great-grandparents and their parents traveled. Bring in pictures for your report.

Directions

Following are some questions about automobiles. Select three questions or write your own. Write each question at the top of a clean sheet of paper. Answer the question using your research books and Web sites. Each question will form a paragraph for your report. Then write a conclusion for each question. This conclusion will be your topic sentence for each paragraph. Add details from your notes to complete each paragraph.

1. Discuss the history of the automobile.

2. What were early cars like? How were they different from cars today?

3. How does an automobile engine work? How does the power get from the engine to the wheels?

4. How has the automobile changed the way people live?

5. Write about some of the obstacles owners of cars faced when cars were first invented.

6. Write about Henry Ford (see our jumpstart).

Books

Keywords: *Automobiles; Cars.*

Loves, June. *Cars.* Brookmall, PA: Chelsea House, 2001.

Macaulay, David. *The Way Things Work.* London: Dorling Kindersley, 1988.

Richards, Jon. *Cutaway Racing Car.* Brookfield, CT: Copper Beech Books, 1998.

Schmittroth, Linda, Mary R. McCall, and Bridget Travers. *Eureka.* New York: UXL, 1999.

Zumerchik, John, ed. *Macmillan Encyclopedia of Energy.* New York: Macmillan, 2001.

Internet

The Great Idea Finder	http://www.ideafinder.com/history/inventions/story054.htm	A general history of the invention of the automobile, with links to more specific sites.
Smithsonian Institution	http://www.si.edu/resource/faq/nmah/earlycars.htm	"Early Cars; A Fact Sheet for Children."
How Stuff Works	http://www.howstuffworks.com/engine.htm	Learn how a car engine works.
Autoworld Brussels	http://www.autoworld.be/en/3-1.htm	Automobile timeline.
Auto Museum	http://www.automuseum.com/History.html	Brief history of the automobile.

Other Resources

A video tour of the Museum of Automotive History: http://www.themuseumofautomobilehistory.com/Films/index.html

Take a look at some of the newest cars on the street and some that are coming in the future: http://www.theautochannel.com/cybercast/americandriver/index.html?EVENTS

Watch videos of racing in action: http://www.theautochannel.com/cybercast/speedwayheat/index.html?EVENTS

For the Teacher

Lesson plans for the history of automobiles, grades three through eight: http://www.teachervision.com/lesson-plans/lesson-4819.html

Students design their own racecars from recycled materials: http://www.thirteen.org/edonline/lessons/racecar/index.html

---

Joke

Q: What part of an automobile is most likely to cause an accident?

A: The nut behind the wheel!

BALD EAGLE

> ## Something Extra
> Watch an eagle on an online live camera at
> http://www.wa.gov/wdfw/viewing/wildcam/eaglecam/

Thinking About the Topic

As the symbol of our country, the bald eagle should be bold and free. It lives high in an aerie and soars over large distances, watching, hunting, and inspecting its territory. But the bald eagle has become a threatened species. Learn where the bald eagle lives and why it is our national symbol.

Directions

Using several resources, answer question 1 and two other questions below. Write each question at the top of a separate page. Take notes on the pages you create. Your notes should be written in complete sentences. Each question will become a paragraph in your report. After you have found the answers, draw a conclusion about your information. Each conclusion will be the topic sentence for a paragraph.

1. Where does the eagle live? Describe the parts of the country, its preferred nesting site, and how it gets its food.

2. How do eagles raise their young?

3. Learn about other types of eagles.

4. How did the eagle become the symbol of our country?

5. What is being done to protect the bald eagle?

Books

Keyword: *Eagles; Bald eagle*

Becker, John E. *Bald Eagle.* San Diego: Kidhaven, 2002.

Gerholdt, James E. *Bald Eagles.* Edina, MN: Abdo & Daughters. 1997

Gibson, Gail. *Soaring with the Wind: The Bald Eagle.* New York: Morrow Junior Books. 1998.

Patent, Dorothy H. *Eagles of America.* New York: Holiday House. 1995.

Raintree Steck-Vaughn Illustrated Science Encyclopedia. Austin, TX: Raintree Steck-Vaughn, 1997.

Richardson, Adele. *Eagles.* Mankato, MN: Creative Education, 1998.

Internet

Hope Rutledge	http://www.baldeagleinfo.com/	American bald eagle, with excellent photos, history, preservation. Some information on other eagles.
National Wildlife Federation	http://www.nfl.org/wildalive/eagle/index.html	Focus on the bald eagle.
Eagle Cam	http://www.wa.gov/wdfw/viewing/wildcam/eaglecam/	Watch an eagle nest live!

Other Resources

Watch a video of an eagle in action online: http://www.nwf.org/wildalive/eagle/audiovideo.html

Video clips of eagles laying eggs, hatching, and feeding, from Northeast Utilities System: http://www.nu.com/eagles/eaglevid.asp

Check out the local library for videos about the eagle.

For the Teacher

Lesson plan utilizing online videos: http://can-do.com/uci/lessons98/Eagle.html

Daffy Definitions

Bird of prey—An eagle that goes to church every week.

BATS

Something Extra

Something Extra

How much do you know about bats? Take the Bat Quiz at
http://www.lhs.berkeley.edu/BATQUIZ/B10.html

Learn and retell a Native American story for your class, "How Bat
Learned to Fly," *in How Chipmunk Got Tiny Feet* by Herald Hausman

Thinking About the Topic

The bat has gotten a bad rap, but we love any animal that can eat 600 mosquitoes at night! Bats can scare you in the dark when they seem to fly right toward your face—then swerve away just in time to miss you. Whew! Learn other facts about this flying night creature.

Directions

There are several good books and Web pages where you can find out about this unusual animal. Select question 1 and two other questions below. Write each question at the top of a separate page. Each question will become a paragraph in your report. After you have found the answers, draw a conclusion about the information. Your conclusion is the topic sentence for the paragraph. Add other details from your notes.

1. Describe the bat.

2. How are bats born, and how does the mother bat care for her young?

3. How does the bat get its food? What does it eat?

4. Where does the bat live, and what are some of its habits?

5. Who are the bat's enemies, and how does it defend itself?

Books

Keywords: *Bats; Desmodus rotundus; Rodents.*

Bair, Diane. *Bat Watching*. Mankato, MN: Capstone, 2000.

Earle, Anne. *Zipping, Zapping, and Zooming*. Let's Find Out About Science. New York: Scott Foresman, 1995.

Gibbons, Gail. *Bats*. New York: Holiday House, 2000.

Harrison, Virginia. *The World of Bats*. Milwaukee, WI: G. Stevens, 1989.

Raintree Steck-Vaughn Illustrated Science Encyclopedia. Austin, TX: Raintree Steck-Vaughn, 1997.

Ruff, Sue. *Bats*. New York: Benchmark Books, 2000.

Internet

Bat Cam	bci.batcon.org/index.html	This live cam photographs bats and updates every minute.
Bat Conservation	www.batconservation.org/content/bathouse/bathouse.htm	Information about bats—and how to adopt a bat.
Bat News Articles	dailynews.yahoo.com/fc/Yahooligans/bats	News articles. Good info for your report.
Bats Bats Everywhere	members.aol.com/bats4kids	Nine big bat facts.
The Bat Cave	www.torstar.com/rom/batcave/cave/index.html	Photos and information—all in the bat cave. Myths about bats included.
Bat World	www.batworld.org	Excellent site for finding out about bat care and conservation.

Other Resources

Bat Video Online: www.geographia.com/malaysia/batsqt1.mov

Online audio and video clips at Seahorse Park: www.poost.nl/seahorse/picts/media/zp7.qt

Bat Adventures. (video). Audubon's Animal Adventure Series. Wynnewood, PA: Library Video Co., 1997.

For the Teacher

Build a bat house and use the forms and information here to help this conservation organization with research: www.batconservation.org/content/bathouse/bathouse.htm

Listen to *Stellaluna* by Janell Cannon (San Diego: Harcourt Brace Jovanovich, 1993) with your class (audiocassette), or read the book aloud.

Joke

A vampire bat came flapping in from the right covered in fresh blood and parked himself on the cave's roof to get some sleep. Soon all the other bats smelled the blood and began hassling him about where he got it. He told them to shut up and let him get some sleep, but they persisted until he finally gave in.

"OK, follow me." He flew out of the cave with hundreds of bats behind him. Down through a valley they went, across a river, and into a forest of trees. Finally he slowed down and all the other bats excitedly milled around him.

"Do you see that tree over there?" he asked? "YES, YES, YES!!" the bats all screamed in a frenzy.

"Well, I didn't!" the vampire bat said.

BEES

> ### Something Extra
>
> See the world through a bee's eye at
> http://cvs.anu.edu.au/andy/beye/beyehome.html

Thinking About the Topic

Has anyone ever said you are as busy as a bee? Bees work so hard, they must think work is fun. Each bee has a special job to do, and they spend all their time working. The busy bee buzzes to and fro, from the flowers to the hive. When it meets another bee, it stops to do a little dance. Bees are fun to watch. They will not bother you unless you bother them. But be careful! If you run across clover in bare feet, you might get stung!

Directions

Using several resources, answer question 1 and two other questions below. Write each question at the top of a separate page. Take notes on the pages you create. Your notes should be written in complete sentences. Each question will become a paragraph in your report. After you have found the answers, draw a conclusion about your information. Your conclusion will be the topic sentence for the paragraph.

1. Describe the bee. Include its body, its habitat, and the way bees talk to each other.

2. What is the role of the queen bee?

3. Describe the different jobs within a beehive.

4. There are many kinds of bees, including killer bees, honeybees, and carpenter bees. Choose a particular type of bee and compare it to the others.

5. How do bees make honey? What is it for?

Books

Keywords: *Bees; Honeybee; Africanized honeybee; Insects.*

Cole, Joanna. *Magic School Bus Inside a Beehive.* New York: Scholastic, 1996

Gibbons, Gail. *Honey Makers.* New York: Morrow, 1997.

Hartley, Karen and Chris Macro. *Bees.* Des Plaines, IL: Heinemaann, 1998.

Holmes, Kevin J. *Bees.* Mankato, MN: Bridgestone, 1998.

Jeonesse, Gallimard, Ute Fuhr, and Raoul Sautai. *Bees.* New York: Scholastic, 1997.

Internet

University of California Riverside	http://bees.ucr.edu/	Information about killer bees.
National Honey Board	http://www.honey.com/kids/facts.html	Honey bee facts.
University of Kentucky	http://www.uky.edu/Agriculture/Engomology/entfacts/struct/ef611.htm	All about carpenter bees.
The Bee Works	http://www.thebeeworks.com/kids/index.html	Kids' page describes the waggle dance, pollination, and what bees are good for.

Other Resources

Online videos of bees being trained, from the University of Montana: http://biology.dbs.umt.edu/bees/video.htm

Search the library catalog for a video your school or local library might have.

Bees. Bug City video series. Wynnewood, PA: Schlessinger Media, 1998.

For the Teacher

Lesson plan on identifying bees and wasps: http://ag.arizona.edu/pubs/insects/ahb/lsn16.html

Bee projects for early elementary students: http://www.abcteach.com/Themeunits/Bees/beesTOC.htm

---

Jokes

Q: How do bees make money?
A: They cell their honey!

Q: Why do bees hum?
A: Because they don't know the words!

JAN BERENSTAIN AND STAN BERENSTAIN

Something Extra

Download Berenstain Bear bank checks and create your own business with your friends. Check online at http://www.randomhouse.com/kids/berenstainbears/activities

Thinking About the Topic

The authors of the famous Berenstain Bears, Stan Berenstain and Jan Berenstain, have been married for many years. They have four grandchildren. In 1962, the Berenstains published a book about a family of bears titled *The Big Honey Hunt*. If Papa Berenstain had been getting older, he would be almost 70 years old now. Ask your parents if they remember reading the Berenstain Bear books when they were young.

Directions

To write about a person, get to know about what he or she does. Before you begin your report, read at least two Berenstain Bear books. Study the illustrations. Then find information about the authors. When you are ready, select question 1 and two other questions below. Write one question at the top of each page. Each question will become a paragraph in your report. Draw a conclusion from the answers you find. The conclusion will be your topic sentence. For example, the conclusion to question 1 might be, "Stan and Jan Berenstain are the authors and illustrators of many Berenstain Bear books."

1. Who are Stan Berenstain and Jan Berenstain? How do they work together to write their books?

2. Why did they become both writer and illustrator? How did they learn about writing and drawing?

3. How did they create the Berenstain family? Where do the Berenstains get ideas?

4. Why do you think the Berenstain Bear books are so popular? What do you like best about these books?

Books

Keywords: *Berenstain, Stan; Berenstain, Jan.*

"Berenstain, Stan and Jan." In *Biography for Beginners*. Pleasant Ridge, MI: Favorable Impressions, 1995.

"Berenstain, Stan and Jan." In *Something About the Author, Volume 64*. Detroit: Gale, 1991.

Berg, Julie. *The Berenstains: The Young at Heart.* Edina, MN: Abdo & Daughters, 1994. Distributed by Rockbottom Books.

Biography Today, Author Series, Volume 3. Detroit: Omnigraphics, 1997.

Woods, Mae. *Stan & Jan Berenstain.* Children's Authors. Edina, MN: Abdo, 2001.

Internet

Bear Country Online	http://villa.lakes.com/mariska/bears/	Fan pages.
Fifth Book of Junior Authors	http://www.edupaperback.org/authorbios/ Berenstain_StanJan.html	Excerpt from a book.
Official Berenstain Bears Site	http://www.berenstainbears.com/	Good information. Be sure you look here.
The Berenstains	http://teacher.scholastic.com/authorsandbooks/ authors/beren/bio.htm	Information from the publisher.

Other Resources

Barn Theater—Berenstain Bear Online Movies: http://www.berenstainbears.com/

E-mail your questions to the authors at sbandjb@rcn. Be very specific and polite.

There are over 30 videos of the Berenstain Bears. Enjoy a few at school, rent one from a video store, or watch some on television.

For the Teacher

Teacher lesson plan for *Berenstain Bears' No Guns Allowed:* http://www.randomhouse.com/ teachers/guides/noguns.html

Bibliography: http://falcon.jmu.edu/~ramseyil/berenstainbib.htm

Stan and Jan Berenstain Resource File: http://falcon.jmu.edu/~ramseyil/berenstain.htm

---

Have fun with activities, from coloring books to puzzles: http://www.berenstainbears.com/

THE BERENSTAIN BEARS

Something Extra

The Berenstain Bears Online Coloring Pages:
http://www.berenstainbears.com/colormain.html

Thinking About the Topic

Mama and Papa Berenstain live in a treehouse with their two children. Oh, wouldn't it be fun to live there? Stan and Jan Berenstain are the famous authors who write these books. Write about the Berenstain family or about Mama and Papa Bear or the children. You may even choose to write about the Berenstains' home and neighbors. What fun!

Directions

For your book character report, read at least two or three Berenstain Bear books. If you decide to write about the Bear Scouts, choose the books about them. When you think you know them well, it will be time to answer your questions. Write your information in complete sentences. Write one question at the top of each page. Answer question 1 and select two other questions below. Your questions will become the paragraphs in your paper.

1.   Who are the Berenstain Bears? Describe them.

2.   Where do they live? What is their home like? Who are their neighbors?

3.   Who are the Bear Scouts? Describe one of their adventures.

4.   What do they do that makes you enjoy reading about them?

5.   Why do you think children have loved the Berenstain Bears for so many years? Give examples.

6.   What do you like best about these books? Why?

Books

Keywords: *Berenstain Bear; Bear Scouts; Jan or Stan Berenstain.*

Bibliography of Berenstain Bear Books: http://www.randomhouse.com/kids/berenstainbears/catalog/. Read several books by the authors.

"Jan and Stan Berenstain." In *Biography for Beginners.* Pleasant Ridge, MI: Favorable Impressions, 1995.

Woods, Mae. *Stan & Jan Berenstain.* Children's Authors. Edina, MN: Abdo, 2001.

Internet

Berenstain Bears' Official Page	http://www.berenstainbears.com/	Start here.
Berenstain Bears Country	http://villa.lakes.com/mariska/bears/	Great and fun page.
Random House Berenstain Bear Pages	http://www.randomhouse.com/kids/ berenstainbears/	From Random House publisher. Good info and activities.
The Berenstains	http://teacher.scholastic.com/authorsandbooks/ authors/beren/bio.htm	Information about the authors.

Other Resources

It is a good idea to ask the author questions. Be very polite. E-mail Stan Berenstain and Jan Berenstain at http://www.berenstainbears.com/beiform.html or write to them at Random House.

Berenstain Bear videos are available at libraries, schools, and video stores.

Berenstain Bears Theater—online movies: http://www.berenstainbears.com/theater.html

For the Teacher

Random House for Teachers: http://www.randomhouse.com/teachers/authors/index.html

Money Matters Unit: http://www.randomhouse.com/kids/parents/money.html. This unit and the Berenstain Bear checks could be fun to learn about money. Have the students operate a small store.

Download Berenstain Bear checks at http://www.randomhouse.com/kids/berenstainbears/ activities/

Read-aloud: *The Berenstain Bears' Trouble with Money*. New York: Random House, 1983.

Read Aloud, Fast!

See that bare Berenstain bear?

See that bare Berenstain bear?

See that bare Berenstain bear?

BOYS CHOIR OF HARLEM

> ## Something Extra
> Bring in a CD or audiocassette recording of the Boys Choir of Harlem to share with your classmates.

Thinking About the Topic

Love to sing? If so, this topic is for you. Imagine yourself singing in a choir so famous that nearly everyone has heard of it. Over 150,000 people see the Boys Choir of Harlem live in concert each year. Millions watch them on television. They even won the important National Medal of Arts from the National Endowment for the Arts. These boys are stars! To stay in the choir, they must work hard. They need self-discipline, and they must follow the rules. Learn more about them. By the way, there is also a Girls Choir of Harlem. There are other famous children's choirs or musical groups that you can write about. Los Angeles has an excellent choir.

Directions

Find out about the Boys Choir of Harlem. The library is a great place to begin. Look for magazine or newspaper articles about the boys at your library. Visit Web sites to learn more information or to hear the group sing. Your local library may have a CD or tape you can check out. Choose question 1 and two others. Use several sources to answer each question. Draw a conclusion about each answer. The conclusion will be your topic sentence.

1. What is the Boys Choir of Harlem? Tell a little about the history of the choir.

2. How do boys get selected for the choir? What do they have to do to stay in the choir?

3. Only 35 out of 500 boys tour the country each year. How are they chosen? What is life like for them while on tour?

4. What do you think it would be like if you could join the choir? How would it change your life?

Books

Keywords: *Boys Choir of Harlem; Choir; Singing.*

Collier, Bryan. *Uptown.* New York: Henry Holt, 2000.

Smith, Charles R. *Perfect Harmony: A Musical Journey with the Boys Choir of Harlem.* Boston: Hyperion, 2002. (If you decide to write on this topic, have the librarian get this book for you.)

World Book Encyclopedia (or any other encyclopedia).

Internet

Alumni of the Choir	http://www.boyschoirofharlem.org/ AlumniCAH/alumni.htm	Choir history.
Endowment for the Arts	http://arts.endow.gov/artforms/Music/ Boys.ram	Very good site for additional information. Look at the rules the boys have to follow.
Musical program	http://www.koger.sc.edu/harl2.html	A little about the group, plus a program
Official site of the Harlem Boys Choir	http://www.boyschoirofharlem.org/	Take your time here.
Smithsonian Magazine article	http://www.smithsonianmag.si.edu/ smithsonian/issues99/dec99/choir.html	Be sure to read this article. It has a lot of good information.

Other Resources

Amazing Grace with Bill Moyers (video). Produced and directed by Elena Mannes. A production of Public Affairs Television, Inc. Watch the boys on video.

Endowment for the Arts: http://arts.endow.gov/artforms/Music/Boys.ram. Excellent information. Listen to the choir sing.

Sound of Hope (sound recording). New York: Eastwest Records, 1994.

See a list of the choirs' recordings at http://www.boyschoirofharlem.org/bchshop/index.html

Write to the Boys Choir at Choir Academy of Harlem, 2005 Madison Avenue, New York, NY 10035-1298. Ask the questions clearly and they will answer.

For the Teacher

Plan a talent day for your students. Kick off the show by allowing the student who selects this topic to make an oral report. Show the talented Boys Choir of Harlem singing. (A good example is the easy to obtain video, *Amazing Grace with Bill Moyers*. A recent Emeril Christmas program also featured the group. Try foodtv.com.) Students love to share their own talents. Maybe the music teacher can have a group perform.

Share the poems and pictures in Charles Smith's *Perfect Harmony: A Musical Journey with the Boys Choir of Harlem* (Boston: Hyperion, 2002).

Joke

Jason: I'm always breaking into song!

Steve: You wouldn't have to break in if you used the right key in the first place.

BRIDGES

> **Something Extra**
>
> Create a bridge using toothpicks. Make it strong enough to carry more than its own weight.
>
> *Bridge Stress—Hands on!:*
> http://www.pbs.org/wgbh/buildingbig/lab/forces.html

Thinking About the Topic

Bridges provide a way across a river or road. They have to be strong to carry cars, trains, and trucks all day long. Have you ever wondered how they can be so strong when they do not seem to have much support? Here is your chance to find out.

Directions

Skim through a book about bridges or read an encyclopedia article so you can decide how you want to begin. You could choose a particular bridge, like the Golden Gate bridge in San Francisco. You might write about a type of bridge, an arch, a suspension, or a beam. You might choose to write about an architect who designs bridges. You could even write about the history of bridges, for example, the beautiful covered bridges.

When you have chosen your topic, write three questions you would like to answer. The first question should state your case, for example, "What is a suspension bridge?" After you take notes from different resources (books, Internet sites, videos), draw a conclusion about your answer. Each conclusion will become the topic sentence for a paragraph. Your notes will provide the paragraph detail support. Before you begin, show your questions to your teacher. Write open-ended questions. They should NOT have *yes* or *no* answers. Questions should lead you to the discovery of new information.

GOOD QUESTION: What makes the arch bridge so strong?

POOR QUESTION: Is the arch bridge strong?

Books

Keywords: *Bridges; Building bridges—Juvenile Literature; Transportation.*

Hill, Lee Sullivan. *Bridges Connect.* Minneapolis, MN: Carolrhoda, 1997.

Kline, Michael P. *Bridges: Amazing Structures to Design, Build & Test.* Charlotte, VT: Williamson Publishing, 1999.

Oxlade, Chris. *Bridges.* Building Amazing Structures. Crystal Lake, IL: Heinemann Library, 2000.

Parker, Janice. *The Science of Structures.* Chicago: Children's Books, 2001.

Ricciuti, Edward R. *America's Top 10 Bridges.* Woodbridge, CT: Blackbirch, 1998.

St. George, Judith. *The Brooklyn Bridge: They Said It Couldn't Be Built.* New York: Putnam, 1982. (There are several books on a particular bridge. Use the catalog.)

Wilson, Forrest. *Bridges Go From Here to There.* Washington, DC: Preservation Press, 1993.

Internet

How Bridges Work	http://www.howstuffworks.com/bridge.htm	You will want to bookmark this site for future visits.
Bridges—by Discovery	http://www.discovery.com/stories/technology/buildings/bridges.html	From the Discovery channel.
Building Big—Bridges	http://www.pbs.org/wgbh/buildingbig/bridge/index.html	PBS has a great site. Good information about structure.

Other Resources

Bridges (video). By David Macaulay. South Burlington, VT: WGBS Boston Video, 2000.

Music and Words—London Bridges: http://.niehs.nih.gov/kids/lyrics/london.htm

For the Teacher

Building Big for Educators: http://www.pbs.org/wgbh/buildingbig/educator/index.html

Pollard, Jeanne. *Building Toothpick Bridges: Math Project Series.* Parsipanny, NJ: Dale Seymour, 1985.

Put your Truss in Building Bridges: http://gby.org/edu/ntti/lessons/archive/bridges.html. A lesson plan by a master teacher.

Think It Over

Have you ever heard people say, "We'll cross that bridge when we come to it?" What do you think they mean when they say it?

MARC BROWN

> ### Something Extra
>
> Write to Marc Brown; maybe he will send an autographed picture of himself or Arthur.
>
> Marc Brown
> c/o Little, Brown and Company
> 3 Center Plaza
> Boston, MA 02108

Thinking About the Topic

Marc Brown has written and illustrated more than 30 Arthur books. He likes to visit with children in schools and at bookstores. His character, Arthur, is so popular that he has his own TV show. Mr. Brown has hidden his children's names in his books. Find Marc Brown's children's names in his books.

Directions

To write about a person, you should get to know something about what he or she does. Before you begin, read several of Marc Brown's books. Study his illustrations. When you are ready, choose question 1 and two others below. Write one question at the top of each page. Each question will be a paragraph in your report. Draw a conclusion from the answers you find. The conclusion will be your topic sentence. For example, the conclusion for question 1 might be, "Marc Brown is a popular author and illustrator."

1. Who is Marc Brown? Find out a little about his life. Where does he live? What does he enjoy? How does he spend his time?

2. Why did Marc Brown become a writer and illustrator?

3. Where does Marc Brown get ideas for his books?

4. What do you like best about Marc Brown's stories and illustrations?

5. Why do you think makes Marc Brown's books so popular?

Books

Keywords: *Marc Brown; Authors.* (If you are looking for information *about* Marc Brown, use his name as a subject. Otherwise, you will find books by him, not about him.)

"Marc Brown." In *Biography for Beginners, 1998.* Pleasant Ridge, MI: Favorable Impressions, 1998.

"Marc Brown." In *Something About the Author, Volume 80*. New York: Gale, 1995.

Woods, Mae. *Marc Brown*. Edina, MN: Abdo, 2001.

Internet

Marc Brown	http://harcourtschool.com/activity/book_buddy/author/marc_brown.html	Publisher information about the author.
Marc Brown	http://www.pbs.org/wgbh/arthur/marc_brown/index.html	You will love this site about Marc Brown and Arthur.
Telling Stories with Pictures	http://www.decordova.org/decordova/exhibit/stories/brown.html	Information about the illustrations.

Other Resources

Arthur's Baby (video). New York: Random House, 1997.

E-mail questions at http://www.pbs.org/wgbh/arthur/feedback/index.html

Watch Arthur on PBS or rent the videos. You school or local library may have several.

For the Teacher:

Marc Brown Lesson Plans: etrc33.louisiana.edu/edres/lessons/elementary/lesson3.htm

Marc Brown: Teacher's Resource: falcon.jmu.edu/~ramseyil/mbrown.htm

Teacher's Corner: http://www.pbs.org/wgbh/arthur/teachers/resources/guides.htm

The Arthur chapter books are great for students to read and discuss in pairs.

Bet You Can . . . Say

Audiences applaud the author of Arthur Aardvark. (Repeat three times, fast!)

BULLIES

> ## Something Extra
> Stories, poems, and artwork by victims: http://www.bullying.org/

Thinking About the Topic

Have you ever known a bully? A bully likes to pick on people who are weaker or different. A bully might make fun of someone. Maybe he or she thinks it is funny to steal someone's glasses. In the background the other kids may laugh, but secretly they're thinking, "I'm glad it's not me he's [or she's] picking on!" Nobody likes bullies. They torment weaker people and are frightening and mean. Remember, the bully is not brave, he or she just finds humor in scaring others. You may find it interesting to see what makes the bully "tick." And what you can do to stop a bully.

Directions

Select or write three questions about your topic. Answer question 1 and any other two questions below. Write each question at the top of a sheet of paper. Answer the question using your research sources (books, Internet, videos). Then write a conclusion for each question. This conclusion will be your topic sentence for each paragraph. Add the details from your notes to your paragraph.

1. Discuss several reasons children might become bullies.

2. What are some reasons children might be picked on? Can you guess why? (Do NOT name names in your report.)

3. How can you tell who is a bully?

4. What are three things a person can do to stop bullies? What is good about each of them? What are the drawbacks?

5. Who else could stop the bullying? What are some ways they can help?

Books

Keywords: *Bullying; Aggressiveness; Cliques; Behavior—Juvenile.*

Gall, Susan B., ed. *Gale Encyclopedia of Childhood and Adolescence.* Detroit: Gale, 1998.

Johnson, Julie. *Bullies and Gangs.* Brookfield, CT: Copper Beech Books 1998.

Polland, Barbara K. *We Can Work it Out; Conflict Resolution for Children.* Berkeley, CA: Tricycle Press, 2001.

Sanders, Pete. *What Do You Know About Bullying?* Brookfield, CT: Copper Beech Books, 1996.

Sifakis, Carl. *Encyclopedia of American Crime.* 2nd ed. New York: Facts on File, 2001.

Internet

Orange County Sheriffs Department	http://www.duila.org/project.htm	What is a gang? What can you do about it?
Bully B'Ware	http://www.bullybeware.com/moreinfo.html	What is bullying? What happens to bullies? What happens to victims?
City University, London	http://www.student.city.ac.uk/~rc313/bullying.html	Stand up to bullying. Ways to stick up for yourself.

Other Resources

One way to stop bullying: http://www.talkingwithkids.org/ads.html

Ex-President Clinton talks about violence in schools: http://www.talkingwithkids.org/ads.html

A bully discusses his past: http://www.bullying.org/andrew.ram

For the Teacher

Several lesson plans on dealing with conflicts and bullies: http://www.edhelper.com/cat80.htm

Gang resistance, education, and training: http://www.atf.treas.gov/great/greatbro/lessons.htm

Resources to help teachers and counselors combat bullying and school violence: http://www.counselorandteachertips.com/

Joke

Nick was cornered by a bully on his way to school.

Bully: Give me a quarter!

Nick: I don't have a quarter. Do you have change for a dollar?

BUTTERFLIES

Something Extra
Something Extra Make a paper butterfly hatch from a chrysalis: http://www.hhmi.org/coolscience/butterfly/index.html Make a butterfly optical illusion: http://butterflywebsite.com/Articles/constructlist.cfm?type=kids

Thinking About the Topic

Can that chubby little caterpillar really turn into a beautiful butterfly? It does not seem possible! If you are lucky enough to find a caterpillar or a chrysalis, you might be able to watch a butterfly emerge. How lucky you are if you have seen monarch butterflies resting in trees. They look like leaves. If you did not know they were there, they would be hidden from you. Write about this beautiful insect. You may even like to find out more about a butterfly that you have seen in your neighborhood.

Directions

Read about the butterfly. Have three pieces of paper. Write one question at the top of each page. Answer question 1 and choose any two other questions below. Write your information in complete sentences.

1. Describe the butterfly.

2. What is the life cycle of the butterfly?

3. What are the differences between a butterfly and a moth?

4. How would you raise a butterfly?

5. How do monarchs migrate? Track the monarch who lives in your area of the country.

6. What plants would you use if you want butterflies to live in your garden? Why?

Books

Keywords: *Butterflies—Juvenile literature; Insects; Monarch butterfly.*

Gibbons, Gail. *Monarch Butterfly*. New York: Holiday House, 1989.

Legg, Gerald. *From Caterpillar to Butterfly*. Lifecycles. Danbury, CT: Franklin Watts, 1998.

Pascoe, Elaine. *Butterflies and Moths*. Woodbridge, CT: Blackbird Press, 1997.

Richardson, Adele D. *Butterflies: Pollinators and Nectar Sippers.* Mankato, MN: Bridgestone Books, 2000.

Royston, Angela. *Life Cycle of a Butterfly.* Des Plaines IL: Heinemann First Library, 1998.

World Book Student Discovery Encyclopedia. Chicago: World Book, 2000.

Internet

Enchanted Learning Software	http://www.enchantedlearning.com/crafts/insects/	Insect crafts.
Northern Prairie Wildlife Research Center	http://www.npsc.nbs.gov/resource/distr/lepid/bflyusa/bflyusa.htm	See pictures of the butterflies in your state.
Thornton Jr. High School Honors Academy	http://www.insecta-inspecta.com/butterflies/monarch/index.html	Life cycle and migration routes. Good information on monarch butterflies.
Iowa State University	http://www.ent.iastate.edu/imagegal/lepidoptera/monarch/monarchonalf.html	Pictures of butterfly and caterpillar, and link to article on hazards to monarchs.

Other Resources

Magic School Bus: *Butterflies!* (video). New York: KidVision, 1999.

Monica the Monarch (CD-ROM): http://www2.cybernex.net/~dbenz/moncd.htm

Butterfly Gardening: http://www.butterflywebsite.com/

Monarch Raising: http://home.wi.rr.com/monarchraising. See Kim's Butterflies.

Butterflies. Bug City video series. Wynnewood, PA: Schlessinger Media, 1998.

For the Teacher

Monarch Watch: http://www.monarchwatch.org/class/index.htm

California Teaching Units for the Monarch Butterfly: http://tlc.ai.org/monarch.htm

Adopt a Classroom Monarch Watch Project: http://monarchwatch.org/conserve/adopt.htm Depending on where you live, this may be a wonderful class project.

Joke

Q: Why did John butter his toast and throw it at his sister?

B: To watch the butter fly!

GEORGE WASHINGTON CARVER

> ## Something Extra
>
> Enjoy the George Washington Carver coloring book at
> http://www.usda.gov/oo/colorbook.htm

Thinking About the Topic

Some people become famous for what they can do. They are good ball players or dancers or singers. George Washington Carver was special. He became famous for being smart and for his inventions. When he was a child and he wanted paint, he mixed his own from plants and clay. When he was hungry, he ate seeds. When he needed shoes, he learned to make them, too. After George Washington Carver grew up, he began to use his knowledge of plants to help other people. When their crops would not grow, he figured out why. When the people had too many peanuts, he came up with 300 uses for them. He devoted his whole life to helping the poor people of the South.

Directions

Using several resources, answer question 1 and two other questions below. Write each question at the top of a separate page. Take notes on the pages you create. Your notes should be written in complete sentences. Each question will become a paragraph in your report. After you have found the answers, draw a conclusion about your information. Each conclusion will be the topic sentence for a paragraph.

1. Tell about George Washington Carver's early life.

2. How did George Washing Carver get an education?

3. What are some of the things he invented? Why did he invent them?

4. What did George Washington Carver do that helped people most? Describe this.

5. Why is George Washington Carver a hero of black history?

Books

Keywords: *Carver, George Washington; Inventors; African American Heroes.*

Contemporary Black Biography, Volume 4. Detroit: Gale, 1993.

Hacker, Carlotta. *Great African Americans in History.* New York: Crabtree, 1997.

Knight, Judson. *African American Biography.* Farmington Hills, MI: UXL, 1999.

Kramer, Barbara. *George Washington Carver: Scientist and Inventor.* Berkeley Heights, NJ: Enslow, 2002.

Nicholson, Lois P. *George Washington Carver.* Brookmall, PA: Chelsea House, 1994.

Rustad, Martha E. H. George Washington Carver. Mankato, MN: Capstone Press, 2002.

World Book Encyclopedia of Science: Men and Women of Science. Chicago: World Book, 2001.

Internet

Gale Group	http://www.galegroup.com/free_resources/bhm.htm	You can search by word for the person you want.
National Park Service	http:// www.nps.gov/gwca	George Washington Carver National Monument.
Peanut Institute	http:// www.peanut-institute.org/	All about peanuts.
Original Nut House	http://www.originalnuthouse.com/kids/carver.htm	Brief history of George Washington Carver and peanuts.

Other Resources

The George Washington Carver National Monument has a free film video library: http://www.coax.net/people/LWF/carver.htm

George Washington Carver. Inventors of the World video series. Wynnewood, PA: Schlessinger Media, 2002.

For the Teacher

Lesson plans: http://www.encarta.msn.com/schoolhouse/lessons/results.asp?keyword=Black-LessonPlans

This list of black history sites and lesson plans includes several on Carver: http://www.educationplanet.com/search/History/Black_History/

Joke

Q: Why did George Washington Carver wear red, white, and blue suspenders?

A: To hold up his pants.

CATS IN THE WILD

Something Extra

Play Cat Lotto. Can you recognize the different wild cats?:
www.nhm.org/cats/lotto/index.htm

CyberTyger:
http://www.nationalgeographic.com/features/97/tigers/maina.html

You be the zookeeper on National Geographic's interactive site.

Thinking About the Topic

Grrrrr! The big cat building at the zoo is very popular. The cougar sleeps in the sun. The bobcat has a new baby. The lion roars. The leopard paces back and forth. His shiny yellow eyes make the hair on our arms stand up. Big wild animals are fun to watch, but we are very glad there is a fence between us. If big cats are the animals you like, maybe you can learn more about them.

Directions

Answer question 1 and choose two other questions below. Write one question at the top of each page. Choose one cat, maybe the lion or tiger, or write about big cats in general. Or write about the big cats in Africa or Asia. How are they alike? How are they different? Big wild cats include cougars, lions, pumas, and tigers.

1.   What makes a cat a cat? (Find information about the cat family.)

2.   What do big cats eat? How do they get their food in the wild?

3.   How do big cats care for their young?

4.   What parts of your body can you use to make you move like a big cat? Describe the way the cat moves and prowls for food.

5.   How does the zoo take care of the big cats?

Books

Keywords*: Big Cats; Lion; Large Cats; Wild Cats; Cougar; Tiger; Leopard; Jaguars; Ocelots; Zoo; Cats in captivity.*

Cleve, Andrew. *Big Cats: A Portrait of the Animal World.* Portraits of the Animal World. New York: Todtri Productions, 1998.

Fowler, Allan. *Really Big Cats.* New York: Children's Press, 1998.

Lumpkin, Susan. *Big Cats*. New York: Facts on File, 1993.

Simon, Seymour. *Big Cats*. New York: HarperCollins, 1994.

Veron, Geraldine. *On the Trail: Big Cats*. Hauppeage, NY: Barrons, 1998.

Internet

BigCatsOnline	http://dialspace.dial.pipex.com/ agarman/bco/ver4.htm	Evolution, social and hunting behaviors, conservation, and Web links.
Bridgeport Nature Center	http://greatcatsoftheworld.com	Offers good information on many large cats.
HDW's History & Culture of the Wild Cats in Photos	http://hdw-inc.com/wildcatsphotos4.htm#wildphotos	Pictures and basic information.
Natural History Museum of Los Angeles	http://nhm.org/cats	A traveling exhibit on large cats. This Web site has history of cats and lots more.

Other Resources

Big Cats of Kalahari: Animals of Africa (video). Woodland Hills, CA: Celebrity Home Entertainment, 1991.

The Ultimate Guide to Big Cats (video). Santa Monica, CA: Discovery Channel, 1998.

National Geographic has made several films about big cats. Check out the library and video stores for more good videos.

For the Teacher

Natural History Museum of Los Angeles: http://nhm.org/cats/. Teacher curriculum on their Big Cats exhibit site.

Lesson Plans Page: http://lessonplanspage.com/Science.htm. There are several online lesson plans available on animals in parts of the world.

 Joke

Q: What happened when the lion ate the comedian?

A: He felt funny!

Q. What does the lion say to his friends before they go out hunting for food ?

A: Let us prey.

CHILDREN IN INDIA

> ## Something Extra
>
> A well-known kids' writer in India, Venu Variath, has been in the field of children's literature for the last 20 years. Enjoy the children's stories and games at www.kuttu.com/
>
> Learn a game Indian children play and teach it to your class.

Thinking About the Topic

India is far away. But many families come from India to make their home in the United States. What do they eat? How do they dress? How is their religion different from yours? It is interesting to learn about people who may be different from us. Have fun finding out.

Directions

Read about India in an encyclopedia, then decide how you want to tackle this topic. Do not try to write everything about the children of India. Choose one or two things you would like to know. The best resource would be someone who has come to America from India. Perhaps there is someone in your classroom. Interview that person. Once you decide on a plan, write three open-ended questions about your topic. The first question should serve as background. For example, "Where is India?" Each question will be a paragraph in your report. After you use different resources to answer each of your questions, write a conclusion for each and let the conclusion be your topic sentence.

GOOD QUESTION: What is school in India like?

POOR QUESTION: Do children in India go to school?

Be sure to consider the following topics as questions: games, schools, Hinduism, books and authors, places to visit, music, customs, native costumes, the importance of colors (red wedding dress, golden temple), music, or what it may be like to come to America to live.

Books

Keywords: *India; Children of India; Hinduism—Juvenile Literature.*

Ganeri, Anital. *Journey Through India.* Journey Through. Topeka, KA: Troll, 1999.

Gray, J. E. B. *Tales from India.* Carey, NC: Oxford University Children's Press, 2001.

Heres, Jules. *The Children of India.* Minneapolis, MN: Carolrhoda, 1993.

India. Children of the World. Milwaukee, WI: G. Stevens, 1988.

Kalman, Bobbie. *India: The Culture.* The Lands, Peoples, and Cultures. New York: Crabtree, 2001.

Landau, Elaine. *India.* True Books. Danbury, CT: Children's Press, 2000.

Littlefield, Holly. *Colors of India.* Colors of the World. Minneapolis, MN: Lerner, 2000.

Parker, David. *Stolen Dreams: Portraits of Working Children.* Minneapolis, MN: Lerner, 1998.

Internet

Appukids	http://www.appukids.com/	Site about India's children, games, history, and education.
Child Labor	http://hdrc.undp.org.in/childrenandpoverty/clbour/wdcw.htm	Children and poverty.
Children of India	http://library.thinkquest.org/J0111929/India/	Customs.
Discover India	http://www.4to40.com/discoverindia/default.htm	India today.
Hindu Net	http://www.hindunet.org/	About the Hindu religion.
Hindu Youth	http://www.hinduyouth.com/india/index.htm	Children and religion.
India	http://www.mrdowling.com/612india.html	Good country information.
Pitara	http://www.pitara.com	News, stories, and games from India and other Asian countries.
The Lonely Planet	http://www.lonelyplanet.com/destinations/indian_subcontinent/india	Information about visiting India.

Other Resources

Interview someone who has lived in India. Be very courteous. Have your questions ready. Write a thank you note after the interview.

What Is Hinduism? Understanding World Religions video series. Wynnewood, PA: Schlessinger Media, 2003.

Visit a Hindu religious service with a friend.

Go to an Indian restaurant and enjoy the food. Talk with the owner about the food and spices.

For the Teacher:

Lesson Plan, India: http://fga.freac.fsu.edu/misc/india.htm. For grade three.

10 Day Lesson Plan: http://faculty.acu.edu/~armstrongl/geography/india.htm

English Translation—Indian Express News: http://www.indianexpress.com/

Listen and Enjoy

Check out an audiotape of Indian music. Really listen to it! How is it different from the music you listen to? How does it make you feel?

CHILDREN IN JAPAN

Something Extra

Learn to eat with chopsticks! Take chopsticks to school and teach your friends to use them at lunch:
http://www.jinjapan.org/kidsweb/cook/intro/intro2.html

Thinking About the Topic

If you dug a hole through the earth to the other side, would you get to Japan? Have you ever wanted to try? Japan is half a world away and very different from the United States, and yet many things are the same in both countries. Explore the differences and similarities.

Directions

Read about Japan in an encyclopedia and decide how you want to tackle this topic. Choose one or two things you would like to know. Use books and Web sites to find your answers. One of the best resources would be someone who has come to America from Japan. If there is someone in your classroom, interview that person. Answer three questions about your topic. Each question will be a paragraph in your report. After you answer each of your questions, write a conclusion for each and let the conclusion be your topic sentence.

1. Describe the land of Japan. How is the land used? What problems do the people of Japan have?

2. Discuss education in Japan. What do Japanese children learn that you do not? What is different about their education from yours? What is the same?

3. What do the Japanese do for entertainment? Compare their activities to what you and your friends do.

4. Describe Japanese food. What do the children eat? How is it different from what you eat?

5. Describe a Japanese custom that is different from yours and compare it to yours.

6. What are some ways children in Japan are different from children in America?

Books

Keywords: *Japan; Japanese; Tokyo—Juvenile Literature; Children in Japan.*

Costain, Meredith. *Welcome to Japan.* Brookmall, PA: Chelsea House, 2001.

Gall, Timothy L., and Susan B. Gall, eds. *Junior Worldmark Encyclopedia of the Nations.* 2nd ed. Detroit: UXL, 1999.

Gresko, Marcia. *Letters Home from Japan.* Farmington Hills, MI: Blackbirch Marketing, 2000.

Kallen, Stuart A. *Life in Tokyo.* Farmington Hills, MI: Lucent, 2000.

Lands and Peoples. Danbury, CT: Grolier, 2001.

Stefoff, Rebecca. *Japan.* Brookmall, PA: Chelsea House, 1998.

Witherick, M. E. *Japan.* Crystal Lake, IL: Heinemann, 2000.

World Book Encyclopedia. Chicago: World Book, 2002.

Internet

Japan Information Network	http://www.jinjapan.org/kidsweb/	What's cool in Japan, basic facts, sports, legends, schools, and more.
Yahooligans	http://www.yahooligans.com/around_the_world/countries/japan/Cultures_and_Traditions/	Japanese culture and traditions.
John Donaldson	http://www.sover.net/~johnd/categories.html	Pictures of Japanese children, schools, kites, and games.

Other Resources

Climb to the top of Mount Fuji: http://www.kids-japan.com/

Quick time videos of Japanese buildings and nature scenes: http://www.kiku.com/qtvr/index.html

Interview a classmate or neighbor who is from Japan.

For the Teacher

Lesson plans on Asian culture: http://www.askasia.org/for_educators/instructional_resources/lesson_plans/less_plan.htm

Access Asia lesson plans: http://www.curriculum.edu.au/accessasia/catalog/lesson.htm

Read aloud the beautiful and sad *Sadako and the Thousand Paper Cranes* by Eleanor Coerr (New York: Putnam, 1977). Have the class make origami paper cranes.

Joke

Alex: Are you taking a ship or a plane to Japan?

Andy: Actually, I thought I'd take a suitcase instead.

CHILDREN IN MEXICO

Something Extra

Write your report. Copy and paste it at http://translation. langenberg.com/. Let this Web site translate it into Spanish.

Learn a few words in Spanish to impress your classmates.

Thinking About the Topic

Hola, los chicos y las chicas. Es divertido aprender acerca de México.
Many families come from Mexico to make their home in the United States. It is one of only two countries that share our borders. You probably know someone who has moved from Mexico. Talk to that person about his or her family and culture. Does this person speak two languages? Ask him or her about it.

Directions

Read about Mexico in an encyclopedia and decide how you want to tackle this big topic. Do not try to write everything about the children of Mexico. Choose one or two things you would like to know. The best resource would be someone who has come to America from Mexico. Perhaps there is someone in your classroom. Ask that person about his or her culture and tell that person about yours. Once you decide on a plan, write three open-ended questions about your topic. The first question should serve as background, for example, "What is Mexico like?" Each question will be a paragraph in your report. After you use different resources to answer each of your questions, write a conclusion for each and let the conclusion be your topic sentence.

GOOD QUESTION: What is school in Mexico like?

POOR QUESTION: Do children in Mexico go to school?

Here are several topics you may want to learn about:

• What do the children of Mexico eat?

• How do they dress?

• Is their religion different from yours?

• What about their holiday celebrations?

• Have fun finding out how children in Mexico may be different from you.

• How are they alike?

Books

Keywords: *Mexico; Children in Mexico; Children around the world.*

Costain, Meredith. *Welcome to Mexico.* Brookmall, PA: Chelsea House, 2001.

Gall, Timothy L., and Susan B. Gall, eds. *Junior Worldmark Encyclopedia of the Nations.* 2nd ed. Detroit: UXL, 1999.

Lands and Peoples. Danbury, CT: Grolier, 2001.

Mexico. By Mary Jo Reilly and Leslie Jermyn. Cultures of the World. New York: Marshall Cavendish, 2002.

World Book Encyclopedia. Chicago: World Book, 2002.

Internet

Mexico for Kids	http://www.elbalero.gob.mx/index_kids.html	This site contains history, games, information about government, and places to visit.
Day of the Dead	http://www.inside-mexico.com/featuredead.htm	Find out about this special holiday.
The Lonely Planet Mexico	http://www.lonelyplanet.com/destinations/north_america/mexico/	About Mexico—from travel publishers.

Other Resources

Interview someone who has lived in Mexico, maybe a classmate or a parent.

Mexican-American Heritage. Produced and directed by Alexandria Productions, Inc. American Cultures for Children video series. Wynnewood, PA: Schlessinger Video Productions, c1997.

Visit a Mexican restaurant and enjoy the food. Talk with the owner about the food and spices.

For the Teacher:

There are many lesson plans on the Web for a classroom study of Mexican culture. Try http://www.atozteacherstuff.com/themes/mexico.shtml

Studying about the children in Mexico (or other countries) presents a golden opportunity to celebrate diversity.

Listen and Enjoy

Check out salsa or another type of Mexican music on audiotape from your library. Listen carefully to the joyful sounds.

CHILDREN IN NIGERIA

> **Something Extra**
>
> Play the Nigerian game of Ayo:
> http://www.motherlandnigeria.com/games/ayo.html

Thinking About the Topic

Long ago and far away, the country that is now Nigeria was part of the Kingdom of Songhay. At the time it was important for gold, spices, and trade. Now it is still an important country for trade, but it trades oil and art. Native Nigerians are black, and they have a very rich culture. Find out about it. Look at their art and listen to their music. You will love it. Then write about children in Nigeria.

Directions

You may want to choose a different African country. Answer the same questions about that country. Read about Nigeria in an encyclopedia, then decide how you want to tackle this project. Are you most interested in school, games, or the way people dress? Choose one or two things you would like to know. If you know someone who has come to America from Nigeria, he or she would be your best resource. Interview that person. Once you decide on a plan, write three open-ended questions about your topic. The first question should serve as background, for example, "What is Nigeria like?" The answer to each question will be a paragraph in your report. Use different resources to answer each of your questions. Write a conclusion for each question and use it for your topic sentence.

1. Describe how children of Nigeria dress, wear their hair, etc. How are their clothes different from the way you dress?

2. Describe the land of Nigeria. In what ways do the people take advantage of their land?

3. Discuss Nigerian schools. Do all children go to school? Why? What do children do if they do not attend school?

4. What do Nigerians do for entertainment?

5. Describe a Nigerian custom that is different from yours, such as marriage, naming children, or death and burial. Compare it to your custom.

Books

Keywords: *Nigeria; West Africa; Children in Africa; Children in Nigeria.*

Freville, Nicholas. *Nigeria.* Brookmall, PA: Chelsea House, 2000.

Gall, Timothy L., and Susan B. Gall, eds. *Junior Worldmark Encyclopedia of the Nations.* 2nd ed. Detroit: UXL, 1999.

Lands and Peoples. Danbury, CT: Grolier, 2001.

Meniru, Teresa—Nigerian children's author

Nnoromele, Salome. *Nigeria.* Farmington Hills, MI: Lucent, 2001.

Parris, Ronals G. *Hausa.* New York: Rosen, 1996.

World Book Encyclopedia of People and Places. Chicago: World Book, 2000. Available online at http://www2.worldbook.com

Worldmark Encyclopedia of Cultures and Daily Life. Detroit: Gale, 1998.

Internet

Consulate General of Nigeria	http://www.nigeria-consulate-ny.org/facts.htm	Basic facts about Nigeria.
Motherland Nigeria	http://www.motherlandnigeria.com/kidzone.html	Nigerian stories, proverbs, jokes, and language.
University Scholars Programme	http://www.scholars.nus.edu.sg/landow/post/nigeria/iboov.html	Beliefs of the Ibo people of Nigeria.
Library of Congress	http://lcweb2.loc.gov/frd/cs/ngtoc.html	"Nigeria—A Country Study." For older students.
International Foundation for Nigerian Children	http://www.ifnc.org/pictures.html	Photographs of Nigerian children.

Other Resources

Listen to Nigerian music: http://www.motherlandnigeria.com/music.html#juju_music

Nigerian medicinal plants: http://www.worldbank.org/globallinks/english/environment.html

See if there is someone from Nigeria to interview. Perhaps someone has visited Nigeria.

For the Teacher

Lesson plans on Africa: http://fga.freac.fsu.edu/academy/

Nigerian lesson plans, including water, desertification, storytelling, and school rules: http://www.uni.edu/gai/Nigeria/Lessons/Nigerian_Lesson_Plans.html

---

Map Fun

Draw a map of Nigeria. Draw pictures to represent some of the important features of the country. Show it to your class.

CLONING

> ## Something Extra
>
> Genes Activity Page:
> http://www.brainpop.com/health/growthanddevelopment/genes/
> activity.weml

Thinking About the Topic

Purr. You cuddle with your kitten. It is so soft and sweet. You wish there were two just the same. But do you really? Scientists have tried for years to make another creature just like the first one. Your kitten is unique. Would it make it less special if there were two? Cloning is very controversial. Some people believe scientists are finding new ways of understanding nature and others believe this is morally wrong. Read about it. Try to understand what cloning is and how it can help scientists.

Directions

Using several resources, answer questions 1 and 5 and at least one other question below. Write each question on the top of a page. Take notes on each answer. Your notes should be written in complete sentences. After you have found the answers, draw a conclusion about your information. Your sentences will form a paragraph. Your conclusion will be the topic sentence for the paragraph.

1.   What is cloning?

2.   How does a cloned animal differ from a natural one? How is it the same?

3.   Would you clone your favorite pet? Discuss the good things and the bad things about it.

4.   Read about Dolly the sheep (or another cloned animal). How is she different from other sheep? What about her babies?

5.   Discuss other uses of cloning rather than duplicating animals or humans. How can this help us?

Books

Keywords: *Cloning; Genetics; Genetic Engineering.*

DuPrau, Jeanne. *Cloning.* San Diego: Lucent, 2000.

Engelbert, Phyllis. *Technology in Action: Science Applied to Everyday Life.* Detroit: UXL, 1998.

Nardo, Don. *Cloning.* Farmington Hills, MI: Lucent, 2001.

New Book of Popular Science. Danbury, CT: Grolier, 2000.

Nicolson, Cynthia Pratt. *Baa! The Most Interesting Book You'll Ever Read About Genes and Cloning.* Tonawanda, NY: Kids Can Press, 2001.

Richardson, Hazel. *How to Clone a Sheep.* New York: Franklin Watts, 2001.

Schmittroth, Linda, Mary R. McCall, and Bridget Travers. *Eureka.* New York: UXL, 1999.

Travers, Bridget, and Fran Locher Freidman, eds. *Medical Discoveries and the People Who Developed Them.* Detroit: UXL, 1997.

Internet

Information Please	http://www.infoplease.com/ipa/A-0193003.html	"Cloning: Facts and Fallacies."
Massachusetts Institute of Technology	http://esg-www.mit.edu:8001/esgbio/rdna/cloning.html	How genes are cloned.
Gene School	http://library.thinkquest.org/28599/cloning.htm	Definition of cloning, and pros and cons.
Eureka ! Science Corp.	http://www.eurekascience.com/ICanDoThat/cloning.htm	History of cloning. Neat site with lots of kid-friendly information.
Time Magazine Pathfinder	http://www.pathfinder.com/TIME/cloning/home.html	All about Dolly, the cloned sheep.

Other Resources

Games and a movie about genes: http://www.brainpop.com/health/growthanddevelopment/genes/

Animated or audio/video introduction to genetics and DNA: http://www.dnaftb.org/dnaftb/

For the Teacher

Lesson plans and standards from the University of Kansas Medical Center: http://www.kumc.edu/gec/lessons.html. Most are for older students but some are for elementary school grades.

Links to a wide variety of genetics sites: http://www.healthwindows.org/body_genetics.asp

---

Map Fun

Q: What would you get if you cloned a 300-pound chicken?
A: The biggest cluck on the farm!

Q: What do you get when you make an exact duplicate of Texas?
A: Clone Star State!

COCA-COLA

> **Something Extra**
>
> Track the stock market growth of Coca-Cola for a period of time. Create a chart.
>
> Compose an advertising campaign for selling your own brand of soft drink. Make a large display.
>
> Time yourself on the Coca-Cola Word Search Puzzle at http://www.geocities.com/Heartland/Pointe/2132/sccppuzzle.html

Thinking About the Topic

Coca-Cola is considered one of the great inventions of all times. Why? Consider your options: write about the history of Coca-Cola, Coke collectibles, advertising campaigns, the inventor, or the growth of the company. You may even conduct a taste test comparing Coke to another soft drink. Set up a table in your class, offer Pepsi and Coke, and take a satisfaction survey. Create a graph of the results of your survey to share with your class. Look up other such surveys and compare your results with those. If you are interested in business and math, write about the company today and track Coca-Cola stock.

Directions

Read about Coke in an encyclopedia, then decide how you want to tackle this topic. Do not try to write about everything. It will be confusing and result in a poorly written paper. Once you decide on a plan (comparing Coke with another company, collectibles, advertising, or Coke history) write three open-ended questions about your topic. The first question should serve as background. For example, "Why do people collect Coca-Cola memorabilia?" Write about some of the collectibles. Each question will be a paragraph in your report. After you use different resources to answer each of your questions, write a conclusion for each and let the conclusion be your topic sentence.

GOOD QUESTION: Why is Coca-Cola considered one of the great inventions?

POOR QUESTION: Is Coca-Cola considered one of the great inventions?

Books

Keywords: *Coca Cola; Inventions; Advertising in America; Collectibles.*

"Coca-Cola." In *Britannica Encyclopedia Online* at http://www.britannica.com/ (or in your library).

Moupin, Melissa. *The Story of Coca Cola*. Mankato, MN: Smart Apple Media, 2003.

Suid, Murry. *Made in America: Eight Great All-American Inventions*. Reading, MA: Addison-Wesley, 1978.

Watters, Pat. *Coca Cola: An Illustrated History*. Garden City, NY: Doubleday, 1978.

Internet

Coca Cola Trivia and History	http://cocacola.com	This site is by Coca-Cola, so spend time here. Look at "About Coca-Cola."
Historic Coke Ads	http://memory.loc.gov/ammem/ccmphtml/colahome.html	From the Library of Congress.
Coca Cola History, Games, Trivia, Advertisements	http://www.geocities.com/Heartland/4269/history.html	Site created by a Coke fan.
The World of Soda Fountains	http://www.candykitchenonline.com/history_of_soda_fountains.htm	A little soda history.
Coca-Cola History and Bottle Collecting Information	http://www2.netdoor.com/~davidroy/cocacola.html	Collectibles and history.

Other Resources

View Coca-Cola ads (online video): http://memory.loc.gov/ammem/ccmphtml/cccap.html

History of Coca-Cola (online video): http://heritage.coca-cola.com/

Write to the Coca-Cola company and ask for their annual report or other information. Or call a local representative. Local phone numbers and e-mails are available online at http://www2.coca-cola.com. Make a display to go with your oral report.

Ask Coca-Cola: http://questions.coca-cola.com/vrep/CokeSay.htm. Write with your questions.

For the Teacher

Coca-Cola Recipes: http://sassman.net/secret/coke_recipes.html

Food Time Line with Links: http://gti.net/mocolib1/kid/food.html

Here is a great math project! Try a taste test in your classroom. Plot customer satisfaction. Have the students write the questions and graph the information

---

Riddle

Q: How many Pepsi drinkers does it take to wallpaper a room?

A: It depends on how thinly you slice them.

COLLECTING

> ## Something Extra
>
> Make a flower press and collect wildflowers:
> http://wildnetafrica.co.za/wildlifestuff/juniorpage/flowers/
> flowers.html

Thinking About the Topic

Coins, baseball cards, fashion dolls, beanie babies, action figures—people of all ages love to collect things. It is exciting to watch your collection grow. What a thrill when you find a missing piece! If you write about your collection, bring it to the classroom to share during your report.

Directions

Pick a certain type of collection such as stamps, coins, baseball cards, or Barbie dolls. Try not to pick anything that is too unusual. You might not be able to find enough information. Choose three questions to answer. Use several books or Web sites to find information for each question. Draw a conclusion from the notes you take. The conclusion will be your topic sentence. Use the other note-taking details to complete each paragraph.

1. What are several reasons people enjoy collecting things?

2. Describe your collectible. What distinguishing features do you look for?

3. What is the history of your collectible? How should you decide what to keep and what not to keep?

4. How could you go about collecting this item? Will the collection ever be complete?

5. Discuss collectors' groups or clubs.

Books

Keywords: Use the subject that interests you—plus *Collectors and Collecting,* for example, *Sports Cards—Collectors and Collecting,* or *Dolls—Collectors and Collecting.*

Lemke, Bob, ed. *Standard Catalog of Baseball Cards.* Iola, WI: Krause, 1998.

Scott Standard Postage Stamp Catalog. Sidney, OH: Scott, 2002.

Yeoman, R. S. *Handbook of United States Coins.* New York: St. Martin's Press, 2002.

Internet

Smithsonian Institution	http://kids.si.edu/collecting/	Collecting for kids, especially coins, rocks, and stamps.
British North American Philatelic Society	http://www.bnaps.org/stamps4kids/pre.htm	Stamp collecting for kids.
University of Kentucky	http://www.uky.edu/Agriculture/Entomology/ythfacts/bugfun/collecti.htm	Insect collecting techniques.
Topps Trading Cards	http://www.topps.com/SportsCollect/index.html	History of sports trading cards.
COA	http://erato.acnatsci.org/conchnet/fun.html	Shell collecting, with facts, jokes, and a quiz.

Other Resources

This is a great opportunity for a visit to a collector's house. Do you know someone who collects stamps or shells? See if you can interview that person. Take good notes if you are going to "quote" your source. Take a camera.

Take a trip to the local post office and talk to someone about stamp collecting.

For the Teacher

The Boy Scouts Collection merit badge could be a starting point for a lesson on collecting: http://www.usscouts.org/usscouts/mb/mb128.html

LessonPlanz has several lessons on collecting, but you'll have to do a keyword search to find them: http://lessonplanz.com/upperelementary.shtml

---

Joke

Joey: The trouble with you, Bennett, is that you are always wishing for the things you don't have.

Bennett: What else is there to wish for?

COMING TO AMERICA

Something Extra

Make a friend of someone whose native language is not English. Have that person tell you about his or her homeland. Visit each other's homes.

Thinking About the Topic

We come from different places, speak different languages,
are different colors, eat different foods,
wear different clothes, have different religions,
follow different customs, yet we are all Americans.

—Thinkquest, http://library.thinkquest.org/CR0212700/final_website/~

Today children from all over the world are coming to America. These children are called immigrants. Except for Native Americans, all Americans have been immigrants. Think about how it would feel to leave your friends and family to go and live in a land where everything is different. Maybe you would never see them again. Learn a little about what it might be like by researching this topic.

Directions

You can research immigrants or narrow your topic to a specific person or group of people. When you are ready, select question 1 and two others below. Write one question at the top of each page. Look in several sources for the answers to your questions. Each question will become a paragraph in your report. Draw a conclusion from the answers you find. The conclusion will be your topic sentence. For example, the conclusion for question 2 might be, "Everything is different in America, so families face many problems when they arrive."

1. What is an immigrant?
2. What are some of the problems families face when they arrive in America?
3. What do the children have to face when they come to America?
4. What are some of the reasons people might leave their homeland? (Be specific and give examples if you write about this question.)
5. What was it like arriving in Ellis Island? What is it like coming across the border from Mexico or Canada?

Books

Keywords: *Immigrants; English as a Second Language; ESL; Immigration.*

I Was Dreaming of Come to America: Memories from the Ellis Island Oral History Project.
Glenview Lake, IL: Scott Foresman, 1997.

Schlesinger, Yaffa. *An Interview with My Grandparent.* New York: McGraw-Hill, 1998.

Strom, Yale. *Quilted Landscape: Conversations with Young Immigrants.* New York: Simon & Schuster, 1996.

Whitman, Sylvia. *Immigrant Children.* New York: Carolrhoda Books, 2000.

Internet

American Immigration	http://www.bergen.org/AAST/ Projects/Immigration/	A tenth-grade class put this page together. Very good information.
Coming to America	http://library.thinkquest.org/ CR0212700/final_website/	Do not miss this site of interviews, recipes, interactivity, and history.
Ellis Island	http://www.ellisisland.org/	Do a little family research if your family members came to America through Ellis Island.
Immigration / Naturalization Service (INS)	http://www.ins.usdoj.gov/	The U.S. government agency that oversees immigration.
The Immigration Journey	http://www.libertystatepark.com /immigran.htm	A little history of how people come to America.
Virtual Tour of Ellis Island	http://www.capital.net/~alta/ index.html	Good information about the immigration process by a middle school class.

Other Resources

Interview someone in your class or neighborhood who is from another country. Take notes.

Citizenship Course Video with Booklet. American Immigration Center. Order online at http://www.us-immigration.com/store/browse/showProduct/304

Immigration. American History for Children video series. Wynnewood, PA: Schlessinger Media, 1996.

Two movies to rent and watch with your family are *Coming to America* and *Green Card.*

For the Teacher

In English, of Course, by Josephine Nobisso (Westhampton Beach, NY: Gingerbread House, 2002), is an excellent read-aloud picture book about multicultural miscommunications and learning to understand the talents of newcomers to America.

Coming to America: http://library.thinkquest.org/CR0212700/final_website/. This is one of the best sites you will find. It includes stories of immigrants (oral histories) and everything you want to know about the process of coming to America. Be sure to use the bibliography.

Have fun translating your own language to another:

http://translation.langenberg.com/

COMMON COLD

Something Extra

Make mucus! As a bonus, you can build some boogers:
http://www.beakman.bonus.com/beakman/mucus/mucus.html.

Thinking About the Topic

"I'b so tired! My dose is all stuffy and I can't breed. I hate habbing a cold!" Everybody gets colds. Usually you will get one two or three times a year. But nobody likes it! If you learn more about the common cold, you may be able to avoid having it. Wouldn't that be nice?

Directions

Following are some questions about the common cold. Select or write three questions. Write each question at the top of a sheet of paper. Answer the question from the research you have done. This will form a paragraph for your report. Then write a conclusion for each question. This conclusion will be your topic sentence for each paragraph. Use the details from your notes to complete the paragraph.

1.   What causes a cold?

2.   What can you do to avoid colds?

3.   Describe three ways to treat a cold.

4.   Adults don't usually get colds as easily as children. Why?

5.   Discuss the differences between a cold and the flu or allergies.

Books

Keywords: *Cold (Disease); Common Cold.*

Bunch, Bryan, ed. *Diseases*. Danbury CT: Grolier, 1997.

Engelbert, Phyllis. *Technology in Action: Science Applied to Everyday Life*. Detroit: UXL, 1998.

Kittredge, Mary. *Common Cold*. Brookmall, PA: Chelsea House, 2000.

New Book of Popular Science. Danbury, CT: Grolier, 2000.

Schmittroth, Linda, Mary R. McCall, and Bridget Travers. *Eureka*. New York: UXL, 1999.

Travers, Bridget, and Fran Locher Freidman, eds. *Medical Discoveries and the People Who Developed Them*. Detroit: UXL, 1997.

Internet

Commoncold, Inc.	http://www.commoncold.org/	Colds. How do you get them? How do you treat them?
Kidsource Online	http://www.kidsource.com/health/the.common.cold.html	Basic facts and prevention of colds.
Kidshealth	http://kidshealth.org/kid/ill_injure/sick/colds.html	Chilling out with colds.
National Institutes of Health	http://www.niaid.nih.gov/factsheets/cold.htm	Fact sheet on colds.

Other Resources

Watch ciliated nasal epithelium sweep away bacteria: http://www-micro.msb.le.ac.uk/video/cilia.html

Ask your own doctor or nurse to talk with you about colds and avoiding them. Treat your conversation like an interview. Have your questions ready and take notes. Don't forget the thank you note. (You might take a camera.)

Ask the school librarian if he or she has a good video you can watch. The librarian may know of one that does not show up when you look at the catalog.

For the Teacher

Have the class make a booklet on "How to Survive the Common Cold": http://www.eduplace.com/rdg/gen_act/survival/survive.html

Introduce Ogden Nash's poem, "The Common Cold." Give extra credit for students who memorize it: http://www.cs.rice.edu/~ssiyer/minstrels/poems/325.html

---

Joke

Q: Which is faster, hot or cold?

A: Hot is faster. You can catch cold.

COMMUNICATING ON THE WEB

Something Extra

A cool kids' site where you can chat with children's authors, help write a progressive story, or learn about travel buddies: http://www.tesan.vuurwerk.nl/diaries/

Thinking About the Topic

Are you interested in how other kids around the world think, act, and talk? Would you like to meet them without leaving home? Do you have a friend who has moved, or have you moved? With e-mail, you can write to people anywhere in the world. You just have to know their e-mail addresses! Give someone your e-mail address, and he or she can write to you. With chat, you can have a live conversation with your friend. If you each have See You See Me cameras, you can see each other via your computer as you chat. What if you do not know anyone to write to? Write your parent at work. You can try a chat room or discussion group. Just be sure it's a safe site for kids!

Directions

Following are some questions about Internet chat and e-mail. Choose one or the other to write about. Select or write three questions. Write each question at the top of a sheet of paper. Answer the question from the research you have done. This will form a paragraph for your report. Then write a conclusion for each question. Each conclusion will be your topic sentence for its paragraph.

1. What do we mean by "communicating on the Web?"

2. How are e-mail, chat, and discussion groups different? The same?

3. How does e-mail (or listservs or chat rooms) work?

4. Discuss the netiquette of chat rooms. What are some things you should do? What shouldn't you do?

5. Show some emoticons and abbreviations often used in e-mail and chat. What do they mean? Why would you use them?

Books

Keywords: *Internet—Juvenile; World Wide Web—Juvenile; Electronic Mail Systems—Juvenile; Communication—Internet.*

Brimner, Larry Dane. *E-Mail.* New York: Children's Press, 1997.

Marshall, Elizabeth L. *A Student's Guide to the Internet.* Brockfield, CT: Twenty-First Century Books, 2001.

Ronney, Anne. *Chilling Out: How to Use the Internet to Make the Most of Your Free Time.* New York: Sterling, 2000.

Wolinsky, Art. *Communicating on the Internet.* Berkeley Heights, NJ: Enslow, 1999.

Internet

Headbone	http://www.headbone.com/	Kids' site for chat, games, and features.
Kids World	http://www.kidsworld.org/	Kids chat with monitors who are other kids from around the world.
KidsCom	http://www.kidscom.com/home_flash.html	Meet other kids from around the world, create your own home page, play games, and chat. Great site!
Kids Chat	http://members.tripod.com/kidchat/	Get help with your homework!

Other Resources

You can ask questions of NASA scientists. You questions may be answered on a Webcast (a report given over the Internet) you can watch from your computer: http://quest.nasa.gov/

Telecommunications. How Things Work video series. Wynnewood, PA: Schlessinger Media, 2002.

For the Teacher

Register your students for online pen pals from around the world at http://www.kidscom.com/friends/keypal/teachers.html

Educators' chat room! Tune in at specified times for prearranged topics: http://teachers.net/chat/

A cautionary site showing what can happen to unwary children: http://www.chatdanger.com

---

Chat

Have a question about your research paper? Log on to our library and chat with a librarian at http://kclibrary.nhmccd.edu

---

CONSUMERS CAN BE KIDS

> ## Something Extra
>
> Think of something that you buy regularly. Create a chart comparing the prices for the item in at least four different stores. (Use the phone if you can't get a ride there. Can you find the item on the Internet? If so, add that price.)

Thinking About the Topic

Researchers say that television viewers up to age eight years old cannot distinguish advertising from regular television programming. In 1997, kids under 12 spent $24 billion of their own pocket money. Those two facts alone show us how important it is for kids to become knowledgeable consumers. If you have your own pocket money, this will be a good topic for you.

Directions

When you are ready, select question 1 and two others below. Write one question at the top of each page. Look in several sources for the answers to your questions. Each question will become a paragraph in your report. Draw a conclusion from the answers you find. The conclusion will be your topic sentence. This is a good topic for you to think about and create your own ideas as well as using what books and the Internet tell you.

1. What is a consumer?

2. What are several ways you can become a smart consumer? **Hint:** Being a smart consumer is not only about buying. What can you do to keep from being ripped off?

3. What do we mean by "truth in advertising?" Find and list rules advertisers should follow when selling to children.

4. Discuss an advertising campaign that you like or do not like. For example, Coca-Cola, no-smoking ads, Barbies, fast food, or Reebok.

Books

Keywords: *Consumers—Juvenile Literature. Advertising to Children; Marketing to Children.*

Acuff, Daniel S., and Robert H. Reiher. *What Kids Buy and Why: The Psychology of Marketing to Kids.* New York: Dimensions, 1997.

Guber, Selina S. *Marketing to and Through Kids.* New York: McGraw-Hill, 1993.

Kids Are Consumers. Kids Make a Difference. Washington, DC: National Geographic Society, 2001.

McNeal, James U. *Kids As Customers: A Handbook of Marketing to Children.* New York: Lexington, 1992.

More Fun, Less Stuff. (Buy online at http://www.newdream.org/award/kids/)

Internet

Advertising and Kids	http://www.iwebquest.com/ responsible/advertising.htm	Excellent information.
Consumer Reports for Kids	http://www.zillions.org/	Have your say about the products you buy.
Kid's Consumer Corner	http://tqjunior.thinkquest.org/ 3643	From *ThinkQuest*. See the "Fast Foods" *ThinkQuest* module, too.
Kids Are Consumers, Too	http://www.state.ma.us/ consumer/Pubs/hol-kids.htm	Advice about wise consuming. Includes a sample letter about getting a bad deal. Know your consumer rights.
Kids Targeted Ads	http://www.newdream.org/ award/kids/	One of the best sites for information.
Rules for Advertising to Kids	http://www.media-awareness. ca/eng/med/class/teamedia/ adrls2.htm	Standard guidelines when advertising for children.
Tobacco Free Campaign	http://tobaccofreekids.org/	This would be a good site to study.

Other Resources

Buy Me That! (video). A kid's guide to food advertising. HBO & Consumer Reports. Chicago: Films Incorporated Video, 1992.

Look for a CD of radio ads. Analyze a few. Play them for your class as part of your report.

Create a marketing campaign for something that both you and your parents use. After reading about advertising, market your product for your age group.

For the Teacher

This topic is perfect for a class unit on consumerism and marketing to children. See http://www.zillions.org/ for surveys and ad campaigns and *Ad Campaign Lesson Plans* at http://website.education.wisc.edu/rla/ADSITE/index.htm

Kids Make a Difference Series. Write National Geographic and get a Teacher's Guide and Assessment Book for *Kids Are Consumers*. Ordering information online at http://national geographic.com

Psychologists Challenge Ethics of Marketing to Children. Background information from Media Channel: http://www.mediachannel.org/originals/kidsell.shtml

Joke

I never worry about money. Why worry about something you don't have?

DAVY CROCKETT

Something Extra

Find a copy of the Disney song, "The Ballad of Davy Crockett," and play it when you give your report. See if you can find a coonskin hat!

Write your own Davy Crockett knock knock joke:

> Knock knock
> Who's there?
> Gravy!
> Gravy who?
> Gravy Crockett!

Thinking About the Topic

> *"Davy! Davy Crockett!*
> *King of the Wild Frontier!"*

Davy Crockett was a real pioneer who has become an American folk hero. He was born in Tennessee over a hundred years ago. He was a statesman, a pioneer, and a frontiersman. He is remembered for his coonskin cap, his famous rifle, his love of the West, and his storytelling. Read his speech to Congress (see the Internet address below) and you will learn the way this backwoodsman talked. Books are your best resource for writing about Davy Crockett. There are plenty of them.

Directions

Davy Crockett will be a great American folk hero to write about. Read a summary of his life in an encyclopedia before you begin your report. Select three questions (including the first) below. Answer each question by using several resources. Draw a conclusion about each answer. The conclusion will be the topic sentence for each paragraph.

1. Who was Davy Crockett? Why is he considered an American hero?
2. What was his early life like?
3. What was the Tennessee Volunteer Militia? Tell about Davy's experiences with them.
4. Davy Crockett was a statesman. Tell about his life in the state legislature and Congress.
5. What did Davy Crocket do that makes us know he loved the West?
6. Davy Crockett ended his life in Texas. Where and how did he die?

Books

Keywords*: Crockett, David.*

Abbott, John S. C. *David Crockett: His Life and Adventures.* Electronic Text Center, University of Virginia Library: etext.lib.virginia.edu/ebooks/subjects/subjects-young.html. Use the table of contents to find the information you need in this online book.

Adler, David A. *A Picture Book of Davy Crockett.* New York: Holiday House, 1998.

Parks, Aileen Wells. *Davy Crockett: Young Rifleman.* Childhood of Famous Americans Series. New York: Aladdin, 1986.

Retan, Walter. *The Story of Davy Crockett Frontier Hero.* Famous Lives. Milwaukee, WI: Gareth Stevens, 1997.

Santrey, Laurence. *Davy Crockett: Young Pioneer.* Mahwah, NJ: Troll, 1989.

Internet

Biography and Timeline	http://www.infoporium.com/heritage/crockbio.shtml	Information about Davy Crockett's life. Timelines are always helpful.
Davy Crockett	http://www.infoporium.com/heritage/crockett.shtml	About his life.
Davy Crockett	http://www.lsjunction.com/people2/crockett.htm	More about Davy.
Davy Crockett	http://www.britannica.com/eb/article?eu=28391&tocid=0	*Encyclopedia Britannica* article

Other Resources

American Tall Tales: Davy Crockett (video). Allen, TX: Lyrick Studios, 1991.

Ballad of Davy Crockett Words and Music: http://www.geocities.com/apembert45/music/Crockett.html

Classic Disney: 60 Years of Musical Magic (sound recording). Burbank, CA: Walt Disney Records, 1997.

Davy Crockett: King of the Wild Frontier (video). (Starring Fess Parker). Burbank, CA: Walt Disney Home Video, 1955.

Speech to Congress: http://www.towson.edu/~duncan/crockett.html

For the Teacher

Sally Ann Thunder Ann Whirlwind Crockett: A Tall Tale, by Steven Kellogg (New York: Morrow, 1995). Read aloud this uproarious tale about Davy Crockett's wife.

The Davy Crockett Almanac and Book of Lists, by William R. Chemerka (Austin, TX: Eakin, 2000). Highly recommended book with facts and bulleted lists. Terrific background for a teaching unit.

> **Quote**
>
> Davy Crockett said when he heard reports of his own death in 1816:
> "I know'd this was a whapper of a lie, as soon as I heard it."

TOMIE DEPAOLA

Something Extra

Strega Nona has nothing on you! Surprise your class with a HUGE crockpot of garlic and butter spaghetti on the day of your report. Make it yourself. Be sure to get permission from your teacher.

Thinking About the Topic

Tomie dePaola is a beloved author and illustrator of children's books. He wrote his first book when he was ten years old. Begin by reading and studying a few Tomie dePaola books. Study his illustrations. Since we are from Texas, *The Legend of the Bluebonnet* is one of our favorite books. But our favorite characters are Strega Nona and Big Anthony.

Directions

You have many options. You can write about dePaola's life or you can focus on the illustrations or the stories. You might even compare Mr. dePaola's art with the illustrations of another author you enjoy. Select three questions below, including question 1. Each of your questions will be a paragraph in your paper. The conclusion you draw will be the title sentence for your paragraph of information.

1.   Who is Tomie dePaola? What does he do? Tell a little about his life.

2.   What jobs has Mr. dePaola had? How do you think they helped him become such a good writer and illustrator?

3.   Where does he get ideas for his stories?

4.   What awards has he won? Why do you think he has won so many awards?

5.   Do you think Mr. dePaola is the best illustrator for his own stories? Why or why not?

Books

Keywords: *dePaola, Tomie* (To find information *about* Mr. dePaola, use a subject search. Otherwise, the books and videos you find will be *by* him.)

Author Talk. Edited by Marcus Leonard. Riverside, NJ: Simon & Schuster, 2000.

Biography for Beginners. Detroit: Omnigraphics, 1998.

Biography Today Author Series, Volume 5. Detroit: Omnigraphics, 1999.

"Creators of Favorite Children's Books Talk About Their Work." In *Meet the Authors and Illustrators, Volume I.* Scranton, PA: Scholastic Paperbacks, 1993.

Elleman, Barbara. *Tomie dePaola: His Art and His Stories*. New York: Putnam, 1999.

Major Authors and Illustrators for Children and Young Adults, Volume 3. Detroit: Gale Research, 2002.

Something About the Author Autobiography Series, Volume 15. Detroit: Gale Research, 1993.

Talking with Artists, Volume I. Edited by Pat Cummings. New York: Macmillan, 1992.

Something About the Author, Volume 108. Detroit: Gale, 1999.

Internet

Children's Reviews	http://www.worldreading.org/	Search dePaola for review by readers.
Tomie dePaola.	http://www.bingley.com/Biography.html	dePaola's own site, includes photographs.
Meet Authors and Illustrators	http://www.childrenslit.com/f_depaola.html	Biography and about his books.
Penguin Putnam Publisher	http://www.penguinputnam.com/Author/index.htm	Biography, book list, photo.
dePaola's Art Online	http://beaconfinearts.com/	A great site featuring his life and work.

Other Resources

Write to Tomie dePaola at his publisher's address. Ask clear questions. Be very courteous.

Listen to a Tomie dePaola radio interview at http://nhpr.org/view_content/415/. This is an excellent way to hear the author talk about his writing.

For the Teacher

Lesson Plan for Tomie dePaola: falcon.jmu.edu/~ramseyil/dePaola.htm

Pine Ridge School Lesson Plans: http://www.pineridge.k12.ca.us/third.htm

Teaching Art: http://www.embracingthechild.com/art.html. Try an art lesson copying dePaola's style. Read *The Art Lesson* aloud.

Declare a Strega Nona Day. Everyone dresses like the people in the town. (You can be Strega Nona or Big Anthony.) Make spaghetti.

All of Tomie dePaola's books are great read-aloud books. They include folktales, legends, myths, and stories that teach a lesson, including the fabulous, magical Strega Nona.

Find Out

See if you can find out how much pasta the average American eats each year.

EMILY DICKINSON

> **Something Extra**
>
> Memorize one of Emily Dickinson's poems and teach it to your class. You can sing Emily Dickinson's poetry to the tune of the theme from *Gilligan's Island.*

Thinking About the Topic

Most children love poetry. One of their favorite poets is Emily Dickinson, who lived during the early nineteenth century, over 100 years ago. She loved to write about nature and is one of the most loved of the American poets. James Whitcomb Riley was another favorite nineteenth-century poet. He liked to write about the fun things he did as a child. Poems for children by Shel Silverstein or Jack Prelutsky are always popular. Some of Emily Dickinson's poems may be difficult, but many you will love, like this one:

> *The spider as an artist*
> *Has never been employed*
> *Though his surpassing merit*
> *Is freely certified.*

Directions

After you choose a poet, select question 1 and two others below. You can apply the same questions to poets other than Emily Dickinson. Write one question at the top of each page. Look in several sources for the answers to your questions. Each question will become a paragraph in your report. Draw a conclusion from the answers you find. The conclusion will be your topic sentence. For example, the conclusion to question 1 might be, "Emily Dickinson was a beloved American poet."

1. Who was Emily Dickinson? Why do people know about her today?

2. Tell a little about Emily Dickinson's life.

3. What kind of poetry did Emily Dickinson write? Why?

4. Why do you think people still love her poems so long after her death?

5. Select one of Emily Dickinson's poems and describe what you think she means.

Books

Keywords: *Dickinson, Emily. Emily Dickinson—Juvenile Literature.*

Dickinson, Emily. *Emily Dickinson: Poetry for Young People.* Poetry for Young People. New York: Sterling, 1994.

Dickinson, Emily. *I'm Nobody! Who Are You?: Poems of Emily Dickinson for Children.* Owings Mills, MD: Stemmer House, 1978.

Dickinson, Emily. *Poems for Youth.* New York: Little, Brown, 1996.

Emily Dickinson: Singular Poet. Minneapolis, MN: Lerner, 2000.

Steffens, Bradley. *The Importance of Emily Dickinson.* Importance Of. San Diego: Lucents, 1998.

Winter, Jeanette, and Emily Dickinson, *Emily Dickinson's Letters to the World.* New York: Frances Foster, 2002.

Internet

Emily Dickinson Poems	http://www.bartleby.com/113/	Over 500 of Emily Dickinson's poems online.
Emily Dickinson	http://www.uta.edu/english/tim/poetry/ed/bio.html	Biography.
Dickinson	http://www.geocities.com/Heartland/Village/1741/dickinson.html	More about her life.

Other Resources

The Belle of Amherst (video). A one-woman show featuring Julie Harris. Learn a little about Ms. Dickinson and listen to her poems.

Singing Time. Performed by Judy Collins. The poems of Emily Dickinson, Robert Browning, and others: http://www.strmedia.com/html/strinf.shtml

For the Teacher

Have the students learn one of Emily Dickinson's poems. Have them try to write a poem describing something in nature in the Dickinson style. Have fun singing them to the tune of *The Yellow Rose of Texas* or the theme from *Gilligan's Island*.

Explore Poetry with Emily Dickinson: http://www.teachervision.com/lesson-plans/lesson-5488.html

---

What do you think Emily Dickinson means by the poem "A word is dead"? Do you agree with her?

> *A word is dead*
> *When it is said,*
> *Some say.*
> *I say it just*
> *Begins to live*
> *That day.*

LEO DILLON AND DIANE DILLON

Something Extra

The Dillons work together to create their artworks. Choose a partner. Select an illustration by Leo Dillon and Diane Dillon. Make a copy of one of their illustrations. Enlarge it on the copier if you need to. Cut out one or two of the most important images, maybe the people or animals. Paste the enlarged cutout on a large piece of art paper and give it a new background. With your partner, pass the artwork back and forth, like the Dillons do when they paint. Copy their art style and color.

Thinking About the Topic

Leo Dillon and Diane Dillon are married to each other. They are artists who illustrate books, posters, and album covers. You may know them from library books like *Why Mosquitoes Buzz in People's Ears* or *Ashanti to Zulu*. Leo Dillon was the first African American to win the Caldecott Medal. Together they have won many awards. Study the illustrations in their books and you will understand why.

Directions

Leo Dillon and Diane Dillon are illustrators. Search the library catalog and find the books they have illustrated. Get to know their beautiful work before you begin. Then, answer question 1 and any other two questions below. Write each question at the top of a sheet of paper. When you have gathered all your information, draw a conclusion about each answer. (For example, the conclusion to question 1 might be, "Leo and Diane Dillon are famous illustrators of children's books.") Each conclusion will become the topic sentence for its paragraph.

1. Who are Leo Dillon and Diane Dillon? What do they do?

2. How did they meet and begin working together? How do they work together to create their art?

3. They illustrate stories, not write them. How do they decide what illustrations would develop the story they are drawing?

4. What awards have the Dillons won? Why do you think they have won so many awards?

5. What do you think is so special or different about their artwork?

6. Compare the Dillons' art with that of another illustrator whose work you like.

7. What is your favorite book with illustrations by Leo Dillon and Diane Dillon? Why do you think the artwork helps you enjoy the story?

Books

Keywords: *Leo Dillon; Diane Dillon; Children's Book Illustrators.*

Preiss, Byron. *The Art of Leo & Diane Dillon.* New York: Ballantine, 1981.

Something About the Author, Volume 106. Detroit: Gale, 1999.

Talking With Artists, Voume I. Edited by Pat Cummings. New York: Macmillan, 1992.

Internet

Amazon.com	http://www.amazon.com	Search for books and read reviews.
Leo and Diane Dillon	http://best.com/~libros/dillon/	Artist biography and art.
Scholastic Author Site	http://www2.scholastic.com/	Search for Dillon to find information about the authors.
L & D Dillon	http://www.bpib.com/l&dillon.htm	Biography and book covers from their artwork.
The Dillons	http://www.locusmag.com/2000/Issues/04/Dillons.html	An interview with the Dillons.

Other Resources

Write the artists at the publisher's site, http://www2.scholastic.com. Ask the questions you have for your report. There is no better resource than the artists. This is called a primary source.

Check the local library for a video recording of *Why Mosquitoes Buzz in People's Ears* (New York: Caedmon Audio, 1984).

For the Teacher

Caldecott Winners from the American Library Association: http://.ala.org/alsc/cquick.html

To Everything There Is a Season: http://teacher.scholastic.com/BookUpdate/toeverything/index.htm. This wonderful book is a great read-aloud and discussion source (both art and text) for almost any grade.

Teaching with Books or Folktale Writing http://teacher.scholastic.com/index.htm

Leo and Diane Dillon: Resources: http://falcon.jmu.edu/~ramseyil/dillon.htm

---

Internet Hunt

What award did *Her Stories,* illustrated by Leo Dillon and Diane Dillon, win? Try google.com

DINOSAURS

Something Extra
At http://www.bonus.com/, choose Explore, then Dinosaurs. Dig up dinosaur fun with games and puzzles.

Thinking About the Topic

Some dinosaurs were larger than elephants; others were as small as a dog. Some could fly like birds; others could swim like fish. What a world it must have been! We no longer have dinosaurs roaming the earth. What happened to them? What was the world like when dinosaurs were around?

Directions

Answer question 1 and any other two questions below. You may write about one particular dinosaur or about dinosaurs in general. If you are writing about just one type of dinosaur, you will have to change the questions a little. Ask your teacher for help.

Write each question at the top of a sheet of paper. Take notes on the question. Write your notes in complete sentences. When you are finished, write a conclusion. Your conclusion will be the topic sentence for the paragraph.

1. What were dinosaurs? Describe them.

2. What was the world of the dinosaurs like? What other animals lived then? What did the dinosaurs eat?

3. What happened to the dinosaurs? Include different theories.

4. Choose a particular dinosaur such as Tyrannosaurus rex, Stegosaurus, Triceratops, or Pteranodon. Compare it to other dinosaurs.

5. How do we know so much about the dinosaurs today?

Books

Keywords: *Dinosaurs* (or use the name of a certain dinosaur); *Extinct animals.*

Benton, Michael. *Dinosaurs.* New York: Kingfisher, 1998.

Harrison, Carol. *Dinosaurs Everywhere!* New York: Scholastic, 1998.

Lessem, Don. *An Encyclopedia of Extinct Animals.* New York: Scholastic, 1999.

Marshall, Chris, ed. *Dinosaurs of the World.* Tarrytown, NY: Marshall Cavendish, 1999.

Osborne, Will. *Dinosaurs: Magic Tree House Research Guide.* New York: Random House, 2000.

Simmerman, Howard. *Dinosaurs: The Biggest, Baddest, Strangest, Fastest.* New York: Antheneum Books for Young Readers, 2000.

Willis, Paul. *Dinosaurs.* Pleasantville, NY: Reader's Digest, 1999.

Internet

The Dino Directory	http://flood.nhm.ac.uk/cgi-bin/dino/	Descriptions and pictures of most common dinosaurs.
Worldbook Encyclopedia	http://www.worldbook.com/fun/ dinosaurs/html/intro.htm	Facts, portraits, and climate information, with some pictures.
Royal Tyrrell Museum	http://www.tyrrellmuseum.com/tour/ index.htm	Pictures and descriptions of the dinosaurs in the museum.
Your local natural history museum		Find your local natural history museum online and find out about the local dinosaur displays.

Other Resources

All About Dinosaurs. Schlessinger Science Library for Children series. Bala Cynwyd, PA: Library Video, 1999.

Crichton, Michael, and David Koepp. *Jurassic Park* (video). Universal City, CA: MCA Home Video, 1994. For family movie night.

Make a visit to the local natural history museum. Visit the dinosaur displays. Talk to the museum curator.

For the Teacher

Lesson plans and worksheets: http://learning-songs.com/free_pages/menu_wkshts/fact_ dino.html

---

Question

Q: What time is it when a dinosaur climbs on your bed?

A: Time to get a new bed.

EDUCATING HOMELESS CHILDREN

> **Something Extra**
>
> Read *Elsa, Star of the Shelter* by Jacqueline Wilson.
>
> Consider having your family or classmates organize after-school volunteer tutoring for homeless children. If you are a pretty good student, you can tutor others.

Thinking About the Topic

Homelessness is a problem in both large cities and small towns. Have you ever known someone who was homeless? When parents do not have jobs and the family is on the move, it is difficult for children to attend school. Have you noticed children who are in your classroom for a month or so and then disappear? They may have been homeless. So, how do we find a way to educate these migratory (Look it up!) children? Whose responsibility is it? Learn more about this sad topic and find out who is working to help these families. See if there is anything you can do to help.

Directions

Select question 1 and two others below. Write one question at the top of each page. Look in several sources for the answers to your questions. Each question will become a paragraph in your report. Draw a conclusion from the answers you find. The conclusion will be your topic sentence. For example, the conclusion for question 1 conclusion might be, "It is very easy for a poor family to become homeless."

1. Who are the homeless?
2. Why is it so difficult for homeless children to do well in school?
3. What laws have helped children of the homeless to get an education?
4. What can the schools do to help these children?
5. What is being done to help educate homeless children in your community? How can you help?

Books

Keywords: *Homeless– Juvenile Literature; Homeless children; Homelessness.*

Ayer, Eleanor. *Homeless Children.* Lucent Books Overview Series. San Diego: Lucent, 1997.

Criswell, Sarah Dixon. *Homelessness.* San Diego: Lucent, 1998.

Stearman, Kaye. *Why Do People Live on the Streets.* Exploring Tough Issues. Austin, TX: Raintree Steck-Vaughn, 2001.

Stewart, Gail. *The Homeless.* The Other America. Farmington Hills, MI: Lucent, 1996.

Vestal, Jeanne. *Homelessness, Can We Solve the Problem.* Issues of Our Times. New York: Twenty-First Century Books, 1995.

Internet

Volunteers of America	http://voa.org/	Find out ways others are helping homeless children and trying to solve the problem of homelessness.
National Student Campaign Hunger and Homelessness	http://www.pirg.org/ nscahh/	Student projects to help.
Education of Homeless Children and Youth	http://nationalhomeless.org/ edchild.html	Good information about the laws and statistics.
National Coalition for the Homeless	http://nationalhomeless.org/	Read the fact sheets about homeless children and families.
University of Colorado Homeless Children	http://csf.colorado.edu/ homeless/courses.html	Links to many Web pages. See subject heading, *Education of and about Homeless Children.*
Homeless Children and Youth	http://www.misd.net/ Homeless/statistics.html	Shocking statistics for your research.

Other Resources

Educating Homeless Children: http://www.ins.usdoj.gov/graphics/services/natz/citizen.htm. NPR has two audiotapes about how America is trying to educate homeless children. Some of the problems are discussed. Easy to understand and very good.

Telephone the Salvation Army or another agency in your town and ask about the children who stay there. How do the children get to school? How long can the family remain at the shelter? Have your questions written down and ready to ask. Be very courteous and professional.

For the Teacher

The Homeless Maze: http://www.geocities.com/ccadurham/maze.html. This group project offers fictionalized situations in which participants assume the identity of a person facing homelessness.

Homeless Education Kit: http://thecity.sfsu.edu/~bahp/homeless_edu_kit.htm. Activities.

Internet Hunt

Use the Searchable Map at the bottom of the page to find a shelter or food bank near you: http://4homeless.hypermart.net/shelters.html

Call and volunteer.

ELECTRICITY

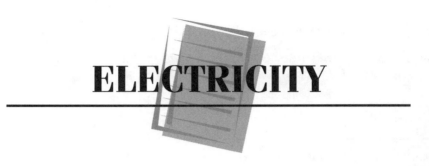

Something Extra

Make a battery from a potato:
http://www.quantumscientific.com/pclock.html or
http://pbskids.org/zoom/phenom/potatobattery.html

Thinking About the Topic

Electricity is all around you. You can see it when you see lightning. You feel it when your hair crackles and flies when you comb it. Electricity is inside the cells in your body. But people were not able to use electricity until they learned how to harness it and store it until it was needed. Learn how they figured it out and how electricity works.

Directions

Select question 1 and two others below. Write one question at the top of each page. Look in several sources for the answers to your questions. Each question will become a paragraph in your report. Draw a conclusion from the answers you find. The conclusion will be your topic sentence. For example, the conclusion for question 1 might be, "Electricity is . . ." Use your notes to create supporting details for each paragraph.

1. What is electricity? How is it made?

2. Describe how electricity gets from the power plant to a light bulb.

3. How would our lives be different without electricity?

4. Describe the types of natural electricity.

5. Tell about the ways electricity was discovered.

Books

Keywords: *Electricity—Juvenile Literature.*

Cole, Joanna. *Magic School Bus and the Electric Field Trip*. New York: Scholastic Press, 1997.

Engelbert, Phyllis. *Technology in Action: Science Applied to Everyday Life*. Detroit: UXL, 1998.

Junior Science on File. New York: Facts on File, 1991– . Looseleaf.

Lauw, Darlene. *Electricity*. New York: Crabtree, 2002.

Macaulay, David. *The Way Things Work*. London: Dorling Kindersley, 1988.

Schmittroth, Linda, Mary R. McCall, and Bridget Travers. *Eureka*. New York: UXL, 1999.

Taylor, Helen. *A Lightning Bolt Is Hotter Than the Sun and Other Facts About Electricity*. Brookfield, CT: Copper Beech Books, 1998.

World Book Encyclopedia. Chicago: World Book, 2002.

Internet

Clark Public Utilities	http://www.clarkpublicutilities.com/kidshome.html	What is electricity? And how can you use it safely?
Science Made Simple	http://www.sciencemadesimple.com/static.html	Learn how static electricity works, and conduct some simple experiments.
Edison International	http://www.edisonkids.com/	Energy heroes; electrical safety; electric cars.

Other Resources

Thomas Edison Biography has a video clip at the bottom of the page: http://www.edison-ford-estate.com/thomas-edison/Ebio.htm#

Static Electricity video clip: http://www.brainpop.com/science/electricity/electricity/index.weml

For the Teacher

Electricity lesson plans for various ages: http://www.proteacher.com/110016.shtml

Science lesson plans for elementary school grades: http://www.physics.rutgers.edu/hex/visit/lesson/lesson_links1.html. Electricity is about halfway down the page.

Jokes

Q: What did the circuit say to the battery?

A: I wuv you watts and watts.

Q: What is the difference between lightning and electricity?

A: Lightning is free!

ENDANGERED SPECIES

Something Extra

Ranger Rick offers information and games about the gray wolf, sea turtle, Siberian tiger, manatee, humpback whale, and crocodile at http://www.nfw.org/wildthornberrys

---

Thinking About the Topic

Have you ever seen a dodo bird? How about a dinosaur? Some animals no longer live on the earth. They are extinct. Other animals may soon be gone unless we do something to save them. There are many groups working to identify and save endangered animals. You can help, too. Find out about endangered species and how you can join in to save these animals.

Directions

Answer question 1 and any other two questions below. Write each question at the top of a sheet of paper. Answer the question from the research you have done. This will form a paragraph for your report. Then write a conclusion for each question. Each conclusion will be your topic sentence for a paragraph.

1. Why are so many animals becoming endangered?

2. Why does it matter that we save endangered species?

3. Pick an animal from the endangered species list. What is special about this animal? What changes have made it become endangered?

4. What changes can be made to help endangered animals?

5. Discuss the role of zoos in saving endangered species.

Books

Keywords: *Endangered Species; Wildlife Conservation* (select an endangered animal to report about).

Allen, Thomas B. *Animals of Africa.* New York: Hugh Lauter Levin Associates, 1997.

Endangered Animals. Danbury, CT: Grolier Educational, 2002.

Endangered Species. Farmington Hills, MI: Greenhaven Press, 2002.

Lessem, Don. *An Encyclopedia of Extinct Animals.* New York: Scholastic, 1999.

Internet

EE Link to Endangered Species	http://eelink.net/EndSpp/specieshighlights-mainpage.html	Endangered species lists.
Kids Planet	http://www.kidsplanet.org/factsheets/map.html	Fact sheets on endangered species throughout the world.
Oakland Zoo	http://www.oaklandzoo.org/atoz/atoz.html	Descriptions of the endangered species at the Oakland Zoo. Some have audio or video files.
Animal Info	http://www.animalinfo.org/rarest.htm	The world's rarest animals.
Endangered Species	http://www.endangeredspecie.com/	Rare species. Good information.

Other Resources

Amazing Animals. Amazing Endangered Animals (video). New York: DK Vision, 1997.

Crichton, Michael, and David Koepp. *Jurassic Park* (video). Universal City, CA: MCA Home Video, 1994.

Endangered & Extinct Animals (video). Wynnewood, PA: Schlessinger Media, 1999.

For the Teacher

Conservation lesson plans from the Environmental Protection Agency: http://www.epa.gov/teachers/

Lesson plans and worksheets: http://abcteach.com/directory/theme_units/animals/endangered_species/

Teachers Pages for Lesson Plans and More: http://www.endangeredspecie.com/Teacher's_Page.htm

---

Limerick

When the fish that goes splishing the fastest
Goes splashing and splishing right past us
Then we almost can't see
He has no company
Of his kind, he just might be the lastest.

ETIQUETTE

Something Extra

Create a skit demonstrating proper behavior in a certain setting, for example at church or on the telephone. Ask a friend to help.

Plan a party for friends or family. Use everything you have learned about party etiquette as you plan.

Thinking About the Topic

Most kids love to go to birthday parties and other celebrations. Believe it or not, attending parties is a great way to practice party manners. Parties are more fun if the partygoers are properly dressed and know how to behave. School, church, and parties all have rules for good conduct. There are even rules for meeting and greeting people, talking on the telephone, and sportsmanship. Find out more.

Directions

Don't try to write about everything. We have listed several situations below. Choose one for your topic, for example table manners, thank you notes, or party manners. Write three questions about that topic. Use three or four resources to help you find the answers. Then draw conclusions from the information you gather. Conclusions will become title sentences.

GOOD QUESTION: What is the best way to answer the phone at home?
BAD QUESTION: Do you just say hello when you answer the phone?

Following are some situations requiring etiquette. You may think of others.

E-mail etiquette (netiquette)	School or church manners
Good sportsmanship	Talking on the phone
Meeting and greeting people	Visiting relatives or adult friends
Party manners	Writing thank you notes

Books

Keywords: *Courtesy; Etiquette for children and teenagers; Manners.*

Barnes, Emilie. *A Little Book About Manners.* Eugene, OR: Harvest House, 1998.

Mitchell, Mary. *Dear Ms. Demeanor: A Young Person's Etiquette Guide to Handling Any Social Situation with Confidence and Grace.* Chicago: Contemporary, 1994.

Packer, Alex J. *How Rude! The Teenagers Guide to Manners, Proper Behavior and Not Grossing People Out.* Minneapolis, MN: Free Spirit, 1997.

Polisar, Barry. *Don't Do That! A Child's Guide to Bad Manners, Ridiculous Rules, and Inadequate Etiquette.* Silver Spring, MD: Rainbow Morning, 1994.

Post, Elizabeth L. *Emily Post Teen Etiquette.* New York: HarperPerennial, 1995.

Internet

History of Etiquette	http://library.thinkquest.org/2993/history.htm	Why do we need good manners?.
Etiquette Question and Answer Tips	http://www.ryangrpinc.com/etiquette_tips_social.asp	FAQs about manners.
Good Sportsmanship	http://kidshealth.org/parent/positive/family/sportsmanship.html	Play sports? This is a good topic.
Writing Thank You Notes	http://drdaveanddee.com/thank.html	Everyone should know this.

Other Resources

Ask Peggy Post: http://magazines.ivillage.com/goodhousekeeping/mail/. Peggy Post will e-mail answers to questions about proper etiquette.

Barney's Best Manners (video). Allen, TX: Barney Home Video. 1993.

Disney Winnie the Pooh Growing Up (video). Burbank, CA: Walt Disney Home Video, 1995.

It's Just Good Manners (video). Atlanta, GA: Mind Your Manners Pub, 1995.

For the Teacher

Kalish, Ginny. *Rachel Rude Rowdy.* Chicago: Children's Books, 1999. Read-aloud for ages eight to twelve.

Lesson Plans: Etiquette: members.aol.com/Donnpages/Sociology.html#Etiquette

M.I.P—Minors In Possession . . . Of Bad Manners. What classroom fun! Great bulletin board display at http://thinkquest.org/library/lib/site_sum_outside.html?tname=2993&url=2993/history.htm

Rude Rage: http://www.dtn-productions.com/dtn/rude_rage_2.htm. Users e-mail notes about rude behavior they have encountered for online posting. Try it in your classroom; Ms. Demeanor may answer.

Kids' Advice to Kids

"Never trust a dog to watch your food." Patrick, age 10

"When your mom is mad at your dad, don't let her brush your hair." Taylia, age 11

"A puppy always has bad breath—even after eating a Tic-Tac." Andrew, age 9

"Never hold a Dustbuster and a cat at the same time." Kyoyo, age 9

"You can't hide a piece of broccoli in a glass of milk." Armir, age 9

"Don't wear polka-dot underwear under white shorts." Kellie, age 11

"Felt-tip markers are not good to use as lipstick." Lauren, age 9

Source: www.cleanjokespage.com/po.html

EXERCISE AND KIDS

Something Extra

Are your classmates fit? Survey them and make the results part of your report online at http://library.thinkquest.org/12153/fit.html

Play the Couch Potato Shuffle Game at http://www.abc.net.au/couch/games.htm#puzzle

Thinking About the Topic

Go outside and play! Quit watching so much television! Get a little exercise! Did you ever hear that? Why do parents want their children exercising? Because exercise prolongs life, we have fewer infections, we feel happier, and we have strong bones. Many children in America are overweight because they do not exercise. If exercise really *can* give us better lives, maybe you should learn more about it.

Directions

Answer question 1 and any other two questions on your topic. After you answer each question using resources you select (books, Internet, videos, etc), draw a conclusion about the answer. Use the conclusion as your topic sentence. For example, the conclusion to question 2 may be, "Kids can get fit without entering organized sports."

1. Why is exercise so important to growing children? What happens to our bodies when we exercise?

2. How do organized sports help kids get enough exercise? Is that enough?

3. Does exercise have anything to do with overall health?

4. Can dieting take the place of exercise for children?

5. What makes you too fat or too thin? Do children worry too much about weight?

Books

Keywords: *Exercise for Children; Physical Fitness for Children.*

Encyclopedia of Health. Tarrytown, NY: Marshall Cavendish, 1995.

Laderer, Mandy. *Fit-Kids: Getting Kids "Hooked" on Fitness Fun!* Hicksville, NY: Allure, 1994.

McGinty, Alice B. *Staying Healthy: Let's Exercise.* New York: PowerKids Press, 1998.

Schwarzenegger, Arnold. *Fitness for Kids Ages 6–10: A Guide to Health, Exercise, and Nutrition.* New York: Doubleday, 1993.

Turck, Mary. *Eating Health for Weight Management.* Nutrition and Fitness for Teens. Mankato, MN: Lifematters, 2001.

Internet

Bodies in Motion: Minds at Rest	http://library.thinkquest.org/12153/	*ThinkQuest* Web page—be sure to look at this.
Kid's Health	http://www.kidshealth.org/kid/index.html	Good information including a section on staying healthy without organized sports.
Get Fit, Don't Quit	http://tqjunior.thinkquest.org/4139/	Personal training schedule.
Welltopia for Kids	http://welltopia.com/kids.htm	Staying well with exercise and good nutrition.
Running	http://www.howstuffworks.com/question485.htm	How a trained athlete can run a marathon, but a couch potato cannot run half a mile.

Other Resources

Hip Hop Animal Rock (video). Wilmington, NC: Educational Records Center, 2000.

Stewart, Georgianna Liccione. *Cool Aerobics for Kids* (sound recording). Long Branch, NJ: Kimbo, 1999.

Chicken Fat-Youth Fitness Video (video). Long Branch, NJ: Kimbo Educational, 1996.

Write to the Presidents Council for Fitness in Children. There are contests and activities for kids.

For the Teacher

Aerobics for Kids Lesson Plan: http://www.lessonplanspage.com/PEAerobicsForKids5.htm

Murphy, Jane. *Stay Tuned: Raising Savvy Kids in the Age of the Couch Potato.* New York: Doubleday, 1996.

National Association for Sport and Physical Education. *National Physical Education Standards K–12.* St. Louis, MO: Mosby, 1995.

---

10 Excuses for Sleeping at School

1. This is just a 15-minute power nap, so I can remember what I learned before we take the test.
2. I was testing my desk for drool resistance.
3. I'm actually doing a Stress Level Elimination Exercise Plan (SLEEP).
4. I wasn't sleeping! I was reviewing the spelling words.
5. This is in exchange for the six hours last night when I dreamed about school!
6. No! Why did you interrupt me? I had almost figured out a solution to the math problem.
7. Boy, that cold medicine my mom gave me last night just won't wear off.
8. Gee, I thought you (the teacher) were gone for the day.
9. I'm just resting my eyes.
10. This is one of the seven habits of highly effective children!

FAIRY TALES

> ## Something Extra
>
> Find a fairy tale told by people in different countries. Compare the versions.
>
> Write a parody of a fairy tale. Read it to your friends and family.

Thinking About the Topic

Long, long ago stories were first told by storytellers. They walked from town to town telling their stories to the villagers. Later, fairy tales were gathered or written down by Charles Perrault and Jacob and Wilhelm Grimm and others. Many of the same stories are told in different countries. You can write about what makes a fairy tale. It may be fun to compare the versions of the same fairy tale, like Cinderella or Snow White, from two or three countries. Or you may want to compare two or three books with the same story, but with the art drawn by different illustrators. Whatever you decide, you will enjoy re-reading these wonderful stories.

Directions

You may want to research a little about the history of fairy tales. Then select question 1 and two others below. Write each question at the top of a page. Look in several sources for the answers to your questions. Take notes. Each question will become a paragraph in your report.

1. What is a fairy tale? Where do fairy tales come from?

2. Why are fairy tales so popular with children and adults?

3. Some people think fairy tales are frightening to young children. Do you agree? Why or why not? Give examples.

4. Write about Hans Christian Andersen or the Brothers Grimm.

5. Write about fairy tales around the world. Compare a single story from two countries.

6. "And they lived happily ever after." Is this true in the stories you read? Talk about the endings of fairy tales.

Books

Keywords: *Fairy tale* (Cinderella, Snow White, or other titles); *Folk literature—Juvenile. Hans Christian Andersen; Grimms' Fairy Tales.*

Hettinga, Donald A. *The Brothers Grimm: Two Lives, One Legacy.* New York: Clarion Books, 2001.

The Oxford Companion to Fairy Tales. New York: Oxford University Press, 2000.

Perrault, Charles. *Perrault's Fairy Tales.* Translated by A. E. Johnson. New York: Dover, 1969.

Internet

Hans Christian Andersen	http://hca.gilead.org.il/	About Hans Christian Andersen and his stories.
Tales of Wonder	http://www.darsie.net/talesofwonder/	A good spot to compare stories from other countries.
Stories, Folklore and Fairy Tales	http://www.cln.org/themes/ fairytales.html	Excellent links to fairy tales and stories from other places in the world.
Hiya.com	http://www.hiyah.com/library. html	Read along with this collection of fairy tales (and games—I like the memory game).
Cinderella Cinderella	http://www.innovativeclassroom. com/Lesson_Plans/lessonplans. asp?id=31	Compare versions of Cinderella from all over the world.

Other Resources

There are many fairy tale films available. Try your local library for individual fairy tales.

Classic Fairy Tales (audio): http://www.classicfairytales.com/. Enjoy reading along with classic fairy tales, Grimm and Andersen stories.

For the Teacher

Read a few fairy tales to the class. Let the students re-tell the story. Discuss the characters or what message the story may have.

Fractured Fairy Tales: http://www.ucalgary.ca/~dkbrown/fft.html. If you want to have fun, share these stories with your students. Have them create a fractured fairy tale.

Multicultural Fairy Tales Lesson Plans: http://www.lessonplanspage.com/LAMultiFairy.htm

---

Telling Time

Q: What time is it when you have 20 dogs and 1 cat?

A: Twenty after 1.

FAMILIES ARE DIFFERENT

Something Extra

Plan a weekly family night. Play board games, order in pizza or cook together, talk!

Thinking About the Topic

Erin's family includes her father and brother. Ryan sometimes lives with his mom and stepfather, at other times with his dad and stepmother and his half-brother and half-sister. We call these blended families. Audrey is adopted and has a brother who is also adopted. Tim's grandparents are raising him. Cassie lives in a foster home. A family can be so many different types of people, but they all have one thing in common. Children and adults are living together, loving and helping each other.

Directions

You may want to research a little about different types of families. Then select question 1 and two others below. Write each question at the top of a page. Use several sources for the answers to your questions. Take notes. Each question will become a paragraph in your report.

1. What is a blended family?

2. Why is family important?

3. List five different things you learn in your family. How do you learn these things?

4. Describe and compare two different kinds of families.

5. Why do families fight? What good does it do? What harm?

6. Should each member of the family have specific chores, or should everyone share them? How is doing chores helpful to growing up?

7. Why might a child suddenly gain brothers and sisters? What problems could this cause? What are the benefits?

Books

Keywords: *Single parent families; Divorce; Adoption; Family—juvenile literature; Stepfamilies; Blended families.*

Hurwitz, Jane. *Coping in a Blended Family.* New York: Rosen, 1997.

LeShan, Eda. *What's Going to Happen to Me?: When Parents Separate or Divorce.* New York: Four Winds, 1978.

Powell, Jillian. *Talking About Adoption*. Austin, TX: Raintree Steck-Vaughn, 2000.

Rogers, Fred. *Divorce*. New York: G. P. Putnam, 1996.

Smook, Rachel Gaillard. *Stepfamilies: How a New Family Works*. Berkeley Heights, NH: Enslow, 2001.

Internet

Kids Health	http://kidshealth.org/kid/feeling/home_family/adoption.html	A kids' guide to adoption.
Kids Health	http://kidshealth.org/kid/feeling/home_family/blended.html	All about blended families.
Dealing with Feelings	http://www.kidshealth.org/kid/feeling/	This is the best choice. Find your topic and see what Kids' Health has to say.
Kid's Turn	http://www.kidsturn.org/kids/main.htm	Dealing with divorce. Letters, books, activities, information.

Other Resources

Watch a video clip about the beanpole composition of families: http://www.unt.edu/cpe/module1/blk7comp.htm

For the Teacher

Lesson plans on blended families: http://cybersleuth-kids.com/sleuth/Education/Lessons/Health/Family_Health/

List of books for teachers: http://www.kidsturn.org/kids/books.htm

Read-aloud: *Dear Mr. Henshaw* by Beverly Cleary. New York: Morrow, 1983.

Joke

Ryan was having a fight with his sister Brittany.

Father: What's going on here?

Brittany: He called me stupid.

Father: Apologize to her.

Ryan. Okay, Brittany. I'm sorry you're stupid.

FOOD ALLERGIES

> **Something Extra**
>
> Try making animal cookies or honey-fudge brownies with no allergens. Recipes at
> http://www.skyisland.com/OnlineResources/cookbook/cookbook.html

Thinking About the Topic

Oh, no! Every time Amy eats strawberries, she gets an itchy rash all over! When James even smells a peanut, he can hardly breathe. If Ryan drinks milk, he gets a terrible stomachache. What is the problem? They have food allergies. But they have to eat! What are they going to do? If you have allergies, this will be a great topic to learn more about. There is a lot of good information available.

Directions

Answer question 1 and any other two questions below. Write each question at the top of a sheet of paper. Answer the question from the books, videos, and Internet pages you have selected. Your notes will form a paragraph for your report. Then write a conclusion for each question. Each conclusion will be the the topic sentence for a paragraph. The notes will become the details.

1. What are allergies? What are some of the causes of allergies?

2. Describe types of allergic reactions.

3. How can you tell if a food has an ingredient you are allergic to?

4. What are some things an allergic person can do to avoid allergenic foods?

5. What are ways the doctor can treat allergies?

6. Write about a specific allergy (like to milk or peanut butter).

Books

Keywords: *Allergy; Food allergy; Allergy in children.*

Dean, Peter M. G. *Coping with Allergies.* New York: Rosen, 1999.

Encyclopedia of Family Health. New York: Marshall Cavendish, 1998.

Silverstein, Alvin, Virginia Silverstein, and Laura Silverstein Nunn. *Allergies.* New York: Franklin Watts, 1999.

Weiner, Ellen, and Moss Freedman. *Taking Food Allergies to School!.* Plainview, NY: Jayjo Books, 1999.

Internet

Food Allergy News for Kids	http://www.fankids.org/FANKid/kidindex.html	Food allergy basics, tips, projects, and games.
Health Touch Online	http://www.healthtouch.com/	Search for *food allergies* for good information about different types of allergies.
Nestlé	http://www.allsands.com/Food/allergyfoodtyp_hd_gn.htm	Read the symptoms and learn what they mean.
Food Allergies for Kids and Teens	http://www.fankids.org/	Select kids or teens. Lots of good information.

Other Resources

Managing Childhood Asthma (video). Garden Grove, CA: Medcom, 1994

Ask the librarian to help you find a video or audiocassette to use for your report.

For the Teacher

Managing food allergies in schools, from the Food Allergy and Anaphylaxis Network: http://www.foodallergy.org/school.html

School project ideas exploring food allergies: http://www.fankids.org/FANKid/School/school.html

---

Joke

Justin: Doctor, do you think strawberries are healthy?

Doctor: They must be! I've never had one as a patient.

FOOD CHAINS IN YOUR BACKYARD

> **Something Extra**
>
> Create your own small backyard ecosystem. See directions at
> http://www.brainpop.com/science/ecology/foodchains/bob.weml

Thinking About the Topic

Every living thing has a part to play if the world is to survive. A first-rate food chain will maintain a proper balance in the ecosystem. If you are interested in the environment, learn more about caring for your own. Learn about the producers, consumers, and decomposers that make up your backyard food chain.

Directions

Read all about food chains. Learn the basic vocabulary. Select or write three questions about your topic. Answer question 1 and any other two questions below. Write each question at the top of a sheet of paper. Answer each question using resources like books, the Internet, or videos. Then write a conclusion for each question. Each conclusion will be the topic sentence for a paragraph. Add the details from your notes.

1. What is a food chain? How is it important?

2. What is an ecosystem? Describe the ecosystem around you.

3. Define producers, consumers, and decomposers. (You may want to have a short paragraph answering question 1, then write a paragraph on each of these new words. Tell what they are, then talk about the role of each and their connection to each other. This would make a great paper.)

4. How have humans affected the food chain?

5. What part can you play to ensure that your ecosystem stays healthy?

6. Draw a food chain chart describing your backyard. Include the producers, consumers (the carnivores and the omnivores), and decomposers. (See the charts in books and online, so you will know how to create a food chain chart.) Make this part of your report.

Books

Keywords: *Food chain; Ecosystem.*

Encyclopedias and specialized encyclopedias can give you good background on this topic. Find them in your library.

Hartzog, John. *Everyday Science Experiments in the Backyard.* New York: Rosen, 2000.

Lauber, Patricia. *Who Eats What?: Food Chains and Food Webs.* New York: HarperCollins, 1995.

Nadeau, Isaac. *Food Chains in a Backyard Habitat.* New York: Rosen, 2002.

Internet

Food Chain	http://www.planetpals.com/foodchain.html	Very good place to begin. Study the chart.
Schoolyard Habitat	http://www.nwf.org/backyardwildlifehabitat	National Wildlife Federation. Helps you create a backyard habitat
Think Quest	http://library.thinkquest.org/11353/food.htm	Hard to find, but the best information. Take your time and type this URL in. Browse the other pages listed at the bottom of the page.

Other Resources

Brainpop: http://www.brainpop.com/science/ecology/foodchains/cassrita.weml.   Animated movies online.

Creepy, Crawly Creatures in Your Back Yard (video). Washington, DC: National Geographic Society, 2001.

Food for Thought (video). Washington, DC: National Geographic Society, 1998.

The Magic School Bus: Gets Eaten (video). By Joanna Cole and Bruce Degen. New York: KidsVision, 1995.

For the Teacher

Chain Food Tag: http://www.nps.gov/olym/teafood.htm. Wonderful activity for your class. If you have a small class, ask a fellow teacher to join in the fun.

Food Web: http://www.LessonPlansPage.com/ScienceWeaveFoodWeb46.htm. Lesson plans.

Beg $50 from the PTO and create a Half-Barrel Pond Ecosystem with your class. See directions and pictures at http://www.jeffcook.com/hbpond.shtml

---

Helping to Balance the Food Chain

At dinner Jane says, "I'm helping maintain the balance of the food chain in my backyard. Would you please pass the frog legs and escargot?"

FOOD RULES

Thinking About the Topic

I eat my peas with honey. I've done it all my life.
It makes my peas taste funny. But it keeps them on my knife.

Has your mother ever said you eat like a pig? Busy families today may not eat together at the dinner table, so children (and sometimes adults) do not always practice good table manners. Proper etiquette is important, especially when eating in a nice restaurant or at the home of friends. You may be surprised at some of the food rules.

Directions

This topic will be fun to learn about. You may want to demonstrate your new knowledge when you give your report. After reading a little, select three questions about table manners you would like to answer. Question 1 is good for introducing your topic. Answer each question and draw a conclusion about your findings. The conclusion will be your topic sentence. For example, the conclusion to question 1 may be, "Table manners are important and make meals more enjoyable for everyone." Use your notes for paragraph details.

1. What do we mean when by table manners? Why is it important that we learn good table manners?

2. Have table manners always been the same as they are now? It might be fun to find out how table manners were different during colonial times or when your great-grandparents were growing up.

3. What are a few of the most important food rules kids should follow?

4. What are the most common errors people make?

5. Are there special rules about eating in a restaurant? What are they?

Books

Keywords: *Table manners; Courtesy; Etiquette; Table etiquette.*

Berry, Joy. *What to Do When Mom or Dad Says . . . "Don't Slurp Your Food."* Danbury, CT: Grolier, 1984.

Giblin, James. *From Hand to Mouth: Or How We Invented Knives, Forks, Spoons And Chopsticks.* New York: Crowell, 1987.

Haduch, Bill. *Food Rules! The Stuff You Munch, Its Crunch, Its Punch, and Why You Sometimes Lose Your Lunch.* New York: Dutton, 1997.

Hoving, Walter. *Tiffany's Table Manners for Teenagers.* New York: Random House, 1989

Kowal, L.A. *The Proper Pig's Guide to Mealtime Manners.* Chandler, AZ: Five Star, 1996.

Wallace, Carol M. *Elbows Off the Table, Napkin in the Lap, No Video Games During Dinner: The Modern Guide to Teaching Children Good Manners.* New York: St. Martin's Griffin, 1996.

Internet

Table Manners for a Typical Evening Meal	http://leaderu.com/isr/lifeinamerica/tablemanners.html	Learning to eat with others.
Table Manners for Children	http://state.ak.us/dec/deh/sanitat/april/manners.htm	A list of good manners for kids.
10 Tips for Tea Party Etiquette	http://www.drdaveanddee.com/tea.html	Be sure to look at the other links at the bottom of this page.

Other Resources

It's Just Good Manners (video). Atlanta, GA: Mind Your Manners Pub. 1995.

Table Manners for Everyday Use (video). Landvision, Inc.: http://tablemannersvideo.com/

Table Manners for Kids: Tots to Teens (video): http://www.angelfire.com/ia/jettefire/tablemanners.html

If you are lucky enough to have grandparents or great-grandparents, interview them about changes in table manners.

For the Teacher

Download English to Pig Latin: http://immigration-usa.com/pig.html. Fun for the entire class.

Gregory, the Terrible Eater, by Mitchell Sharmat (New York: Simon & Schuster, 1980) is available in every school or public library and is a terrific book for read-aloud fun and discussion.

Lesson Plans: Etiquette: http://members.aol.com/Donnpages/Sociology.html#Etiquette

---

Jokes

Q: Why did the pig have ink all over his face?

A: Because it came out of the pen.

Q: What did the pig say at the beach on a hot summer's day?

A: I'm bacon!

HENRY FORD

> ## Something Extra
> Join a fictional family on their road trip in a Model T:
> http://www.hfmgv.org/education/smartfun/welcome.html

Thinking About the Topic

Henry Ford had a knack for understanding machinery and the ability to make things simple. Do you know why Henry Ford is famous? It is not only because of the car that bears his name, but for a new way of doing things, called the assembly line. Find out what an assembly line is and what it did for the automobile. Write about early transportation in the Model T, Henry Ford, assembly lines, or travel during the early twentieth century. All of the topics tie together and will be interesting and will include information about Henry Ford.

Directions

Select or write three questions about your topic. Write each question at the top of a sheet of paper. Answer the question using different resources (books, Internet, videos). Then write a conclusion for each question. Each conclusion will be your topic sentence for a paragraph. Add the details from your notes to the topic sentence.

1. Tell about Henry Ford's early years.

2. How did Ford learn the skills he needed for designing automobiles?

3. Describe the assembly line and tell how Henry Ford thought about this new method of building something. How did it change life for factory workers?

4. What innovations made Ford's Model T so popular?

5. Describe how Henry Ford helped others.

Books

Keywords: *Ford, Henry; Industrialists; Automobiles; Inventors.*

Gourley, Catherine. *Wheels of Time: A Biography of Henry Ford.* Brookfield, CT: Millbrook, 1997.

Malam, John. *Henry Ford: An Unauthorized Biography.* Crystal Lake, IL: Heinemann, 2001.

McCarthy, Pat. *Henry Ford: Building Cars for Everyone.* Berkeley Heights, NH: Enslow, 2002.

Moss, Joyce, and George Wilson. *Profiles in American History*. Farmington Hills, MI: Gale, 1995.

World Book Encyclopedia. Chicago: World Book, 2002.

Wyborny, Sheila. *Henry Ford*. San Diego: Kidhaven, 2002.

Internet

Henry Ford Museum	http://www.hfmgv.org/exhibits/hf/default.asp	Brief biography of Henry Ford and a picture of his quadricycle.
Incwell	http://www.incwell.com/Biographies/Ford.html	Biography of Henry Ford.
Edison-Ford Winter Estates	http://www.edison-ford-estate.com/henry-ford/Fbio.htm	Learn how Ford was inspired to build the Model T.

Other Resources

Henry Ford. Inventors of the World video series. Wynnewood, PA: Schlessinger Media, 2001.

Listen to learn about Henry Ford's quest for success: http://www.entrepreneur.com/av

Spirit of Ford (video): http://www.ford.com/en/ourCompany/heritage/default.htm

For the Teacher

Develop a classroom assembly line to create an automobile: http://www.sos.state.mi.us/history/museum/techstuf/erlyauto/createcar.html

Let the students work in small groups to complete a project. Encourage the use of an assembly line where each person has a job he or she must do.

Look it up

1. What year did Henry Ford create the Model T?
2. How much did it cost to buy the first Model Ts?
3. How long did it take to get across the country driving a Model T Ford?

BENJAMIN FRANKLIN

> ## Something Extra
>
> Make music with Franklin's invention, the Armonica:
> http://www.fi.edu/franklin/musician/virtualarmonica.html

Thinking About the Topic

A small leak will sink a great ship, a stitch in time saves nine, a penny saved is a penny earned: *Poor Richard's Almanack* was full of good advice. But who was Poor Richard? None other than Benjamin Franklin!

Besides writing good advice, Ben Franklin was an inventor and a statesman. What did he invent? Do your research and find out! What is a statesman? It is someone who helps our country work well with other countries. Ben Franklin did this even before the Declaration of Independence was written. He also played an important role in creating that document. What was it? Franklin is one of the most interesting characters in American history. Learn more about him.

Directions

Write each question at the top of a piece of paper. Answer question 1 and any two other questions below in complete sentences. When you finish a question, write a conclusion. The conclusion will be your topic sentence, and the answers will make up your paragraph.

1. Tell about Benjamin Franklin's childhood.

2. Describe two of Franklin's inventions and tell why he invented them.

3. How did Benjamin Franklin help during the American Revolution?

4. How did he come to be a writer? Discuss some of his writings.

5. Why is Benjamin Franklin considered an American hero?

6. What role did Benjamin Franklin play in the writing of the Declaration of Independence?

Books

Keywords: *Franklin, Benjamin.*

Boekhoff, P. M. *Benjamin Franklin.* San Diego: KidHaven, 2002.

Gregson, Susan R. *Benjamin Franklin.* Mankato, MN: Bridgestone, 2001.

Kallen, Stuart A. *Benjamin Franklin (Inventor and Creator)*. Farmington Hills, MI: KidHaven, 2002.

Moss, Joyce, and George Wilson. *Profiles in American History*. Farmington Hills, MI: Gale, 1995.

Parker, Steve. *Benjamin Franklin*. Brookmall, PA: Chelsea House, 1995.

Raatma, Lucia. *Benjamin Franklin*. Minneapolis, MN: Compass Point Books, 2001.

Internet

Spectrum Home and School Magazine	http://www.incwell.com/Biographies/Franklin.html	Biography.
US History Organization	http://www.ushistory.org/franklin/courant/index.htm	Read the Silence Dogood articles that Ben wrote.
US History Organization	http://www.ushistory.org/franklin/index.htm	Experiments, fun and games, Franklin's Philadelphia, and quotes.
Government Printing Office	http://bensguide.gpo.gov	Ben's *Guide to Government for Kids*, arranged by grade level.

Other Resources

Franklin video online, from the Franklin Institute: http://sin.fi.edu/franklin/video/theme.mov

Online video from U.S. History Organization: http://www.ushistory.org/franklin/av/index.htm

Lawson, Robert. *Ben and Me* (video). Burbank, CA: Walt Disney Home Video, 1989.

Have a family night at the movies and watch the musical *1776*.

For the Teacher

Lesson ideas at various grade levels using Ben Franklin's Armonica: http://sin.fi.edu/pieces/dukerich/teacherlessonideas.html

Lesson plans based on the lightning rod and other powers of electricity: http://sin.fi.edu/pieces/hongell/curriculum.htm

Using *Ben's Guide* as a learning tool: http://bensguide.gpo.gov/pt/learning.html

---

Do the Math

On January 17, we wish Ben Franklin a happy birthday. He is over 290 years old. If a generation is 20 years, how many generations ago did Ben Franklin live?

GERMS

> **Something Extra**
>
> Have fun with food safety puzzles, coloring books, games, and songs:
> http://vm.cfsan.fda.gov/~dms/educate.html

Thinking About the Topic

Wash up before you eat! Wash up after you go to the bathroom! Wash up when you go to bed! Wash up when you sneeze! Why do your parents always tell you to wash up? It is because of germs. Germs are parasites that live inside your body. They are tiny little microbes that can cause disease. They are pretty sneaky. So watch out! Planning a career in science? Here is your chance to find out all about those pesky germs you will be studying when you grow up.

Directions

Read all about germs and microbes. Then answer question 1 and any other two questions below. Write each question at the top of a sheet of paper. When you have gathered all your information, draw a conclusion about each answer. (For example, question 2, "There are four main types of germs.") Each conclusion will be the topic sentence for a paragraph. Use the other details from your notes to complete each paragraph.

1.   What are germs? How can doctors see them?

2.   How many types of germs are there? Describe them.

3.   How do germs get around? What do germs do to their host?

4.   What is so gross about germs?

5.   What are a few ways you can protect yourself from germs?

Books

Keywords: *Microbiology—Juvenile; Immunity—Juvenile; Bacteria—Juvenile; Viruses—Juvenile.*

Berger, Melvin. *Germs Make Me Sick.* New York: Harper & Row, 1995.

Colombo, Luann. *Gross But True, Germs.* New York: Little Simon, 1997.

Encyclopedia of Health. Tarrytown, NY: Marshall Cavendish, 1995.

Nardo, Don. *Germs.* San Diego: Kidhaven, 2002.

Internet

Stalking the Mysterious Microbe	http://www.microbe.org	Spend time here! This site for kids has great information.
The Immune System	http://newscenter.cancer.gov/ sciencebehind/immune/ immune01.htm	How does our immune system work?
What Are Germs?	http://kidshealth.org/kid/talk/ qa/germs.html	All about germs. Short definitions.
IndiaParenting	http://www.indiaparenting.com/ raisingchild/data/raisingchild174. shtml	The four kinds of germs.

Other Resources

Why Is Hand Washing Important?: http://www.microbe.org/washup/importance.asp. Online video clips and interactive questions.

Morris the Moose (video). Churchill Entertainment. Racine, WI: Golden Book Video, 1993.

Germs Make Me Sick (sound recording). Melvin Berger. New York: HarperCollins, 1987.

If you have a doctor's appointment, ask the nurse or doctor your questions about germs. Take notes. An interview with an expert is one of the best ways to get information.

For the Teacher

Lesson plans by grade level and subject: http://lessonplanet.com/. Keyword search. You will find plenty here on germs.

Science lessons and experiments: http://ofcn.org/cyber.serv/academy/ace/sci/elem.html. Especially for teachers

How to Lose a Million Bacteria Game: http://vm.cfsan.fda.gov/~cjm/millprt.html. Class fun.

Doctor Jokes

Patient: Doctor, Doctor, I keep seeing an insect.

Doctor: Don't worry, it's just a bug that's going around!

Patient: Doctor, Doctor, I think I'm a mosquito.

Doctor: Go away, sucker!

There are lots of doctor jokes. Find them online.

GONE FISHING

Something Extra

Anglers have always been teased about their tall fish tales. They have been known to exaggerate the size of the fish they caught. Ask a parent or grandparent for a few "fish tales" you can tell the class as part of your report.

Thinking About the Topic

Fishing has been popular for centuries. Fishing can be done for sport or for food. Today fishing ranges from sitting on the bank of a pond to deep-sea fishing or the fly-fishing. Why do people enjoy fishing? Really, it is just standing around waiting for fish to bite, right? Wrong? Learn more about this form of recreation. Anglers have rules they must abide by. They have to learn about the environment. They have to choose the proper equipment that will help them catch the type of fish they want. For you anglers, we know you will enjoy this report. Then plan a fishing day with your folks.

Directions

Narrow your topic to a particular type of fishing. When you are ready, select question 1 and two others below. Write one question at the top of each page. Look in several sources for the answers to your questions. Each question will become a paragraph in your report. Draw a conclusion from the answers you find. The conclusion will be your topic sentence. For example, the conclusion for question 2 might be, "The proper fishing equipment can make a fishing trip more fun."

1. Describe the type of fishing you do (fly-fishing, deep-sea fishing, lake or pond fishing)

2. What equipment do you need to be an angler? (Describe it.)

3. What are some fishing hot spots? Why do fish like these special places?

4. What rules or laws should an angler know? What is "catch and release?"

5. What can fishing teach us about nature? Does learning about fishing help you enjoy it more?

Books

Keywords: *Fly fishing; Fishing—Juvenile literature; Sport fishing; Angling.*

Bailey, Donna. *Fishing.* Austin, TX: Steck-Vaughn, 1991.

Bailey, John. *Young Fishing Enthusiasts.* New York: DK Publishing, 1999.

Drinkard, G. Lawson. *Fishing in a Brook: Angling Activities for Kids.* Salt Lake City, UT: Gibbs Smith, 2000.

Love, Ann, and Jane Drake. *Fishing*. Illustrated by Pat Cupples. Toronto: Kids Can, 1999.

Paull, Frankie, and Bob Carrie Jackpine. *Cool Fishin' for Kids Age 5 to 85*. Superior, WI: Savage, 2001.

Internet

If you want to write about fishing in your home state, use keywords: *Fishing kids (Texas).*

The Young Angler	http://www.nebworks.com/kids/angler.htm	Information for kids who want to fish.
Kids Pages for Fishing	http://www.ncfisheries.net/kids/fish.htm	All about fishing, including the rules.
Ethical Angling	http://www.texasgulfcoastfishing.com/ethic.htm	This is a good site to learn about the rules of fishing.
Beginner's Guide to Fishing	http://family.go.com/raisingkids/learn/activities/feature/famf79fish/	Information from gear to techniques.

Other Resources

Fishing Page: http://www.kdfwr.state.ky.us/fisherie.htm. Listen to the audio called *Take a Kid Fishing.*

The video store has several selections about fishing. Take a trip to the store or library. You can also learn from the fishing shows on cable TV.

For the Teacher

Fishing with Family: http://fishing.about.com/cs/familyfishing/index_2.htm. Excellent selection for information about fishing.

Joke

John and Joseph were digging for fishing bait. Uncovering a many-legged creature, John showed Joseph.

"No, he won't do for bait," Joseph said. "He's not an earthworm."

"He's not?" John asked. "Well, what planet is he from?"

HABITAT FOR HUMANITY

Something Extra

Make a Bienvenue Bebe bag for newborns in Haiti:
http://www.familycares.org/familycares/projects/baby_bags.shtml

---

Thinking About the Topic

Many people in the United States are poor. They need basic things like food, clothing, and a home to live in. You will be amazed at what you can do to help! Have you ever seen a dripping faucet? Drip, drip, drip. Put a cup under that drip and in a short time, the cup will be filled with water. Volunteering is like that. You can only do a little bit, but when many people do their little bit, it becomes a whole lot! One way families can volunteer is through Habitat for Humanity. Find out what this group does for needy families. See if this group is active in your town. Ex-President Jimmy Carter is very active in this group. You may want to write about his work as a volunteer.

Directions

Habitat for Humanity is one way to help others. You might choose a different social services group, such as a soup kitchen, a homeless shelter, a food pantry, or a nursing home. Use books and the Internet to answer question 1 and two others.

1. What is Habitat for Humanity?

2. How does it help change lives?

3. Describe what the group does. Find someone who has volunteered and interview that person.

4. Volunteer with this group. You might volunteer with a parent, a scout organization, or a religious organization. Describe your experiences.

5. Research other ways to volunteer in your community. Write about them.

Books

Keywords: *Habitat for Humanity; Student Service; Volunteerism.*

Fuller, Millard. *More Than Houses: How Habitat for Humanity Is Transforming Lives and Neighborhoods.* Nashville, TN: Word Pub, 2000.

Hoose, Phillip. *It's Our World, Too!: Stories of Young People Who Are Making a Difference* Gordonsville, VA: Farrar, Straus & Giroux, 2002.

Lewis, Barbara. *Kids Guide to Service Projects: Over 500 Service Ideas for Young People Who Want to Make a Difference.* Minneapolis, MN: Free Spirit, 1995.

Suen, Anastasia. *Habitat for Humanity.* New York: PowerKids Press, 2002.

Internet

Habitat for Humanity Homepage	http://www.habitat.org/	Learn how, where, and why these houses are being built.
Habitat for Humanity Canada	http://www.habitat.ca/	Read about the people who receive the homes and those who build the homes in Canada.
Action without Borders	http://www.idealist.org/kt	Learn what other kids are doing to help others. Check out what volunteer opportunities there are in your state.
Kids Can Make a Difference	http://www.kids.maine.org/	Learn what kids are doing to help end hunger and poverty in their communities and around the world.

Other Resources

Videotape on using vinyl in habitat for humanity housing: http://c3.org/partnerships/pfh/video.html

Watch a house go up in 30 seconds: http://www.artsci.wustl.edu/~marton/Images/AdZemel.html

Interview someone at Habitat for Humanities. Have your questions ready before you call.

For the Teacher

Service learning lesson plans for all ages: http://www.goodcharacter.com/SERVICE/webresources.html

Education Planet's links for volunteering: http://www.educationplanet.com/search/Environment/Volunteering/

Links to volunteerism Web sites from the U.S. State Department: http://usinfo.state.gov/usa/volunteer/other.htm

---

Joke

Q: Where can you always find a helping hand?

A: At the end of your arm!

HARRY POTTER

Something Extra

Make up a new game with rules, similar to Quidditch. Explain it to your friends and have them play it with you.

Start your own *Hogwart's Journal* about your friends, school, and secrets.

Thinking About the Topic

The famous Harry Potter attends Hogwarts School for Witchcraft and Wizardry. His classmates and teachers know he is destined for greatness. If you are a Harry Potter fan, you may want to write about this book character. You may even want to write about his Muggles family or another book character.

Directions

You will not be able to write about Harry until you have read at least one of the books. Remember, you are writing about *a character* in a book. Select three questions from the list below, including question 1. Use several books or other resources to answer your questions. Each of your questions will be a paragraph. Draw a conclusion. For example, the conclusion for question 1 might be: "Harry Potter is the title character in the book series by J. K. Rowling." The conclusion will be the paragraph title sentence.

1. Who is Harry Potter? Describe him. What kind of person is he?

2. Describe the Muggles family Harry lives with. What is Harry's life like with them? Why do you think they are so mean to Harry Potter?

3. Tell about Hogwarts School for Witchcraft and Wizardry. What is Harry's life like there?

4. What do you like best about Harry Potter and his friends? Describe one of their adventures.

5. Read the book, then see the movie, *Harry Potter and the Sorcerer's Stone.* Were you pleased or disappointed with the movie? Which do you like best, the movie or the book? Why?

Books

Keywords: *Rowling, J.K.; Harry Potter; Authors—Juvenile Literature.*

Biography for Beginners. Detroit: Omnigraphics, 2000.

Fraser, Lindsey. *Conversations with J.K. Rowling*. New York: Scholastic, 2001.

J.K. Rowling. Who Wrote That? Broomall, PA: Chelsea House, 2002.

Rowling, J. K.—*Harry Potter and the Sorcerer's Stone. Harry Potter and the Chamber of Secrets. Harry Potter and the Prisoner of Azkaban. Harry Potter and the Goblet of Fire.*

Something About the Author, Volume 109. Detroit: Gale, 1999.

Internet

Bloomsbury Magazine	http://www.bloomsburymagazine.com/harrypotter/	A little about Harry, the author J. K. Rowling, and the books.
Harry Potter at Scholastic	http://www.scholastic.com/harrypotter/	From Scholastic books. Slow, but worth it.
Harry Potter Lexicon	http://www.i2k.com/~svderark/lexicon	This is a great site. It includes all kinds of information to help you. We like the timelines and Quidditch rules.
Official Harry Potter Site	http://harrypotter.warnerbros.com/	You will need Flash on your computer for this multimedia site.
The Unofficial HP Site	http://www.harrypotterfans.net	Chat, calendar, book reviews, Quidditch rules, encyclopedia "potterica."

Other Resources

Write to J. K. Rowling, c/o Scholastic Inc., 555 Broadway, New York, NY 10012-3999.

Harry Potter and the Sorcerer's Stone (video). Burbank, CA: Warner Home Video, 2002.

Harry Potter and the Chamber of Secrets (video). Burbank, CA: Warner Home Video, 2003.

Harry Potter: http://harrypotter.warnerbros.com/home.html Video trailers from Warners.

For the Teacher

Harry Potter books will be great "chapter" read-alouds. Declare a *Harry Potter Day* and have the students dress as their favorite characters. (You be Headmaster.) Play one of the games described in the books. Arrange long tables in the cafeteria and lunch with the "teachers" at the head, just like Hogwarts School.

Lesson plan for Harry Potter books: http://www.angelfire.com/co3/teachhpotter/index.html

---

Potter Games

1. *Harry Potter Games Online:* http://www.harrypotterfans.net/fun/games.html
2. Crossword puzzle: http://www.surfnetkids.com/popup.htm

HUNGER IN THE UNITED STATES

Thinking About the Topic

It is sad to think that there are children in America who go to bed hungry. But it is true. Try to find out more about this subject. You may want to find information about hunger in America in general, or consider writing about your own community. See what can you do to help children who are hungry. Help start a food drive at your school. Churches and schools have a list of families who need help. Houston has a restaurant run by the homeless, called Soup and More. Does your city have one you can visit?

Directions

When you are ready, select question 1 and two others. Write one question at the top of each page. Look in several sources for the answers to your questions. Each question will become a paragraph in your report. Draw a conclusion from the answers you find. The conclusion will be your topic sentence. Add details to the paragraph from your notes.

1. Who are the "hungry children" in your community? How can you help them?

2. Discuss organizations in your community that help poor families.

3. Children who do not have an adequate diet can be at risk. In what ways?

4. Find statistics about how many children in America are hungry. Discuss.

5. What programs do the schools have that help hungry children?

Books

Keywords: *Hunger in America—Juvenile; Poverty in America—Juvenile; Food Banks.*

Bridges, Jeff, comp. *Cooking Up an End to Childhood Hunger in America.* New York: Time, 2001.

Grant, Bruce. *A Furious Hunger: America in the 21st Century.* Carlton, VIC: Melbourne University Press, 1999.

Lyons, Mary E. *Feed the Children First: Irish Memories of the Great Hunger.* New York: Atheneum Books for Young Readers, 2002.

Meltzer, Milton. *Poverty in America.* New York: Morrow, 1987.

Internet

End Hunger Network	http://www.endhunger.com/Children.html	Look closely at "How Children Are Affected."
Who's Hungry in America?	http://64.224.98.61/whoshungry/hunger_study_intro.html	Take a look around this site, especially at "Childhood Hunger."
Kids Can Make a Difference	http://www.kids.maine.org/	Newsletter, statistics, facts, and ideas for kids.
America's Second Harvest	http://www.secondharvest.org/childhunger/childhunger.html	Statistics, what you can do, programs to help stop hunger.

Other Resources

This is a very good topic to talk about with your local church or organization that works with families in trouble. Call the Salvation Army or another local organization that cares for the homeless. Ask questions about the care children get at these places. Write your questions down and have paper and pencil ready for the interview. **Hint:** A thank you note is always welcomed. Possible questions to ask them:

- How many families do you feed each day?

- What percentage of the people you feed are children?

- Why do families come to you? What happens to make a family not able to take care of itself?

- How long can a family stay with you? (or at a soup kitchen, How long will you continue to feed a family?)

For the Teacher

- Have your class organize a food project for Thanksgiving or another holiday. Let the children plan every step from phoning to delivery. They can identify local homeless families or deliver directly to a local organization.

- Children's Hunger Relief Fund: http://www.chrf.org/. Help your class collect money so a child can eat for a year.

- *Feeding Minds—Stopping Hunger*: http://www.feedingminds.org/. Lesson plan ideas by grade level.

- *Food History Lesson Plans*: http://www.gti.net/mocolib1/kid/food2a.html. Includes hunger.

Joke

Q: What did the mother ghost tell the baby ghost when he ate too fast?

A: Quit goblin your food.

HURRICANES AND TORNADOES

Something Extra

Make a hurricane: http://www.ucar.edu/40th/webweather/tornado/tornadoes.htm

---

Thinking About the Topic

The fastest winds in the world are often found in hurricanes and tornadoes. They are strong enough to pick up cars, trucks, and even houses! In the past, a hurricane could kill thousands of people! They would not even know it was coming. In our time, meteorologists study and predict hurricanes and tornadoes. However, they still cannot prevent them or redirect the powerful winds.

Directions

Choose to report about tornadoes or hurricanes. Answer three questions on your topic. Take notes from several resources. Draw a conclusion from the answers you find. The conclusion will be your topic sentence. Add details to the paragraph from your notes. Add pictures of storm damage from the newspaper or Internet to your report.

1. Describe a tornado. Include speed, sound, and damage done.

2. Where do most tornadoes happen? When? What causes them?

3. Describe a hurricane. How do hurricanes form? Where and when? How do they get their names?

4. Write about one famous hurricane.

5. Tell about hurricane hunters or tornado chasers.

Books

Keywords: *Hurricanes; Weather; Natural Disasters; Storms; Tornadoes.*

Allaby, Michael. *Tornadoes and Other Dramatic Weather Systems.* London: Dorling Kindersley, 2001.

Berger, Melvin, and Gilda Berger. *Do Tornadoes Really Twist? Questions and Answers About Tornadoes and Hurricanes.* New York: Scholastic, 2000.

Challoner, Jack. *Hurricane and Tornado.* London: Dorling Kindersley, 2000.

Claybourne, Anna. *Tornadoes.* Brookfield, CT: Copper Beech, 2000.

Morgan, Sally. *Read About Hurricanes.* Brookfield, CT. Copper Beech, 2000.

New Book of Popular Science. Danbury, CT: Grolier, 2000.

Newton, David E., Rob Nagel, and Bridget Travers, ed. *UXL Encyclopedia of Science.* Detroit: UXL, 1998.

Summer, Ray, ed. *World Geography.* Pasadena, CA: Salem, 2001.

Internet

Miami Museum of Science	http://www.miamisci.org/hurricane/	How do hurricanes work? How are they tracked?
FEMA	http://www.fema.gov/kids/hurr.htm	Hurricane names, classification, tracking, and hunters
Environment Canada	http://www.ns.ec.gc.ca/weather/hurricane/kids.html	How do hurricanes work? What should you do if you are in the path of one? Includes games.
National Severe Storms Laboratory	http://www.photolib.noaa.gov/nssl/tornado1.html	Great photographs!
Sky Diary	http://skydiary.com/kids/	Hurricanes, tornados, lightning, and storm chasing.
NOAA	http://www.nws.noaa.gov/om/reachout/kidspage.shtml	Hurricanes, winter storms, tornadoes, floods—facts, precautions, true stories.

Other Resources

Film clip on weather: http://www.brainpop.com/science/weather/weather/index.weml

Hurricanes and Tornadoes. Weather Fundamentals video series. Wynnewood, PA: Schlessinger Media, 1998.

Video clips of hurricanes and tornados, from FEMA: http://www.fema.gov/kids/v_lib.htm

Virtual tour of a hurricane, from NASA: http://kids.earth.nasa.gov/archive/hurricane/tour.html

For the Teacher

Lesson plans for hurricanes, tornados, and other disasters: http://www.engineering.usu.edu/jrestate/lessons/lesson.htm

http://lessonplancentral.com/lessons/Weather/hurricanes/

http://www.cln.org/themes/hurricanes.html

Limerick

There was a young boy named Alfredo
Who was caught in a raging tornado.
When the wind put him down
He was way out of town
And had to walk back to Laredo.

INVENTIONS AND INVENTORS

Something Extra

Fun and games from the U.S. patent office:
http://www.uspto.gov/go/kids/kidsgames.html

Work on an invention of your own. Most inventions happen because someone thinks of a way to make a job easier. What would make your life easier? Maybe a kitchen gadget or a small tool. Try inventing it.

Thinking About the Topic

Some people become famous for what they can do. They are good ball players or singers or actors. Inventors are different. They become famous for creating something we have never had before. When George Washington Carver wanted to paint, he could not afford to buy paints. So he made his own from paint from clay and plants. William Wright and Orville Wright repaired bicycles, but they really wanted to fly. They invented the airplane, using some bicycle parts. When Alexander Graham Bell wanted to be able to talk to someone without going over to that person's house, he invented the telephone.

Directions

There are two ways you can approach the subject of inventions. You can write about either an invention or an inventor. Once you have chosen your topic, using several resources, answer question 1 and two other questions below. Write each question at the top of a separate page. Take notes on the pages you create. Your notes should be written in complete sentences. Each question will become a paragraph in your report. After you have found the answers, draw a conclusion about your information. Your conclusion will be the topic sentence for the paragraph. Use the rest of your notes for details.

1. If you decide to write about an invention, your first question should be "How did we get _____?" (the bicycle, the radio, the can opener)

2. What got your inventor interested in the invention?

3. Describe the problem he or she was trying to solve and attempts to solve them.

4. Did this person also invent other things? What and why, or why not?

5. How did this invention benefit the world?

Books

Keywords: *Inventions and Inventors* (or search for your inventor or invention by name).

Jeffries, Michael, and Gary A. Lewis. *Inventors and Inventions.* Facts America Series. New York: Smithmark, 1992.

Kane, Joseph. *Famous First Facts: A Record of First Happenings, Discoveries, and Inventions in American History.* New York: H. W. Wilson, 1997.

New Book of Popular Science. Danbury, CT: Grolier, 2000.

World Book Encyclopedia of Science: Men and Women of Science. Chicago: World Book, 2001.

Internet

Mining Company	http://inventors. miningco.com/	Look up inventors by name or by their inventions.
U. S. Government Patent Office	http://www.uspto.gov/ go/kids/	Kids' pages, with puzzles, games, and challenges about inventions.
Girl Tech	http://www.girltech. com/invention/IN_ menu_frame.html	Inventions by or for girls.
The Invention Dimension!	http://web.mit.edu/ invent/	Sites for kids—great links for kids. Also, look at what other kids have invented.

Other Resources

Video clip about Thomas Edison's inventions: http://www.edison-ford-estate.com/thomas-edison/ Ebio.htm#

Connections 3 (video): [Journey on the Web]. A production of The Learning Channel. New York: Manufactured and distributed by Ambrose Video Publishing, 1997.

Have the librarian help you find a video on inventions. Your library should have some.

For the Teacher

Lesson Plans that teach students to come up with an invention: http://Inventors. miningco.com/cs/lessonplans/lessonplans

"Teaching through invention" lesson plans: http://www.educationworld.com/a_lesson/ lesson240.shtml

---

Find the Answer

Who invented Gatorade? Why was it developed?

HELEN KELLER

Something Extra

See your name in Braille and other Braille games:
http://www.afb.org/braillebug/Games.asp

Learn sign language and play this game:
http://www.iidc.indiana.edu/cedir/kidsweb/gameschamber.html

Thinking About the Topic

Have you sometimes pretended you were blind and tried to walk with your eyes closed? Do you act like you are deaf when you want to ignore your Mom? Just think what it would be like if you were really blind and deaf at the same time! Helen Keller lost her vision and hearing at an early age, but she still learned to talk and read. She and her teacher, Anne Sullivan, did something for blind and deaf people that will always be remembered.

Directions

To report on Helen Keller, answer three of the questions below on your topic. Take notes from several resources. Draw a conclusion from the answers you find. The conclusion will be your topic sentence. Add details to the paragraph from your notes.

1.   Tell about Helen Keller's early life. What was her relationship with Anne Sullivan?

2.   Describe Helen's life after her loss of sight and hearing.

3.   How did Helen learn to communicate?

4.   Describe some of the things Helen did to help others.

5.   What did Helen do for fun? How is that different from what sighted people do?

Books

Keywords: *Keller, Helen; Braille.*

Bredeson, Carmen. *Presidential Medal of Freedom Winners.* Springfield, NJ: Enslow, 1996.

Graff, Stewart, and Polly Anne Graff. *Helen Keller: Crusader for the Blind & Deaf.* New York: Young Yearling, 1991.

Hurwitz, Joanna. *Helen Keller: Courage in the Dark.* New York: Random House, 1997.

Keller, Helen. *The Story of My Life*. Garden City, NY: Doubleday, 1905.

World Book Encyclopedia of People and Places. Chicago: World Book, 2000. Available: http://www.worldbook.com.

Internet

RNIB Factsheet	http://www.rnib.org.uk/wesupply/fctsheet/keller.htm	The life of Helen Keller.
American Foundation for the Blind	http://www.afb.org/info_documents.asp?CollectionID=1&KitID=9	Photographs of Helen Keller.
In Search of the Heroes	http://www.graceproducts.com/keller/life.html	Brief biography of Helen Keller.
The Miracle	http://www.time.com/time/time100/heroes/profile/keller01.html	From *100 Heroes* page, facts about Keller's life.

Other Resources

Video clip of Helen Keller and Anne Sullivan demonstrating how Helen learned to speak: http://www.britannica.com/women/ind_mediagallery.html

Miracle Worker (video). Santa Monica, CA: MGM Home Entertainment, 2001.

For the Teacher

Several lesson plans on blindness, for older children: http://www.DistinguishedWomen.com and http://www.hollows.org/resources/lesson_plan/lesson_plan.htm

Lesson plan teaching the use of Braille: http://www.educationworld.com/a_tsl/archives/00-1/lesson0013.shtml

National Information Clearinghouse on Children Who Are Deaf-Blind: http://www.tr.wou.edu/dblink/biblio.htm

---

Joke

Joe: What would happen if I cut off your ear?

Sam: I wouldn't be able to hear.

Joe: What would happen if I cut off your other ear?

Sam: I wouldn't be able to see.

Joe: Why couldn't you see if I cut off both your ears?

Sam: My hat would fall down over my eyes.

MARTIN LUTHER KING JR.

> ## Something Extra
>
> Make a teeny tiny book about Martin Luther King Jr.:
> http://www.geocities.com/Heartland/6459/mlk.html

Thinking About the Topic

Sticks and stones can break my bones but words will never hurt me! When someone is mean to you, you want to fight back, don't you? But fighting back makes them angrier. It is difficult to make peace again. Martin Luther King Jr. had every reason to be angry. He decided it was best for his people to fight back in a peaceful way. He organized them to fight peacefully for equal rights for African Americans. His enemies still found ways to put him in jail. He became an American hero.

Directions

Using several resources, answer question 1 and two other questions below. Write each question at the top of a separate page. Take notes on the pages you create. Your notes should be written in complete sentences. Each question will become a paragraph in your report. After you have found the answers, draw a conclusion about your information. Your conclusion will be the topic sentence for the paragraph.

1. Who was Martin Luther King Jr.?

2. What was Martin Luther King Jr.'s early life like?

3. What did Martin Luther King Jr. and his followers do when they were angry? How did they fight back?

4. What happened to Martin Luther King Jr.? What effect did he have on the Civil Rights movement?

5. Do you consider Martin Luther King Jr. an American hero? Why or why not?

Books

Keywords: *King, Martin Luther, Jr.; Civil Rights Workers; African American History.*

Contemporary Black Biography. Farmington Hills, MI: Thomson, 1992– .

Knight, Judson. *African American Biography.* Farmington Hills, MI: UXL, 1999.

Lambert, Kathy Kristensen. *Martin Luther King, Jr.: Civil Rights Leader.* Broomall, PA: Chelsea House, 1993.

Moss, Joyce, and George Wilson. *Profiles in American History*. Farmington Hills, MI: Gale, 1995.

Schaefer, Lola M. *Martin Luther King, Jr.* Mankato, MN: Capstone Press, 1999.

Internet

Kulture Zone	http://www.kulturezone.com/kidz/calendar/mlk/index.html	Listen to King's famous "I have a Dream" speech.
Buckman School	Buckman.pps.k12.or.us/room100/timeline/kingframe.html	Timeline.
Seattle Times	http://www.seattletimes.com/mlk/index.html	Biography of MLK.
The Power of Speech	*The Power of Speech* (video)	See MLK make his famous speech, "I have a dream."

Other Resources

Hear excerpts from Dr. Martin Luther King Jr.'s speeches: http://www.archervalerie.com/mlk.html.

Martin Luther King Jr.: The Man and the Dream (video). New York: A & E Home Video, c1999.

Our Friend, Martin (video). Los Angeles: 20th Century Fox, 2000.

Power of Speech (video). Princeton, NJ: Films for the Humanities and Sciences, 1994.

For the Teacher

A collection of lesson plans for various grade levels: http://atozteacherstuff.com/themes/mlk.shtml

MLK activities for young children: http://www.childfun.com/themes/mlk.shtml

Links to worksheets, puzzles, and games to reinforce lessons on Martin Luther King Jr.: http://www.educationplanet.com/articles/mlk.html#child

MLK Lesson Plans and Links: http://www.education-world.com/a_lesson/lesson046.shtml

World of MLK for Teachers: http://martinlutherking.8m.com/

Find Out

What did MLK talk about in his "Letter from the Birmingham Jail?"

LIBRARIES

Something Extra

Take a trip to your local public library and get your own library card.

Read *The Librarian from the Black Lagoon* by Mike Thaler to a first-grade class during their story time.

Thinking About the Topic

Librarians like to say, "Libraries bring you the world." What do they mean by that? Libraries are changing every day. Visit your library and really look at what is going on. Every job has its own language. Learn some of the language of the library. Write about the services libraries provide for teachers and students.

Directions

When you are ready, select question 1 and two others. Write one question at the top of each page. Look in several sources for the answers to your questions. Each question will become a paragraph in your report. Draw a conclusion from the answers you find. The conclusion will be your topic sentence.

1. Where did libraries come from? Who started the first library? Why?

2. How are libraries organized? Describe two different collections in your library.

3. Who works in a library? What are their jobs?

4. How has the Internet changed the job of the librarian? What information do you get online rather than in books?

5. What is a virtual library? How is it different from your school library?

6. A shortage of librarians is predicted for the future. If you wanted to be a librarian, what education would you need? What do you think your job would be like?

Books

Keywords: *Libraries—Juvenile Literature.*

Cart, Michael. *In the Stacks: Short Stories About Libraries and Librarians* Woodstock, NY: Overlook Press, 2002.

Hill, Lee Sullivan. *Libraries Take Us Far.* Minneapolis, MN: Carolrhoda, 1998.

Johnston, Marianne. *Let's Visit the Library.* New York: Rosen, 2000.

Kent, Zachary. *Andrew Carnegie: Steel King and Friend to Libraries.* Springfield, NJ: Enslow Publishers, 1999.

"Libraries." *World Almanac* or *World Book Encyclopedia.*

Vogel, Elizabeth. *Meet the Librarian.* New York: PowerKids Press, 2002.

Internet

Library of Congress	http://www.loc.gov	Visit the Library of Congress online and see what is available. This library really does offer the world.
Your Own Library	There are many libraries online. Look up your school or local library online and see what is available to you on the Web. Did you find book lists? Subject guides? Author information? The library catalog? A magazine database? A calendar? Anything else?	

Other Resources

Interview the librarian at your school. Have your questions ready. You might tape record the session.

There are several videos about libraries. See if your librarian can help you find one.

Dora the Explorer: Dora's Backpack Adventure (video). Hollywood, CA: Paramount, 2002.

For the Teacher

Read-aloud: *The Library Card* by Jerry Spinelli. Scranton, PA: Scholastic, 1998.

Take a trip to the library for a group interview of the librarian and the library helpers.

Have your class help the librarian "read" the library shelves.

The Perfect Excuse!

or

Why my book has not been returned to the library!

- I left it in my truck and my truck was in an accident and got towed to the garage and I won't be able to get to the garage until this weekend.
- My mother took it camping and lost it.
- I never had that book!
- My cat peed on it and it smells too bad.
- It flew out the car window on the freeway and was devoured by an 18 wheeler!
- My little sister tried to read it when she was taking a bath.

LICE (HEAD LICE)

Something Extra

Play Head Games, read poetry, and enter the monthly poster contest at *Headlice.org*: http://www.headlice.org/

Thinking About the Topic

Scratch! Scratch! Scratch! When school begins each year, tiny little creatures visit the classroom. They love everyone. The school nurse hates them. Your parents despise them. They are the size of a sesame seed. They love it when you share a comb with a friend. What are they? LICE! COOTIES! YUK!

Directions

For your report on head lice answer question 1 and any two others below. Write each question at the top of a separate page. Take notes on the pages you create. Your notes should be in complete sentences. Each question will become a paragraph in your report. After you have found the answers, draw a conclusion about the information. (For example, the question 5 conclusion might be: "You can get rid of lice by _____.") Your conclusion will be the topic sentence for the paragraph. Your notes will be the details for the paragraphs.

1. Describe the tiny louse. (Remember, louse is one, lice are more than one.)

2. Describe the life cycle of lice.

3. What do lice eat, and where do they get their food?

4. How can lice be spread from one person to another?

5. How do we get rid of head lice?

Books

Keywords: *Lice; Pediculosis.*

Caffey, Donna. *Yikes, Lice.* Morton Grove, IL: Albert Whitman, 1998.

Copeland, Lennie. *The Lice-Buster Book: What to Do When Your Child Comes Home with Head Lice!* Boston: Warner, 1996.

Hayes, Cheri. *There's a Louse in My House: A Kid's Story About Head Lice.* New York: Jayjo, 2001.

"Lice." *World Book Encyclopedia.*

Merrick, Patrick. *Lice.* Naturebook's Creepy Crawlers Series. New York: Child's World, 2000.

Internet

Why Lice Aren't So Nice	http://kidshealth.org/kid/ill_injure/ sick/lice.html	Kids Health Organization. Very good site about lice, what they are, and how to get rid of them.
Having a Lousy Week?	http://pbskids.org/arthur/grownups/ lice/index.html	Information from Arthur.
Headlice.org	http://www.headlice.org/	Check out the FAQs and the animations. For parents and kids.
Head Lice Info	http://www.hsph.harvard.edu/ headlice.html	Harvard University fact sheet about head lice. Take your time; the answers are very clear. This is a good site.

Other Resources

The NPA's *All Out Comb Out.* Order online at http://www.headlice.org/catalog/catalog4.htm

Licemeister. An instructional video.

Head Lice to Dead Lice: Safe Solutions for Frantic Families (video). Weston, MA: Sawyer Mac Productions, 1997.

For the Teacher

Harvard School of Public Health: http://www.hsph.harvard.edu/headlice.html. Background information for adults about head lice.

Head Lice Information: http://www.headliceinfo.com. Try "Know Your Enemy." Order *Head Lice to Dead Lice* (video with five-step plan for getting rid of lice).

Centers for Disease Control: http://www.cdc.gov/ncidod/dpd/parasites/headlice/factsht_head_ lice.htm

Zollman, Pam. *Don't Bug Me!* New York: Holiday House, 2001. Great read-aloud book. Megan Hollander has to collect 25 different species of bugs. And she hates bugs!

Joke

Mom, the teacher says I have headlights.

ABRAHAM LINCOLN

Something Extra

Online crossword puzzle created by Marshall Elementary School:
http://www.marshall-es.marshall.k12.tn.us/jobe/lincoln.html

Thinking About the Topic

Have you ever thought school was too much work? Or that your parents want you to do too many chores? Just think what life was like 150 years ago when Abe Lincoln was young. He helped his family with clearing forests and farming! Swing the axe, clear the forest, plant the crops, stack the logs to build a house. Abraham Lincoln grew up working hard, and when he went to school, it was only for a few weeks at a time. He became the fifteenth American president.

Directions

For your report on Abraham Lincoln answer question 1 and any two other questions below. Write each question at the top of a separate page. Take notes on the pages you create. Your notes should be in complete sentences. Each question will become a paragraph in your report.

1. Describe Abraham Lincoln's early life.

2. Was Lincoln an educated man? Tell about his education.

3. What were some of Lincoln's early jobs?

4. Discuss Lincoln's family.

5. Tell about how Lincoln became president. What did he believe in?

6. What famous address did Lincoln give? Discuss what he said.

7. What makes Abraham Lincoln great? How did he affect the way this country grew?

Books

Keywords: *Lincoln, Abraham; Presidents of the United States.*

Bashfield, Jean F. *Profiles of the Presidents: Abraham Lincoln.* Minneapolis, MN: Compass Point Books, 2002.

Bowler, Sarah. *Abraham Lincoln: Our Sixteenth President.* Chanhassen, MN: Child's World, 2001.

D'Aulaire, Ingri, and Edgar Parin D'Aulaire. *Abraham Lincoln*. Garden City, NY: Doubleday, 1957.

Grabowski, John F. *Abraham Lincoln: Civil War President*. Brookmall, PA: Chelsea House, 2001.

Oberle, Lora Polack. *Abraham Lincoln*. Mankato, MN: Bridgestone Books, 2002.

Raatma, Lucia. *Abraham Lincoln*. Minneapolis, MN: Compass Point Books, 2000.

Internet

Smithsonian Institute	http://americanhistory.si.edu/presidency/home.html	Pictures of the presidents and some of the possessions; summary of their terms.
Spectrum Home and School Magazine	http://www.incwell.com/Biographies/Lincoln.html	Biography.
White House	http://www.whitehouse.gov/history/presidents/al16.html	Biography emphasizing his years as president.
Berwick Academy	http://www.berwickacademy.org/lincoln/lincoln.htm	Illustrated timeline, created by kids.

Other Resources

Video clips of Abraham Lincoln's life, from the Illinois Humanities Council: http://lincoln.lib.niu.edu/aboutbiovideo.html

Songs from Abraham Lincoln's era: http://lincoln.lib.niu.edu/sound.html

President Abraham Lincoln (video). Irving, TX: Nest Entertainment, 1993.

For the Teacher

How the Berwick Academy studied Lincoln and created a Web page: http://www.berwickacademy.org/lincoln/how.htm

Lesson plans about Abraham Lincoln, crafts, and games for grades K–6: http://www.proteacher.com/090158.shtml

---

Joke

Q: What is the difference between George Washington and Abraham Lincoln?

A: Lincoln lived in Washington, but Washington never lived in Lincoln.

YO-YO MA

> ## Something Extra
>
> Making sounds with string:
> http://www.sci.mus.mn.us/sound/nocss/activity/ssl9.htm

Thinking About the Topic

Have you ever wanted something so much that you were willing to do anything to have it? Even practice for hours and hours each day? That is what outstanding classical musicians like Yo-Yo Ma have to do. But even after all that practicing, they need something more. They need an extra spark that makes them special. Yo-Yo Ma is a famous cellist who works hard and practices long hours. You can see him performing with orchestras on television. Yo-Yo Ma has done a television commercial for Apple computer. Have you seen it?

Directions

To write your report about Yo-Yo Ma, answer question 1 and any two other questions below. Write each question at the top of a separate page. Take notes on the pages you create. Each question will become a paragraph in your report. After you have found the answers, draw a conclusion about the information. Your conclusion will be the topic sentence for the paragraph. Add details to each paragraph from your notes.

1.   Who is Yo-Yo Ma? What does he do that makes him famous today?

2.   What is a typical day like for Yo-Yo Ma?

3.   Why is it important for someone who plays so well to continue to practice?

4.   Yo-Yo Ma has what we call charisma. What does this mean? Watch a video of Mr. Ma and see if you agree. (Look for humor, good storytelling ability, eye contact with the audience, and that something extra that makes you enjoy his music.)

5.   How is Yo-Yo Ma a good role model for budding musicians?

Books

Keywords: *Ma, Yo-Yo; Cellists; Ma, Yo-Yo—Biography—Juvenile literature.*

DeRemer, Leish Ann, ed. *Contemporary Musicians.* Detroit: Gale, 2002.

Grolier Library of North American Biographies. Danbury, CT: Grolier, 1994.

Harris, Laurie Lanzer, ed. *Biography Today.* Detroit: Omnigraphics. Serial.

Ma, Marina. *My Son Yo-Yo*. Ann Arbor: University of Michigan, 1995.

Ma, Yo-Yo. *Along the Silk Road*. Seattle: University of Washington Press, 2002.

Marzollo, Jean. *My First Book of Biographies*. New York: Scholastic, 1994.

Internet

Yo-Yo Ma's Home Page	http://www.yo-yoma.com/	Biography, music, film clips, schedule.
Sony	http://www.sonyclassical.com/artists/ma/bio.html	Biography.
Silk Road Project	http://www.silkroadproject.org/	Crossing cultures, fostering creativity. The Silk Road Project is Yo-Yo Ma's pet project. Hear a little audio, too.
Yo-Yo Ma	http://www.pbs.org/wnet/gperf/feature1/html/feature_bio1.html	Biography from PBS.

Other Resources

Watch a video clip of *The Music Garden*: http://sonyclassical.com/music/63203/films/media/MusicGarden_dir.mov

Listen to Yo-Yo Ma talk about the soul of the tango: http://sonyclassical.com/music/63122/

Hear part of Yo-Yo Ma's *Silk Road Journeys; When Strangers Meet* at http://www.sonyclassical.com/music/89782/ (or rent it out from your local video store).

For the Teacher

Lesson plans on Asian culture: http://www.askasia.org/teachers/Instructional_Resources/Lesson_Plans/index.htm

Have your music class listen to Yo-Yo Ma. What makes his music so special? (A video would be even better and would capture his personality and love of music.)

Teacher's guide to the *Silk Road Project*: http://teachers.silkroadproject.org/

Joke

Q: How do you make a cello sound beautiful?

A: Sell it and buy a violin.

MARTIAL ARTS

Something Extra

Ask someone (maybe yourself) to perform a kata for the class before your report.

Thinking About the Topic

When Bruce Lee fells an enemy with a flying sidekick or Chuck Norris splits a tree stump in half with the side of his hand, they're practicing martial arts. Martial arts are far more than brute force. You would know that if you have ever taken a course and practiced the exercises. What else are they?

Directions

Answer question 1 and any two other questions below. Write each question at the top of a separate page. Take notes on the pages you create. Your notes should be in complete sentences. Each question will become a paragraph in your report. After you have found the answers, draw a conclusion about the information. Your conclusion will be the topic sentence for the paragraph. Add details from the notes you take.

1. Where and how did martial arts originate?

2. Discuss two different martial arts. How are they different? The same?

3. Describe a martial arts competition. What happens? How do competitors get points? Where can they go from there?

4. What are the benefits of martial arts?

5. If you have taken a martial arts class, tell about your school and classes. Demonstrate your talent.

Books

Keywords: *Judo; Karate; Tae Kwon Do; Jujitsu; Aikido; Kung Fu.*

Collins, Paul. *Judo*. Broomall, PA: Chelsea House, 2001.

Corcoran, John, and Emil Farkas. *Original Martial Arts Encyclopedia*. Los Angeles: Pro-action, 1993.

Knotts, Bob. *Martial Arts*. New York, Children's Press, 2000.

Metil, Luana, and Jace Townsend. *The Story of Karate from Buddhism to Bruce Lee*. Minneapolis, MN: Lerner, 1995.

Morris, Neil. *Karate*. Chicago: Heinemann, 2001.

Morris, Neil. *Tae Kwon Do*. Chicago: Heinemann, 2001.

Zannos, Susan. *Fitness Stars of the Martial Arts: Featuring Profiles of Bruce Lee, Chuck Norris, Cynthia Rothrock, and Carlos Machado*. Bear, DE: Mitchell Lane, 2000.

Internet

Black Belt Kids	http://w3.blackbeltmag.com/bbkids/	History, tips, and features on martial artists.
International Judo Foundation	http://www.ijf.org/htmls/main.html	Photos and rules.
About.com	http://martialarts.about.com/library/weekly/aa092799.htm	Compares the different martial arts.
Warrior Information Network	http://www.winjutsu.com/ninjakids/index.html	History, techniques, vocabulary.

Other Resources

Jackie Chan Adventures; The Power Within (video). Culver City, CA: Columbia Tristar, 2001.

Video clips of aiku jujitsu: http://jujitsu.geddis.org/movies/descriptions.html

Animated throwing techniques of judo: http://judoinfo.com/animate.htm

For the Teacher

Web site for health and PE teachers: http://pe.central.vt.edu/

Martial Arts e-zine: http://tutor.hypermart.net/martialarts_ezine7199.htm

---

Joke

Did you hear about the girl who studied judo in case a boy should kiss her and try to run away?

MODERN ART

Something Extra
Create your own painting online: http://www.kidpix.com/kid_paint.html

Thinking About the Topic

Cave people painted crude pictures of hunts or battles on cave walls. We call this prehistoric art. In the 1600s, artists made very accurate paintings of people and landscapes. That is called Renaissance art. During the twentieth century, painters started creating pictures that did not always look like anything at all. They were painting what they felt. We call this modern art. Some modern artists were Picasso, Miro, Calder, and Kandinsky. (You could write about the artist, the style, or modern art.) Try one of the modern art styles yourself. It is not as easy as it seems!

Directions

Choose a style of modern art to investigate. You might try cubism, surrealism, or abstractionism. Or write about an artist of the period. Investigate three questions, beginning with "What is modern art?" Answer each question using several resources. Watch a video if you can—or take a trip to your local museum. A talk with your local art teacher or artist would be very helpful. Be sure to allow your teacher to read your "open-ended questions" so you know they will lead to good information. Be sure to talk about what you feel when you see these paintings.

GOOD QUESTION: How does the artist use color and shapes to illustrate feelings?

POOR QUESTION: Does the artist use color to illustrate feelings?

Books

Keywords: *Modern art; Cubism; Painting, modern; Picasso;* add *Juvenile.*

Barnes, Rachel. *Abstract Expressionists.* Crystal Lake, IL: Heinemann, 2002.

Bolton, Linda. *Surrealists.* Crystal Lake, IL: Heinemann, 2002.

Krull, Kathleen. *Lives of the Artists: Masterpieces, Masses and What the Neighbors Thought.* San Diego: Harcourt Brace, 1995.

MacDonald, Patricia A. *Pablo Picasso: Greatest Artist of the 20th Century.* Woodbridge, CT: Blackbirch Marketing, 2001.

Mason, Paul. *Pop Artists.* Crystal Lake, IL: Heinemann, 2002.

Wallis, Jeremy. *Cubists.* Crystal Lake, IL: Heinemann, 2002.

Internet

National Gallery of Art	http://www.nga.gov/kids/kids.htm	Explore art in an interactive dimension. Includes stories and music.
Metropolitan Museum of Art	http://www.metmuseum.org/explore/artists.asp	Explore the life, times, and work of various artists, some modern.
Museum of Modern Art	http://www.moma.org/onlineprojects/artsafari/safari_menu.html	Go on a virtual art safari!
Kids Art	http://www.kidsart.com/topten.html	Kids' top ten artists, art museums, music for abstract art, and more.
ThinkQuest	http://library.thinkquest.org/J001159/artstyle.htm	Styles of art and some of the artists.

Other Resources

Interview your art teacher or a local artist, or visit the local art museum or gallery. Study the works there. What do you see? Try to find a poster to share with your class.

Crayola Activity Center, with music: http://www.crayola.com/kids/index.cfm

Interactive exploration of the UC Berkeley Art Museum: http://www.bampfa.berkeley.edu/education/kidsguide/welcome/welcomekids.html

For the Teacher

A multitude of art lesson plans from Crayola: http://www.crayola.com/educators/lessons/index.cfm

Internet School Library Media Center links to art education sites for K–12: http://falcon.jmu.edu/~ramseyil/arteducation.htm

---

Jokes

Q: What do you call a painter who paints crushed soda cans?

A: A pop artist!

Q: Did you hear about the two little boys who found themselves in a modern art gallery?

A: "Quick," one said. "Let's run before they say we did it!"

MONKEYS

Something Extra

Gather your whole family on a beautiful day and go to the local zoo. Take lots of pictures. A picture of you in front of the monkey cage will be a good addition to your report. Make a funny face! Two monkeys in one picture!

Thinking About the Topic

Look at a picture of a monkey. Does it look like your cousin or your uncle? Monkeys, apes, and other primates look so much like people that we love to watch their antics. Sometimes it is fun to pretend we are monkeys and act just like them. There are several kinds of monkeys in the world. Choose a special breed to write about—or write about monkeys in general.

Directions

Write one question at the top of each page. Answer question 1 and choose two other questions from the list below. You may want to learn more about them. Choose one monkey, maybe the spider monkey, or write about monkeys in general. You may want to compare the monkeys in Africa, Asia, or South America. How are they alike? How are they different?

1. What is a monkey?

2. How do monkeys live in the wild? What do they eat? How do they protect themselves?

3. What are the differences between old world monkeys and new world monkeys?

4. Would a monkey make a good pet? Why or why not?

5. Is a zoo a good home for a monkey? Explain your answer.

Books

Keywords: *Monkeys; Animals in captivity; Primates; Spider monkeys.*

Jeunesse, Gallimard, and James Prunier. *Monkeys and Apes.* New York: Scholastic, 1999.

Llewellyn, Claire. *Chimps Use Tools.* Brookfield, ON: Copper Beech Books, 1999.

Maynard, Thane. *Primates: Apes, Monkeys and Prosimians.* New York: Franklin Watts, 1994.

The World Book Student Discovery Encyclopedia. Chicago: World Book, 2002.

Internet

Jane Goodall Institute's Center for Primate Studies	http://www.cbs.umn.edu/chimp/faq.html	Facts about chimpanzees.
Singapore Zoo	http://www.szgdocent.org/pp/p-main.htm	Detailed facts and pictures, for older children.
Wisconsin Regional Primate Research Center	http://www.primates.com/welcome.htm	Fantastic photographs of monkeys, lemurs, and apes.
Primates at the Zoo	http://www.houstonzoo.org/mammals/primset.htm	Information about zoo care of monkeys.

Other Resources

Monkey Business and Other Family Fun (video). Washington, DC: National Geographic Kids, 1996.

Amazing Monkeys and Apes (video). New York: DK Vision, 1997.

Hear the sounds some monkeys and apes make! http://www.indiana.edu/~primate/prpimates.html

Visit the local library or video store for several tapes about monkeys.

Call the local zoo and ask about care of the monkeys. Have your questions ready for your interview.

For the Teacher

A social studies lesson on the ecosystem: http://www.Atozteacherstuff.com/lessons/GreatKapokTree.shtml

Teach the song, "The Three Little Monkeys," to improve motor skills: http://askeric.org/Virtual/Lessons/Arts/Music/MUS0009.html

---

Jokes

Q: Why did the monkey fall out of the tree?

A: Because he was dead.

Q: Why did the squirrel fall out of the tree?

A: Because he was stapled to the monkey.

MONOPOLY GAME

Something Extra

Create a monopoly game of your town and the places you know or of places in your school and your classroom. Be sure to include the principal's office and gym. Take the game to school and play it with classmates. A large poster board would be just the right size. Use drawings or photographs. Use the money and pieces from your own Monopoly game for the game.

Thinking About the Topic

Just imagine, the Monopoly game is over 65 years old. It is still the best-selling board game. Over 200 million Monopoly games have been sold. Your grandparents played Monopoly with your great-grandparents when they were children. Plan a family evening of Monopoly. What fun to write about the history of a game! There are not as many books and Web sites as other topics have, but you will find plenty of information for a very interesting report.

Directions

Select question 1 and two others below. Write one question at the top of each page. Look in several sources for the answers to your questions. Each question will become a paragraph in your report. Draw a conclusion from the answers you find. The conclusion will be your topic sentence.

1. Who invented the Monopoly game? Tell a little about the history of Monopoly.

2. What are a few tips for being a better player, and why do they work?

3. Describe a few of the new versions of Monopoly. Compare them to the original. (**Hint:** Disney has a new Monopoly game.)

4. What do Monopoly game collectors buy? Describe their collections. Why?

5. Why do you think Monopoly has lasted so many years? Why do you enjoy it?

Books

Keywords: *Monopoly game; Board games; Games.*

Brady, Maxine. *The Monopoly Book: Strategy and Tactics of the World's Most Popular Game.* New York: D. McKay, 1976.

Oakley, Ruth. *Board and Card Games.* New York: Marshall Cavendish, 1989.

Orbanes, Philip. *The Monopoly Companion: The Player's Guide: The Game from A to Z, Winning Tips, Trivia.* Avon, MA: Adams Media, 1999.

Parlett, David Sidney. *The Oxford History of Board Games*. New York: Oxford University Press, 1999.

World Book, World Almanac, encyclopedias of games, or any other encyclopedias and dictionaries.

Internet

Monopoly Game	http://www.monopoly.com/	History, news, official rules, and tips and tricks.
Hasbro World	http://www.hasbro.com	Search term: monopoly, then browse links.
Monopoly Collectors	http://www.cabinfever. org/cf_monopoly.html	Look at the different Monopoly versions. Includes Monopoly history and trivia.

Other Resources

Monopoly (computer file). Beverly, MA: Hasbro Interactive, 1999.

Jumanji (video). Check out this fun movie and you will see what a real board game is about! This is a good movie for family night.

Interview your grandparents. Ask about family entertainment when they were children. If they played Monopoly or other board games with their parents (your great-grandparents), ask them to tell you about it.

For the Teacher

An art project could be to have teams create different board games and cards to go with them. What fun!

Have a board game day on the next rainy day or Friday afternoon. Have several students bring games to school. Choose teams of four. Have fun! Be sure to include Monopoly. Each team should get to play two or three different games. Post the winners. Continue on the next rainy day.

Internet Hunt

After 35 years, Monopoly has issued a new piece to play with. What is it? Look online for the answer.

Music

Something Extra
Juice Bottle Jingles! Play music on bottles filled with different amounts of water: http://www.lhs.berkeley.edu/shockwave/jar.html

Thinking About the Topic

A, B, C, D, E, F, G . . . do you know the alphabet song? Of course you do. "Old MacDonald Had a Farm" taught you animal sounds. "There Were Ten Little Monkeys on the Bed" helped you count backwards. Music stays in your head and helps you remember things. As you get older, you learn to enjoy other kinds of music, even music without words.

Directions

Write three questions, developed from from the list below, about the topic you choose. Be sure to define your topic. For example, if you decide to write about a specific musical instrument, your first question might be, "What is a French horn?"

1. Describe some of the earliest musical instruments and their sounds.

2. Describe a family of musical instruments: woodwinds, brass, strings, or percussion.

3. Describe how an instrument works.

4. Choose a favorite musician or composer and describe his or her music.

5. Write about Boy Scout songs, rhythm and blues, rock and roll, hymns, classical, folk, country, jazz, or gospel.

Books

Keywords: *Woodwind Instruments; Stringed Instruments; Brass Instruments; Musicians; Blues (Music); Gospel Musicians; Musical Instruments; Music Appreciation.*

Ardley, Neil. *Music.* London: Dorling Kindersley, 2000.

Blue, Rose. *History of Gospel Music.* Broomall, PA: Chelsea House, 2001.

Bredeson, Carmen. *Ten Great American Composers.* Berkeley Heights, NJ: Enslow, 2002.

Lommel, Cookie. *History of Rap Music.* Broomall, PA: Chelsea House, 2001.

Macaulay, David. *The Way Things Work.* London: Dorling Kindersley, 1988.

Witman, Kathleen L. *CDs, Super Glue & Salsa: How Everyday Products Are Made.* Farmington Hills, MI: UXL, 1996.

World Book Encyclopedia. Chicago: World Book, 2002.

Internet

ThinkQuest	http://library.thinkquest.org/15413/	Musical instruments, games, and history.
Rock and Roll Hall of Fame	http://www.rockhall.com/home/default.asp	News and exhibits vary. Check it out!
Schoolhouse Rock	http://www.apocalypse.org/pub/u/gilly/Schoolhouse_Rock/HTML/schoolhouse.html	Lyrics to "Grammar Rock," "Multiplication Rock," "Science Rock," and "History Rock."
Essentials of Music	http://www.essentialsofmusic.com/	Six main eras of music history, including some audio files, and biographies of 70 composers.
In Harmony with Education	http://www.menc.org/guides/IHWE/ihwes1.html#instruments	Make your own musical instruments.

Other Resources

Videos, audios, and interactive learning on *Music: The Unspoken Word,* by ThinkQuest: http://library.thinkquest.org/C0113187/splash2.html

Listen to the sound of different musical instruments! http://www.Lehigh.EDU/zoellner/encyclopedia.html

Musical Instruments. The Way Things Work video series. Wynnewood, PA: Schlessinger Media, 2002.

For the Teacher

A great selection of resources for teachers, including lesson plans, lyrics, and associations: http://www.isd77.k12.mn.us/resources/staffpages/shirk/k12.music.html#classroom

Have your students make their own simple musical instruments, such as maracas, drums, and a tambourine; for younger children: http://familycrafts.about.com/cs/musicalcrafts/index.htm

National Association for Music Education has some valuable lessons on the art and science of music, for older children: http://www.menc.org/guides/IHWE/ihwet1.html

---

Joke

Q: Why did Grandpa put wheels on his rocking chair?

A: He wanted to rock and roll!

MYSTERY AND DETECTIVE STORIES

Thinking About the Topic

Both children and adults love mystery books. Solving the puzzle before the author reveals the answer is part of the fun. What makes a mystery exciting? Are there rules about writing a mystery or detective book? Consider the *Boxcar Children, Nancy Drew, Encyclopedia Brown, or The Hardy Boys*. There are many children's mystery books. Are you reading your parents' books yet? If you are a good reader, try *The Cat Who . . .* books by Lillian Jackson Brawn. Koko, a Siamese cat, helps uncover clues.

Directions

When you are ready, select question 1 and two others below. Write one question at the top of each page. Look in several sources for the answers to your questions. Each question will become a paragraph in your report. Draw a conclusion from the answers you find. The conclusions will be your topic sentence. The details from your notes will be the paragraphs.

1. What is a mystery or detective story?

2. Describe the history of the mystery or detective story.

3. Good mysteries include a crime, suspense, suspects, a victim, a detective, an alibi, red herrings, and clues. Discuss each mystery story element.

4. Learn about mystery rules. Then examine a particular mystery series you have read, like the Nancy Drew or Hardy Boys books. How do they follow the "rules?"

Books

Keywords: *Detective and mystery stories—Juvenile Literature.*

Bowers, Vivien. *Crime Science: How Investigators Use Science to Track Down the Bad Guys.* Buffalo, NY: Firefly, 2001.

Dixon, Franklin W. *The Hardy Boys Detective Handbook.* New York: Grossett & Dunlap, 1972. (The way detective stories were solved long ago.)

Gorman, Ed. *The Fine Art of Murder: The Mystery Readers Indispensable Companion.* New York: Galahad, 1995.

Herbert, Rosemary, ed. *The Oxford Companion to Crime and Mystery Writing*. New York: Oxford University Press, 1999.

Penzler, Otto. *The Crown Crime Companion: The Top 100 Mystery Novels of All Time*. New York: Crown, 1995.

Use the *World Book* or another encyclopedia to find more information. Ask the librarian for help.

Internet

History of the Kid's Mystery Book	http://kids.MysteryNet.com/history	You'll need this for question 4. It has the rules.
Kids Love a Mystery	http://www.KidsLoveAMystery.com	Some interactivity for readers.
Mystery	http://tqjunior.thinkquest.org/5109	ThinkQuest. Spend time looking at this site for kids.
Mystery Net	http://mysterynet.com	Good information.

Other Resources

See if your local library has mystery videos, like those about the Hardy Boys or Encyclopedia Brown. Watch and take notes when you see clues, red herrings, etc. Include these in your paper.

Interview a mystery reader. (Maybe your teacher.) Why does that person like mysteries? What authors does he or she like best? Why?

For the Teacher

Lesson Plan: *Elements of a Mystery*: http://www.people.memphis.edu/~jsiegel/courses/BLOCK/www/myst5.html

Read-aloud: Choose a good mystery your students will enjoy. Let them hunt for clues as you read. Let the students write down or vote on who they think the "culprit" is.

Find a copy of *Father Ronald A. Knox' Detective Story Decalogue*. (The 10 Commandments for the classic mystery writer.) It is online at http://home.ican.net/~radix/twixt/knoxrule.html. Discuss the rules with your class. Encourage the students to decide whether the book they read uses these rules to play fair with the reader.

Food for Thought

Fool the reader—yet play fair. Every mystery writer tries to do this. What do you think it means? What does the writer do to make this happen?

NEWBERY AWARD

> ## Something Extra
> After reading several Newbery books, create a match game for your classmates.
> Match titles and authors or titles and one-sentence plots.

Thinking About the Topic

Each year since 1922, Newbery winners and honor books have been selected. They are selected as the best of children's literature. Many of these books have become classics. That means that your mom and dad may have read them, you will read them, and your children will probably read them, too. If you are an avid reader, this may be the topic for you.

Directions

You have options with this report. You can write about the award or you can write about one of the award-winning books. Either way, start your report with a paragraph of information about the Newbery Award (question 1). Use several resources to answer your three questions. Draw a conclusion for each question. For example, the conclusion for question 1 might be, "The Newbery Award is given for the most distinguished American children's book of the year."

1. What is the Newbery Award?

2. What important group gives this award each year? How do they select the winner?

3. Who was John Newbery? What book(s) did he write?

4. What elements are the committee members watching for in a Newbery winner?

5. Name one book you read and tell why you think it won the Newbery Award.

6. If you write about a Newbery book, be sure you focus on WHY it may have won the award.

Books

Keywords: *Newbery Medal* (look by particular author).

Hege, Claudette. *Newbery and Caldecott Trivia and More for Every Day of the Year.* Englewood, CO: Libraries Unlimited, 2000.

Kingman, Lee. *Newbery and Caldecott Medal Books, 1966–1975.* Boston: Horn Book, 1977.

Kingman, Lee. *Newbery and Caldecott Medal Books, 1976–1985.* Boston: Horn Book, 1986.

Kunitz, Stanley J. *The Junior Book of Authors*. New York: H. W. Wilson, 1951– (and others in the series).

Newbery and Caldecott Medal Books, 1976–2000: A Comprehensive Guide to the Winners. Chicago: American Library Association, 2001.

Newbery Medal Books, 1922–1955. Boston: Horn Book, 1957.

Townsend, John Rowe. *John Newbery and His Books: Trade and Plumb-Cake Forever, Huzza!* New York: Scarecrow, 1994.

Internet

Newbery Medal Home Page	http://www.ala.org/alsc/newbery.html	From the American Library Association. They select the award winners.
Newbery Award	http://ils.unc.edu/award/nhome.html	University of North Carolina. Find answers here.
Newbery Medals	http://www.literature-awards.com/ newbery_medal_award_winners.htm	Literature awards. This site has a listing of every Newbery winner and a link to information about it.

Other Resources

Many of the Newbery Award-winning books have been made into videos. They can be ordered online or found in local libraries.

For the Teacher

Mock Newbery Award Group: http://www.homestead.com/epmnewbery/Newbery2000.html. This group of 25 kids reads new books and tries to predict who the winner of the award will be.

Gillespie, John T. *The Newbery Companion: Booktalk and Related Materials for Newbery Medal and Honor Books (Newbery Companion)*. Englewood, CO: Libraries Unlimited, 2001.

Who Wrote That?

America's Longest River	By Misses Hippy
Breaking the Law	By Kermit A. Krime
Broken Beds	By Squeak E. Springs
Don't Hurt Me!	By I. Bruce Easley
Errors and Accidents	By Miss Takes and Miss Haps
Appreciation for Art	By Drew Lousy

These funny titles and others are at
http://members.tripod.com/LEADER_7/funnyjokes.html

THE NIGHT SKY

Something Extra

Find out when the local astronomy club meets. Join them with your family for a wonderful evening outing viewing the night sky.

Thinking About the Topic

From the earliest time, people have been interested in the heavens. The night sky has to be enjoyed away from city lights. Do you ever lie under the stars at night? If so, you know the feeling of being a single small human in a huge, wonderful world. Can you find the Big Dipper? Can you spot other constellations? Have you ever seen a falling star? If this interests you, you are in for a treat as you learn more about the changing night sky.

Directions

When you are ready, select question 1 and two others below. Write one question at the top of each page. Look in several sources for the answers to your questions. Each question will become a paragraph in your report. Draw a conclusion from the answers you find. The conclusion will be your topic sentence.

1. What are stars? What else can we view in the night sky?

2. Why is the night sky constantly changing?

3. What instruments are needed to study the sky? Describe them.

4. Describe recent discoveries in the night sky.

5. Who are the people who study the sky, and what education do they have?

6. Write about your favorite star (or the Milky Way).

Books

Keywords: *Astronomy—Juvenile Literature; Constellations; Stars.*

Croswell, Ken. *See the Stars: Your First Guide to the Night Sky.* Honesdale, PA: Boyds Mill Press, 2000.

Dickinson, Terence. *Exploring the Night Sky: The Equinox Astronomy Guide for Beginners.* Willowdale, ONT: Firefly Books, 2001.

Mitton, Jacqueline. *The Scholastic Encyclopedia of Space.* New York: Scholastic Reference, 1999.

Schaaf, Fred. *40 Nights to Knowing the Sky: A Night-by-Night Skywatching Primer*. New York: Henry Holt, 1998.

Internet

What Do You See in the Night Sky?	http://school.discovery.com/schooladventures/ skywatch/index.html	Everything from observation tips to sky stories.
Star Child	http://starchild.gsfc.nasa.gov/docs/StarChild/ StarChild.html	NASA's site for children.
Astronomy for Kids	http://www.dustbunny.com/afk/index.html	Great information. Visit Sky Maps and see what is going on in the sky "right now."
Light Pollution	http://www.lightpollution.it/dmsp/	The night sky—light pollution. Interesting site for older students.

Other Resources

The Night Sky: http://concam.net/. View the night sky via this live cam.

View *NASA.gov* online for great information and video clips.

Get your family to participate in a trip to visit a planetarium. Take notes.

Aurora: Rivers of Light in the Sky (video). Anchorage, AK: SkyRiver Films, 1994.

For the Teacher

Have a class family evening to study the night sky. Hot dogs, marshmallow roasting—what fun! Maybe the parents will help you organize the evening.

A field trip to the local planetarium would be a real treat.

Sky Poetry: http://www.wsanford.com/~wsanford/exc/s-p_teacher_resources.html. A nice bibliography for teachers of older students.

Excellent teacher's plans from the Sudekum Planetarium: http://www.sudekumplanetarium. com/shows/WS/

Joke

Q: What candy bars do you eat in space?

A: Milky Ways and Mars bars.

NUTRITION

Something Extra

Are your classmates fit? Have them take this online survey to find out. Create a table and chart the results as part of your research: http://library.thinkquest.org/12153/fit.html

Virtual Cow Tipping: http://www.ieatcrayons.com/ (No, you won't have to go into the field with the cow.)

Thinking About the Topic

You are what you eat! What a funny thought. But it may be true. Proper food and exercise can keep you healthy. Certain foods have healing effects. For example, if you place a sterile gauze pad saturated with honey over a wound, then put a dry gauze pad on top of the first one, it will help heal an open cut. Every mother knows that homemade chicken soup combats the common cold. Learn more about helpful foods and exercise. If you want to be an Internet Nutrition Sleuth, answer the questions online at http://www.kidfood.org/sleuths/work_sh.html.

Directions

Answer question 1 and any other two questions from the list below on your topic. After you answer each question using books or the Internet, draw a conclusion about the answer. Use the conclusion as your topic sentence.

1. Why is what we eat so important? How does good nutrition help us?

2. What is a food pyramid? How can you use it to stay healthy? Create a pyramid of healthy foods for yourself. Include it in your report.

3. What is the truth about fast foods? Healthy or not? Do a little research into the fast foods you like best.

4. Find information about food myths.

5. What are a few foods that keep you well or help you heal? How?

Books

Keywords: *Nutrition—Juvenile; Food composition; Diet.*

Encyclopedia of Health. Tarrytown, NY: Marshall Cavendish, 1995.

Haduch, Bill. *Food Rules! The Stuff You Munch, Its Crunch, Its Punch, and Why You Sometimes Lose Your Lunch.* New York: Dutton, 2001.

Leedy, Loreen. *The Edible Pyramid: Good Eating Every Day.* New York: Holiday House, 1994.

Lynn, Sara, and Diane James. *What We Eat: A First Look at Food.* Chicago: World Book/Two-Can, 2000.

Internet

10 Healthy Tips for Kids	http://www.crees.org/family/nutrition/10tips.html	Tips for you.
Kid's Health	http://www.kidshealth.org/kid/stay_healthy/fit/what_time.html	How do you stay fit? Nutrition and exercise information.
Kids Food Cyberclub	http://www.kidfood.org/	Basic information about nutrition.
The Food Pyramid	http://www.nal.usda.gov:8001/py/pmap.htm	What should you eat each day?
The Truth About Fast Foods	http://tqjunior.thinkquest.org/4485/frames.htm	Good information for comparing fast food places.

For the Teacher

Ask Eric Lesson Plans—Nutrition: http://www.askeric.org/cgi-bin/lessons.cgi/Health/Nutrition

Feeding Kids Newsletter: http://nutritionforkids.com/Feeding_Kids.htm. Articles and ideas for adults.

Pro Teacher Lesson Plans—Nutrition: http://www.proteacher.com/120001.shtml

Read *Gregory the Terrible Eater* to the class and use the lesson plan ideas at http://www.askeric.org/cgi-bin/printlessons.cgi/Virtual/Lessons/Health/Nutrition/NUT0002.html

Read-aloud books about food. Bibliography at http://www.kidfood.org/books/books.html

---

Joke

My family eats from the three basic food groups: canned, frozen, and take-out.

WIFE: Honey, how would you like a steak, potatoes, and apple pie?
HUSBAND: No, I'm too tired. Let's eat at home.

OCTOPUS

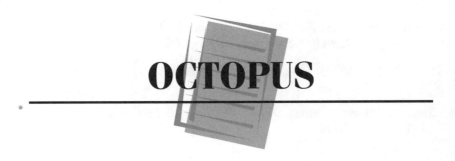

> **Something Extra**
>
> Many people around the world eat octopus. Try it at your house. Help your mom or dad prepare octopus for dinner. (Squid is a good substitute if you can't find octopus.) Recipes are online at http://thebite.com/thebite/squid.html

Thinking About the Topic

The octopus is surely one of a kind. It has eight legs, three hearts, and many suction cups. It could really give you a big hug. There are several kinds of octopuses. You may want to write about the common octopus, which lives in Florida, or the giant octopus, which lives off the West Coast.

Directions

Using several resources, answer question 1 and two other questions below. Write each question at the top of a separate page. Take notes on the pages you create. Your notes should be written in complete sentences. Each question will become a paragraph in your report. After you have found the answers, draw a conclusion about your information. (For example, the conclusion for question 5 might be: "The octopus lives in _____.") Your conclusion will be the topic sentence for the paragraph.

1. Describe the octopus. What family of fish does it belong to?

2. Where does the octopus live? What does it eat? How does it get food?

3. Discuss the unusual behavior of the octopus.

4. Describe octopus mating. How does the female octopus take care of her young?

5. How does the octopus defend itself from enemies?

Books

Keywords: *Octopus; Sea life.*

Cerullo, Mary. *The Octopus: Phantom of the Sea.* New York: Cobblehill, 1997.

Hirschi, Ron. *Octopuses.* Minneapolis, MN: Carolrhoda, 2000.

Kite, Patricia. *Down in the Sea: The Octopus.* Morton Grove, IL: Albert Whitman, 1993.

Lauber, Patricia. *The Octopus Is Amazing.* New York: Crowell, 1990.

Zochura-Walske, Christine. *Giant Octopuses.* Minneapolis, MN: Lerner, 2000.

Internet

Cephalopod Page	http://is.dal.ca/~ceph/TCP/index.html	Our favorite for information and photos. Articles by experts.
Cephalopods	http://www.aqua.org/animals/species/procto.html	Facts about cephalopods, including the octopus.
Marine Lab in Florida	http://www.marinelab.sarasota.fl.us/OCTOPI.HTM	Excellent information.
Octopus	http://www.pbs.org/wnet/nature/octopus/	Good information from PBS.
The Giant Octopus	http://www.npca.org/marine_and_coastal/marine_wildlife/octopus.asp	About this large octopus breed.
The Octopus Show	http://www.germantown.k12.il.us/html/octopus.html	Second-grade project about the octopus. You could do this, too.

Other Resources

Octopus-octopus (video). Undersea World of Jacques Cousteau. Beverly Hills, CA: Pacific Arts, 1989.

The Ultimate Guide: The Octopus (video). Santa Monica, CA: The Discovery Channel, 2001.

Visit or call the local aquarium or zoo. Ask your questions of the specialist there.

For the Teacher

Octopus Behavior: http://is.dal.ca/~ceph/TCP/behavior.html

Oceans Learning Page: http://www.learningpage.com/free_pages/menu_wkshts/plans_oceans.html

Raising an Octopus: http://is.dal.ca/~ceph/TCP/rearing.html (Wow! What a class project.)

Teacher lesson plans at DiscoverySchool.com (use *search term OCTOPUS*): http://school.discovery.com/

Joke

Q: What did the boy octopus say to the girl octopus?

A: I want to hold your hand, hand, hand, hand, hand, hand, hand.

PANDAS

| **Something Extra** |
| Make a giant panda mask, do a crossword puzzle, or make fortune cookies: http://pandas.si.edu/htdocs/kids/index.htm |

Thinking About the Topic

Giant Pandas are big and furry and look so cuddly. You would love to hug them. Maybe you had better not! There are only a few pandas in American zoos. In fact, you won't see a panda unless you go to a special zoo. China gave two pandas to the National Zoo in Washington, D.C. You may want to write about them. Did you know that there is also another kind of panda known as the Red Panda?

Directions

Read about the panda. Then get three pieces of paper. Choose question 1 and any other two questions below. Write each question at the top of a piece of paper. Take notes on the questions in complete sentences. Write a conclusion for each question. This conclusion will be the topic sentence for your paragraph, and the notes will be the paragraph.

1. What is a panda? Describe it.

2. Describe the panda's ecosystem.

3. Why are pandas an endangered species? What can be done to prevent them from becoming extinct?

4. How do pandas differ from other bears?

5. Is it a good idea to keep pandas in zoos? Why or why not?

6. Write about the pandas in the Washington, D.C., or San Diego, California, zoo.

Books

Keywords: *Giant Panda; Pandas; Lesser Panda; Endangered Species; Bears.*

Leeson, Tom. *Giant Panda.* Woodbridge, CT: Blackbirch, 2000.

New Book of Popular Science. Danbury, CT: Grolier, 2000.

Presnall, Judith Janda. *The Giant Panda.* Farmington Hills, MI: Lucent, 1998.

Raintree Steck-Vaughn Illustrated Science Encyclopedia. Austin, TX: Raintree Steck-Vaughn, 1997.

Rutten, Joshua. *Red Pandas.* Mankato, MN: Child's World, 1998.

Internet

National Zoo	http://Pandas.si.edu/htdocs/facts/index.htm	All about pandas.
Giant Pandas	http://www.giantpandabear.com/index2.html	Everything you need to know about the giant panda.
Animal Planet	http://animal.discovery.com/convergence/pandas/video/behavior.html	Pictures, videos, and an audio explanation of real panda behavior.
Panda articles	http://magma.nationalgeographic.com/ngexplorer/0111/articles/aboaj_0111.html	From National Geographic for Kids.

Other Resources

Watch videos of the pandas at the San Diego zoo: http://www.sandiegozoo.org/virtualzoo/videos/index.html

Play Panda Chow: http://magma.nationalgeographic.com/ngexplorer/0111/games/index.html

E-mail the San Diego or Washington, D.C. head zookeeper and ask your questions. Find the e-mail address online.

For the Teacher

Lesson plan for finding Panda information on the Internet, especially for grades three through five: http://www.challenge.state.la.us/k12act/data/giant_panda.html

---

Joke

Q: What is black and white and has wheels?

A: A Giant Panda on roller skates!

PEANUTS

Something Extra

Learn the song "Goober Peas," by A. Pindar. Teach it to your friends.

Activity book to download, with recipes, coloring pages, and a story, from *Virginia-Carolina Peanuts:* http://www.aboutpeanuts.com/kids.html

Thinking About the Topic

Peanuts! What are they? Peas or nuts? Surprise! They are really legumes, so they are closer to peas than nuts! So when your mom tells you to eat your vegetables, maybe you can get away with a handful of peanuts! Be sure to find information about George Washington Carver. He invented over 300 uses for peanuts. (See our jumpstart on him.)

Directions

Decide on your exact topic. Then get three pieces of paper. Choose question 1 and any other two questions below. Write each question at the top of a piece of paper. Take notes on the questions in complete sentences. Write a conclusion for each question. This conclusion will be the topic sentence for your paragraph, and the notes will be the paragraph.

1. Tell about the history of the peanut. Where did it first grow? How did it spread?

2. How does a peanut grow? Where? How is it harvested?

3. Describe several of the uses for peanuts. Do not limit yourself to food!

4. Why are peanuts such a useful food? How do they fit in your diet?

5. Peanuts can be deadly! Find out why. Describe the problem and what can be done about it.

Books

Keywords: *Peanuts (*watch out! You'll get Charlie Brown, too*); Peanut Products; Inventors and Inventions.* (Then look up *Peanuts* or *George Washington Carver.*)

Kramer, Barbara. *George Washington Carver: Scientist and Inventor.* Berkeley Heights, NJ: Enslow, 2002.

Micucci, Charles. *Life and Times of the Peanut.* Boston: Houghton Mifflin, 1997.

Raintree Steck-Vaughn Illustrated Science Encyclopedia. Austin, TX: Raintree Steck-Vaughn, 1997.

Witman, Kathleen L. *CDs, Super Glue & Salsa: How Everyday Products Are Made.* Farmington Hills, MI: UXL, 1996.

Internet

Peanut Institute	http://www.peanut-institute.org/kidsFFT.html	Recipes and research on peanuts.
Skippy Peanut Butter	http://www.peanutbutter.com/	Nutrition facts, allergy facts, crafts, and games about peanut butter.
Original Nut House	http://www.originalnuthouse.com/peanuts/peanuts1.htm	Peanut facts for kids, including nutrition, how peanuts grow, and the four varieties of peanuts.

Other Resources

Watch the birth of a peanut: http://www.houstonpeanuts.com/education.htm

Make peanut butter play dough: http://www.teachnet.com/lesson/art/playdoughrecipes/pbdough.html

See if your climate will support peanuts. If it will, try growing them. They would make a great addition to your report.

For the Teacher

Educational materials from Virginia-Carolina Peanuts: http://www.aboutpeanuts.com/

Planting lesson plans from ProTeacher: http://www.proteacher.com/110013.shtml

Plan a class lesson preparing peanut butter.

Jokes

Q: Why did the elephant quit the circus?
A: He was tired of working for peanuts.

Q: Should I eat peanuts with my fingers?
A: No, you should eat your fingers separately.

PEOPLE I KNOW

Something Extra

Make a five-minute video or picture album for your class showing the people you have interviewed while writing your report. Label any pictures.

Create a timeline of the two friends, family members, or whomever you select as part of your presentation. There are many timelines online to use as samples.

Thinking About the Topic

Writing about people you know will improve your interview and research skills. Use the Internet and books to find interviewing tips, timelines, and any other items that will help with this research. Then, interview two people and draw comparisons between them. How are they alike? Different? How did they get together? Suggestions of people to interview include (1) your mom and grandmother, (2) your dad and his brother, (3) your mom or dad and a friend he or she grew up with, (4) your teacher and minister, (5) a firefighter and police officer. Choose people who have something in common. Be sure to "tie a common thread" from one person to the other. If you find something interesting in books or on the Internet, use it in your opening paragraph. For example, "Books say that mothers and daughters grow more alike as they age."

Directions

A professional interviewer makes an appointment, prepares questions, and arrives on time with a notebook, pencils, camera, and tape recorder. If you select this topic, most of your paper should look like an interview. You will find samples of interviews online. Do a little homework before you begin. Write a paragraph introducing your interviewees.

- **Friends:** How did you meet? Why do you think you have remained friends for so long? What memories do you share from long ago?

- **People of different generations**: What was life like when you were young? What did your family do for fun? What was school like? How are things different now?

- **Teacher and minister:** Why did you choose this career? What do you enjoy most about being a teacher (or minister)? How do you think your careers are alike? Different? What do you like best about your job? What is the hardest part of your job?

- **Oral history option:** Interview the oldest person in your family (or another family). Find out about this person's early life and record your findings. The questions at http://www.rootsweb.com/~genepool/oralhist.htm will help you. Take pictures. Put together a scrapbook as part of your report. Share it with your subject.

Books

Keywords: *Genealogy; Interview Techniques; Family History; Public Speaking.*

Cooper, Kay. *Where Did You Get Those Eyes?: A Guide to Discovering Your Family History.* New York: Walker, 1988

Fletcher, William. *Recording Your Family History: A Guide to Preserving Oral History.* New York: Dodd, Mead, 1986

Otfinoski, Steven. *Speaking Up, Speaking Out: A Kid's Guide to Making Speeches, Oral Reports, and Conversation.* Brookfield, CT: Millbrook Press, 1996.

Perl, Lila. *The Great Ancestor Hunt: The Fun of Finding Out Who You Are.* New York: Clarion Books, 1989.

Internet

Genealogy Today	http://genealogytoday.com/junior/	Very good basic information.
Genealogy: Where to Begin	http://family.go.com/raisingkids/ child/skills/feature/dony0800gene_ start/dony0800gene_start.html	Information about interview techniques is included here.
World Gen Web for Kids	http://www.rootsweb.com/ ~wgwkids/	All about finding out about your family.
Ellis Island	http://www.ellisisland.org/	If your family came into America through Ellis Island, you will love this site.

Other Resources

Family Trees Quick & Easy 5.0 (CD-ROM). Helps you build a family tree; add notes, photos, scanned documents, and sounds; and create Web pages with your family tree.

For the Teacher

An excellent video for a Friday afternoon (no bad language) is *Family Tree.* Burbank, CA: Warner Home Video, 2000. Appropriate for any age.

Genealogy for Children: A Resource for Teachers, Parents and Grandparents, by Liana Brittain. Almonte, ONT: Educational Support Personnel, 1997.

Genealogy for Kids: http://home.istar.ca/~ljbritt. Games, vocabulary, and activities for teachers.

People who make speeches often practice tongue twisters before they go on stage.

A tutor who tooted a flute
Tried to tutor two tooters to toot.
Said the two to their tutor,
"Is it harder to toot
or to tutor two tooters to toot?"

PETS

Something Extra
Coloring pages and mazes from Animal Planet: http://www.planet-pets.com/kids/kidscoloring.htm

Thinking About the Topic

When your cat purrs in your lap, you feel happy. When your dog rolls around on the floor with you, you feel excited. When you whistle to your parakeet and it whistles back, you feel special. When your hamster eats out of your hand, you feel important. But pets can also be hard work. Pets need love and care. Taking care of a pet helps you learn about responsibility.

Directions

Pick a pet and read all about it. Then get three pieces of paper. Choose question 1 and any other two questions below. Write each question at the top of a piece of paper. Take notes on the questions in complete sentences. Write a conclusion for each question. This conclusion will be the topic sentence for your paragraph, and the notes will form the paragraph.

1. Describe the pet you have chosen and your reasons for choosing it.

2. How would you care for this pet? Talk about what your pet needs to be healthy and happy.

3. If the pet can be trained, describe some of the tricks it can learn to do. Describe how you go about teaching your pet. (Use books to find out about training.)

4. Having a wild animal as a pet can cause problems. Write about this. Give examples.

5. Find out about pets and the elderly. How do pets help the elderly?

Books

Keywords: *Pets—Juvenile; Animals as pets;* specific animals like *Dogs, Cats.*

Frost, Helen. *Birds*. Mankato, MN: Capstone, 2001.

Frost, Helen. *Rabbits*. Mankato, MN: Capstone, 2001.

George, Jean Craighead. *How to Talk to Your Dog*. New York: HarperCollins, 2000.

Gutman, Bill. *Becoming Your Bird's Best Friend*. Brookfield, CT: Millbrook Press, 1996.

Hansen, Ann Larken. *Cats*. Minneapolis, MN: Abdo & Daughters, 1997.

Head, Honor. *Guinea Pig*. Austin, TX: Raintree/Steck, 2001.

Head, Honor. *Hamsters and Gerbils*. Austin, TX: Raintree/Steck, 2001.

New Book of Popular Science. Danbury, CT: Grolier, 2000.

Internet

Mining Company	http://exoticpets.miningco.com/	Choose from all sorts of exotic pets, such as prairie dogs, hermit crabs, and tree frogs.
Pet Web Site	http://www.petwebsite.com/pet_information.htm	How to buy and care for the more common pets, such as cats, dogs, horses, and guinea pigs.
American Veterinary Medical Society	http://www.avma.org/care4pets/safelikr.htm	Safety tips for kids.
Pets for Kids	http://www.petsforkids.co.uk/	Care for various common pets such as dogs, rabbits, and rats.
Pets for the Elderly	http://petsfortheeelderly.org/Research1.htm	Find out how having a pet can help an elderly person.

Other Resources

See an online video of a dog getting its teeth brushed: http://www.petdental.com/html/2c_home.htm

See How they Grow: Pets (video). New York: Sony, 1995.

For the Teacher

Lesson plans on insects, including classroom pets: http://www.pedagonet.com/other/lsplns.html

Links to information about pets at home and classroom pets. Scroll down the page for lesson plans: http://edtech.kennesaw.edu/web/pets.html

---

Jokes

Q: How do you catch a runaway dog?

A: Hide behind a tree and make a noise like a bone!

PABLO PICASSO

Something Extra

After reading about Picasso and studying his different styles, try to create a painting, perhaps in the cubist style. If you prefer, use clay and create a Picasso-like sculpture.

Thinking About the Topic

What a funny painting by the famous artist Picasso! Why are both eyes on the same side of his face? And what is the arm doing over there? That person is all blue. What does it mean? Pablo Picasso had a unique style that has fascinated people for years. He created what was called the cubist style.

Directions

Read about Picasso. Then get three pieces of paper. Choose question 1 and any other two questions below. Write each question at the top of a piece of paper. Take notes on the questions in complete sentences. Write a conclusion for each question. This conclusion will be the topic sentence for your paragraph, and the notes will be the paragraph.

1.   Describe Picasso's early life.

2.   What makes Picasso's art unique? (Study some of Pablo Picasso's paintings.)

3.   What is cubism? Who are other artists who painted in this style?

4.   Pick one particular Picasso painting and tell about it. *The Blue Room* is one you may like. How does it make you feel?

5.   Create a picture in Picasso's style. Explain the things you did and why.

Books

Keywords: *Picasso, Pablo—Juvenile Literature; Cubism; Modern Art.*

Grolier Library of International Biographies. Danbury, CT: Grolier, 1996.

Krull, Kathleen. *Lives of the Artists: Masterpieces, Messes (and What the Neighbors Thought).* San Diego: Harcourt Brace, 1995.

Lowery, Linda. *Pablo Picasso.* Minneapolis, MN: Carolrhoda, 1998.

MacDonald, Patricia A. *Pablo Picasso: Greatest Artist of the 20th Century.* Farmington Hills, MI: Blackbirch Marketing, 2001.

Internet

Picasso	http://home.xnet.com~stanko/	See some of Picasso's works and read a little about his life.
Cyber Nation	http://cyber-nation.com/victory/ quotations/authors/quotes_ picasso_pablo.html	Great quotations from Picasso.
Kids Art	http://www.kidsart.com/topten. html	Kids' top ten artists, art museums, music for abstract art, and more.
Boston MFA Picasso Online	http://www.boston.com/mfa/ picasso/	Museum tour of Picasso exhibit. Be sure to look at the timeline. Enter the exhibition to see all the paintings.

Other Resources

Video clips from a film on Matisse and Picasso: http://www.matisse-picasso.com/production/ videoclips.html

Take a trip to the local art museum and look at the works of Picasso.

Interview your art teacher. Ask about Picasso and what he or she thinks his works mean. Ask the teacher to tell you about cubism.

For the Teacher

Thumbnail pictures of most of Picasso's works, as well as his biography, at *On-Line Picasso Project*: http://www.tamu.edu/mocl/picasso/

Your class might enjoy creating a peace mural, like Picasso's *Guernica:* http://www. kids-guernica.org/

Lesson plans from the National Gallery of Art, based on Picasso's paintings: http://www.nga. gov/education/picteach.htm

Pintura: http://www.eduweb.com/pintura/a1.html. Have fun being an art detective.

Limerick

When his paintings were met with derision,
Picasso, with cubist precision,
Put a nose on the cheek
And an ear on the beak
And succeeded with his composition

POCAHONTAS

Something Extra

Read the Pocahontas serialized storybook online:
http://disney.go.com/Kids/pocastory/

Thinking About the Topic

It's amazing! They wear such strange clothes! They build big walls to keep everything out. They come to a land of plenty and do not know how to find food. Pocahontas must have thought the English who came to her America 400 years ago were very strange indeed. As she got to know them, Pocahontas tried to help the English. Later she married one of the strangers and became friends with another.

Directions

Read about Pocahontas. (Do not depend on the Disney film to give you the information you need.) Choose question 1 and any other two questions below. Write each question at the top of a piece of paper. Take notes on the questions in complete sentences. Write a conclusion for each question. This conclusion will be the topic sentence for your paragraph, and the notes will be the details in your paragraph.

1. Describe Pocahontas's early life. Where did she live? What was life like then?

2. How did Pocahontas get to know the new settlers? How did she help them?

3. Tell the story of Pocahontas and John Smith. Why did John Smith go away?

4. How did Pocahontas come to live among the settlers? What happened to her then?

5. Why is Pocahontas an American hero?

Books

Keywords: *Pocahontas; Powhatan Women; Native Americans* (Use *Juvenile Literature* to get easier books.).

Edwards, Judith. *Jamestown, John Smith and Pocahontas in American History.* Berkeley Heights, NJ: Enslow, 2002.

Fritz, Jean. *The Double Life of Pocahontas.* North Bellmore, NY: Marshall Cavendish, 1991.

Holler, Anne. *Pocahontas: Powhatan Peacemaker.* Broomall, PA: Chelsea House, 1992.

Moss, Joyce, and George Wilson. *Profiles in American History.* Farmington Hills, MI: Gale, 1995.

Internet

Association for the Preservation of Virginia Antiquities	http://www.apva.org/history/pocahont.html	Detailed and accurate biography of Pocahontas, for older children.
American History Ring	http://members.tripod.com/~AlanCheshire/indes-24.html	Pocahontas chronology.
David Morenus	http://www.geocities.com/matoaka1595/poca_main.html	Biography of Pocahontas by one of her descendants.

Other Resources

Pocahontas (video). Burbank, CA: Walt Disney Home Video, 1995.

Slide show by Fairlane Elementary students (maybe your class can do this, too): http://www.towson.edu/csme/mctp/StudentProjects/pocohontas/TitlePage.html

For the Teacher

Lesson plans on Native Americans, with one specifically about Pocahontas: http://www.proteacher.com/090076.shtml

Native American lesson plans, including many craft activities: http://members.aol.com/MrDonnHistory/American.html#NATIVE

Match These

These four men played important roles in Pocahontas's life. Who were they? Draw lines to match them.

Her father	Captain John Smith
Her father's captain	Chief Powhatan
An adventurer	Kocoum
Her husband	John Rolfe

POETRY

> **Something Extra**
>
> Memorize an Emily Dickinson poem. Sing it to your class to the tune of the *Beverly Hillbilly's* theme song.

Thinking About the Topic

Clouds appear
and bring to men a chance to rest
from looking at the moon.
—Bashó, 1644–1694

Bashó wrote that Haiku over 400 years ago. He traveled around Japan and recited haiku that described the way he viewed the world. Wow! Rhythm, meter, imagery, and rhyme are all poetry concepts. Poems can be funny, sad, or romantic. They describe a feeling in only a few words. Choose a poet (Jack Prelutsky; Shel Silverstein; X. J. Kennedy; Emily Dickinson; Robert Frost) or a poetry style (Haiku, sonnets, limericks, nursery rhymes, song lyrics) to write about. Write your own poems.

Directions

When you are ready with a topic, write three questions. Using several sources, draw a conclusion from the information you find. The conclusion will be your topic sentence for each paragraph. Your first question should be, "What is poetry?" If you are writing about a poetry style, be sure to write your questions about the style, for example, What is haiku? What is the history of haiku poetry? Questions are important. Ask your teacher to check yours before you begin.

GOOD QUESTION: Why do young children love poetry?

POOR QUESTION: Do young children love poetry? (The answer is simply yes. See?)

Books

Keywords: *Poetry—Juvenile Literature*; *Poetry—Authorship*; *Poetry—Collections*.

Burkholder, Kelly. *Poetry*. Vero Beach, FL: Rourke Press, 2001.

Fletcher, Ralph. *Poetry Matters: Writing a Poem from the Inside Out*. New York: HarperCollins, 2002

Hopkins, Lee Bennett. *Pass the Poetry, Please!* 3rd ed. New York: HarperCollins, 1998.

Janeczko, Paul B. *How to Write Poetry*. New York: Scholastic Reference, 1999.

Ryan, Margaret. *How To Read and Write Poems*. New York: Franklin Watts, 1991.

Internet

The Poet's Shelf	http://www.kyrene.k12.az. us/schools/brisas/sunda/ poets/poet.htm	Visit this site and see the biographies of 12 American poets. See "Poetic Devices."
A Good Poem Will Give You Goosebumps	http://www.educationworld. com/a_curr/curr399.shtml	Read Kenn Nesbitt's easy-to-understand article about poetry.
Poetry Pals	http://www.geocities.com/ EnchantedForest/5165/ index1.html	K–12 poetry project. Good place to start. Types of poetry are described.
Poetry from the Library of Congress	http://www.loc.gov/poetry/	Poetry lists: listen and watch poets reading their own poems.
Giggle Poetry	http://www.gigglepoetry. com/	Learn more about poems and enter the poetry contest.

Other Resources

Arthur's Famous Friends (video). New York: Random House Home Video, Sony Wonder, c2000.

Favorite Poem: http://www.favoritepoem.org/. Video and audio of Americans reading their favorites

Prelutsky, Jack. *Pizza the Size of the Sun* (sound recording). Old Greenwich, CT: Listening Library, 1999.

Quip with Yip and Friends (video). Hollywood, CA: Fries Home Video, 1990.

For the Teacher

Haiku—Teaching Japanese Poetry: http://www.education-world.com/a_curr/curr052.shtml

Poetry: http://teacher.scholastic.com/writewit/poetry/index.htm. Teacher's guide and a place where students can publish. By Prelutsky and others.

The Cremation of Sam McGee by Robert Service: http://www.ncte.org/teach/Pipkin31368. html. Read-aloud.

The Place My Words Are Looking for: What Poets Say About and Through Their Work. Selected by Paul B. Janeczko. New York: Bradbury Press, c1990. Thirty-nine poets share their poems.

Enjoy Poetry Online

http://www.prominence.com/java/poetry/

http://home.freeuk.net/elloughton13/scramble2.htm

POP CULTURE: Or Your Parents When They Were Your Age

Something Extra

Make an album containing pictures of your parents and yourself at the SAME ages. It would be neat if you had pictures doing the same activity, biking, swimming, school pictures, etc. Be sure to label each picture. Include each person's name, the place, and the year. Share the album with your classmates and your parents.

Bring Twister or another game that was popular in the 1970s or 1980s to school and play it during recess.

Thinking About the Topic

Do your parents claim life was harder when they were children than it is today? Do they say they had more homework, more rules, they played outside all day long, they had no computers, no videos? Here is your chance to find out. Compare life in your parent's childhood decade (1970s? 1980s?) to your life today.

Directions

Join your parents in taking a trip down memory lane. Popular culture describes what was popular during a period of time. Things like music, books, and food help describe our lifestyle. For example, during the 1960s, some people sang protest songs. This helped them describe how they felt about the Vietnam War. Write about your parents' childhood or compare what life was like during their childhood with your life today. Write three or four questions. Your questions are important. Please ask your teacher to approve your questions before you begin. Draw a conclusion about each answer and let it become your topic sentence for each paragraph.

GOOD QUESTION: What was television like when you were my age? What were your favorite shows? How much time did you spend watching TV?

POOR QUESTION: Did you watch television much when you were my age?

Suggested topics for questions include music, school life, food, books, television/movies, chores, fads, news, toys/games, dance, leisure time, and allowance

Books

Keywords: *The Seventies (or The Eighties); Popular Culture; Lifestyles.*

Communities Across America Today. Washington, DC: National Geographic Society, 2001.

Epstein, Dan. *The 70's. (or The 80's).* 20th Century Pop Culture series. Philadelphia: Chelsea House, 2000.

Gilbert, Adrian. *The Eighties.* Look at Life in. Austin, TX: Raintree Steck-Vaughn, 2000.

Gordon, Lois G. *American Chronicle.* New York: Columbia University Press, 1995.

Grant, R.G. *The Seventies.* Look at Life in. Austin, TX: Raintree Steck-Vaughn, 2000.

Internet

American Cultural History	http://kclibrary.nhmccd. edu/decades.html	Created by the authors of this book, this is a great site to learn what was happening during the twentieth century. Choose your decade.
American Decades Project	http://www.aclibrary.org/ teenroom/decades.asp	Excellent page of links to other information about the decades.
In the Eighties (Also links to In the Seventies)	http://www.inthe80s.com/ http://www.inthe70s.com	Charles R. Grosvener wrote this neat site. Includes music, news, fads, and more. Nice.

Other Resources

Interview your parents. If you decide to compare their childhood with yours, try a chart like this sample. It will make a nice display in addition to your written report.

Topic	**[Insert decade here] (Parents)**	**The Present (You)**
What did you do for fun when you were my age?		
What teacher influenced you most when you were a kid? Why?		
Describe an average Saturday when you were growing up.		
What music did you listen to? How did it make you feel?		

For the Teacher

American Cultural History: http://kclibrary.nhmccd.edu/decades.html. This site by the authors of this book will be very useful in learning the popular culture of each decade.

American Decades Project: http://www.aclibrary.org/teenroom/decades.asp. Excellent page of links to other information about the decades.

Ed Helper: http://www.edhelper.com/cat103.htm. Lesson plans on the 1970s. "Fun in the Seventies" is particularly useful. Includes several suggestions for group projects.

Locate the most popular children's books of the 1970s or 1980s. Read them aloud to your class.

Ask your parents if they learned to "skip" when they were young. If so, have them show you how. Teach your classmates to skip during PE class or recess. It is really fun!

PRESIDENTS

Thinking About the Topic

From George Washington to George W. Bush, American presidents have ruled the country. Many have been great. Choose a president to report about. What was going on in America during the time your president was in office? Be sure to discuss what the president did during his term of office that makes him remembered. You might even write about the White House. Take a virtual tour at http://www.whitehouse.gove/history/life. If you don't want to write about a president, consider writing about the process of electing a president.

Directions

Read about American presidents. If you decide to write about a particular president, be sure your questions focus on his life as president. Write three questions, including number 1 below. Write each question at the top of a piece of paper. Take notes on the questions in complete sentences. Write a conclusion for each question. This conclusion will be the topic sentence for your paragraph, and the notes will be the details in your paragraph.

1. Name and describe the president you selected. When was he in office?

2. What made him decide to become president of the United States?

3. What kind of education did he have? What other jobs did he do?

4. What was happening in America when _____ was president?

5. What decisions did he make that help us remember him as president?

Books

Keywords: *President—Biography; Name of president—Juvenile Literature; Elections in America.* (There are many books on presidents. Ask the librarian if you need help.)

Bausum, Ann. *Our Country's Presidents*. Washington, DC: National Geographic Society, 2001.

World Book of America's Presidents. Chicago: World Book, 2002.

Internet

Smithsonian Museum of American History	http://americanhistory.si.edu/presidency/home.html—pictures of the presidents and some of their possessions, summary of their terms	Description of the site.
White House	http://www.whitehouse.gov/history/presidents/	Brief history of each president, emphasizing his time in the presidency.
Michael Cowen	http://www.fujisan.demon.co.uk/USPresidents/preslist.htm	Lists of presidents by interesting traits, such as who was left handed, month and day of birth, and state of origin.

Other Resources

Video clips of some of the presidents, from Grolier: http://gi.grolier.com/presidents/gallery/pocket.html

Listen to key moments in American history, from Grolier: http://gi.grolier.com/presidents/gallery/sound.html

Search the Library of Congress site for speeches, photographs, and multimedia presentations: http://memory.loc.gov/ammem/amhome.html

For the Teacher

Online teacher's manual for studying the presidency, for grades four and up: http://americanhistory.si.edu/presidency/5b_frame.html

Video clips and lessons by C-SPAN, featuring each of the U. S. presidents: http://www.loc.gov/loc/lcib/9911/cspan.html

Gutman, Dan. *The Kid Who Ran for President* (sound recording). Prince Frederick, MD: Recorded Books, 2001. With his friend as campaign manager and his former babysitter as running mate, 12-year-old Judson Moon sets out to become president of the United States.

Presidential places, media, and gravesites on the Web: http://www.americanpresidents.org/

Truth Is Stranger Than Fiction

http://www.vtliving.com/jokes/jok6.htm.

Look at some of the facts about Kennedy and Lincoln. Wow! Compare your president with any other. Can you find cool matching facts?

RECYCLING

Something Extra

Fun recycling projects: http://www.chetthecheetah.org/kids/funprojects.html

Help form a recycling project at your school.

Thinking About the Topic

Would you believe it? The average American throws away four pounds of trash each day! All that trash is filling up the earth. What can you do about it? Follow the three Rs—Reduce, Reuse, Recycle. If you do it, and convince your family and your school to do it too, you could reduce the trash going to the landfill by tons. That's a lot of trash!

Directions

Read about recycling. This is a sizeable subject. Be sure you refine your topic to something you can handle. Talk to your teacher about it. Choose three questions below to write about. Write each question at the top of a piece of paper. Take notes on the questions in complete sentences. Write a conclusion for each question. This conclusion will be the topic sentence for your paragraph, and the notes will be the details in your paragraph.

1. What is recycling? Why is it important that people recycle?

2. What happens to the trash in your town?

3. Composting is a way you can recycle lawn and kitchen waste. How do you make a compost pile? What does in it? How do you tend it?

4. How are metal, plastic, or glass recycled? What are the advantages of recycling them?

5. How is paper recycled? What differences are there between recycled paper and new paper?

6. How can you recycle? Create a plan and write about it.

Books

Keywords: *Recycling (Waste, etc.); Recycled Products; Waste Paper; Refuse and Refuse Disposal.*

Donald, Rhonda Lucas. *Recycling*. New York: Children's Press, 2001.

Dorling Kindersley Science Encyclopedia. New York: Dorling Kindersley, 1993.

Emmer, Rae. *Community Service*. New York: PowerKids Press, 2001.

Mongillo, John, and Linda Zuidt-Warshaw. *Encyclopedia of Environmental Science*. Phoenix: Oryx Press, 2000.

Royston, Angela. *Recycling*. Austin, TX: Raintree Steck-Vaughn, 1998

Internet

Environmental Protection Agency	http://www.epa.gov/recyclecity/	Welcome to Recycle City!
Thomas Recycling	http://www.thomasrecycling.com/kids.html	Facts about recycling.
Earth 911	http://www.earth911.org/master.asp?s=kids&a=kids/kids.asp	The As to Zs of helping the planet.
Napcor	http://www.napcor.com/kids.html	What kids can do to make a difference.

Other Resources

Interactive environmental site developed by Parkdale Public School: http://www.on.ec.gc.ca/water/greatlakes/classroom/intro-e.html. Video clip on food recycling.

Call a local garbage collection company and ask them how much garbage they collect in a year: http://www.ciwmb.ca.gov/LGCentral/Programs/

For the Teacher

Recycling links for teachers: http://www.earth911.org/master.asp?s=kids&a=kids/links/teacher_links.asp

Recycling lesson plans from Texas A & M University: http://aggie-horticulture.tamu.edu/extension/compostfacility/les.htm

Have a math lesson in which students figure out how much trash they and their families throw out daily. They can weigh their trash at home, compute the class average, and compare it to the national average of four pounds per day. If they measure the volume, it can be used to determine how much space their trash will occupy in a landfill in a year.

Think About It

Q: Which weighs more, a ton of trash or a ton of soap bubbles?

A: They both weigh the same! A ton is a measure of weight.

RODENTS

Something Extra

Coloring pages and pet care: http://www.afrma.org/kidskorner.htm

If you are writing about a hamster or rabbit or white rat because you have one, bring it to school to share during your report.

Thinking About the Topic

Rats and mice! Ugh! To some people, the thought sends shivers down their spines. Other people think they make great pets! Learn more about them and decide for yourself. Hamsters, squirrels, and rabbits are also rodents, just like rats and mice.

Directions

Pick one rodent to write about (rat, mouse, hamster, guinea pig, or rabbit). Then choose question 1 and any other two questions below. Write each question at the top of a sheet of paper. As you read about your rodent, take notes to answer each question. Write the notes in complete sentences. Write a conclusion sentence for each question. This sentence will be the topic sentence for your paragraph, and your notes will form the paragraph.

1. Name several rodents and describe the characteristics of a rodent.

2. How does the rodent live in the wild? What differences are there if it is a pet?

3. What natural enemies does it have? How does it protect itself?

4. If you have a rodent, does it make a good pet? Why or why not? How do you take care of it?

Books

Keywords: *Rodents; Gerbils; Hamsters; Mice as pets; Rodents as Pets; Rabbits.*

Frost, Helen. *Rabbits*. Mankato, MN: Capstone, 2001.

Head, Honor. *Hamsters and Gerbils*. Austin, TX: Raintree/Steck, 2001.

Head, Honor. *Rats and Mice*. Austin, TX: Steck-Vaughn, 2001.

World Book Student Discovery Encyclopedia. Chicago: World Book, 2000.

Internet

Rat and Mouse Club of America	http://www.rmca.org/	Care of pet rats and mice, games you can play with them, and treats to make.
American Fancy Rat and Mouse Association	http://www.afrma.org/kidskorner.htm	Basic pet rat and mouse care, and coloring pages.
KidZone	http://www.kidzone.ws/animals/bats/facts9.htm	Brief facts about bats.
House Rabbit Society	http://www.rabbit.org/kids/	Caring for rabbits.
Detroit Zoological Society	http://www.detroitzoo.org/dzs/april2001/kids.html	Wild rabbits: facts and activities.

Other Resources

Short video clip of a deer mouse and a cotton rat: http://www.cdc.gov/ncidod/diseases/hanta/hanta97/noframes/ratmovie.htm

Interview someone who has a rat, gerbil, or rabbit as a pet. Take good notes or record your interview.

For the Teacher

Lesson plans with an outdoor focus: http://rivervision.com/branchclass/lessonpl.html

Lesson plan on animal classification: http://school.discovery.com/lessonplans/programs/animaladaptations/index.html

Consider a class pet. A gerbil or rabbit is an easy-to-care-for pet. Students get a lot of enjoyment watching animals. Some of them do not have pets at home.

Joke

Q: Why can't a rat's nose be 12 inches long?

A: Because then it would be a foot!

J. K. ROWLING

> ## Something Extra
>
> Make up a new game with rules, similar to Quidditch. Explain it to your friends and have them play it with you.
>
> Start your own *Hogwarts Journal* about your friends, school, and secrets.

Thinking About the Topic

J. K. Rowling is the author of the popular Harry Potter books. Harry Potter attends Hogwarts School for Witchcraft and Wizardry. His classmates and teachers know he is destined for greatness. J. K. Rowling has wowed the world with her books. Where is she from? Where did she get the idea for Harry Potter? What are her plans for future Harry Potter books? If you are a fan, you may want to learn more about her.

Directions

J. K. Rowling is the famous creator of Harry Potter. Children and adults worldwide love these books. Read at least one of the books before you begin (you can also watch the movies). Select three questions below, including question 1. Use several books or other resources to answer your questions. Draw a conclusion for each question. For example, the conclusion for question 1 might be, "Ms. Rowling is the author of the famous Harry Potter books."

1. Who is J. K. Rowling? Tell a little about her life and what made her want to write.

2. Where did the idea for Harry Potter come from? Relate how Harry became a book.

3. What awards has Mrs. Rowling won for Harry Potter books? Why do you think the books have won these awards?

4. What other books are planned for Harry? Why do YOU think these books have so many readers (both adult and children)?

5. What role does Ms. Rowling play in the making of the Harry Potter movies? Is she satisfied that they depict her books as she would like?

Books

Keywords: *Rowling, J.K.; Harry Potter; Authors- Juvenile Literature.*

Biography for Beginners. Detroit: Omnigraphics, 2000.

Biography Today. Detroit: Omnigraphics, 1999.

Fraser, Lindsey. *Conversations with J.K. Rowling.* New York: Scholastic, 2001.

"J. K. Rowling." In *Something About the Author, Volume 109.* Detroit: Gale, 1999.

Shields, Charles J. *Mythmaker: The Story of J.K. Rowling.* Who Wrote That? Series. Broomall, PA: Chelsea House, 2002.

Internet

Rowling	http://www.sffworld.com/authors/r/rowling_jk/	Reviews of the books, information about the author.
J. K. Rowling	http://www.scholastic.com/harrypotter/	About the author and Harry.
Interview with the Author	http://hosted.ukoln.ac.uk/stories/stories/rowling/interview1.htm	Interview and other information.
Chat with the Author	http://www.yahooligans.com/content/chat/jkrowlingchat.html	Read the transcript from a chat with J. K. Rowling.

Other Resources

Write to J. K. Rowling, c/o Scholastic, Inc., 555 Broadway, New York, NY 10012-3999.

Harry Potter and the Sorcerer's Stone (video). Burbank, CA: Warner, 2002.

Harry Potter and the Chamber of Secrets (video). Burbank, CA: Warner Home Video, 2003.

For the Teacher

Teacher Resources: http://falcon.jmu.edu/~ramseyil/rowling.htm

Harry Potter books make great "chapter" read-alouds. The students who have read them will love hearing them again. Those who have not will also enjoy them.

Declare a Harry Potter day and have the students dress as their favorite characters (you can be the headmaster). Play one of the games described in the books. Have a Harry Potter reading festival.

Joke

Q: What do you call a stupid cow that you can "walk through?"

A: *Dumbledore (Dumb-bull-door!)*

SACAGAWEA

Something Extra
Word scramble: http://www.phillyburbs.com/sacagawea/activities.shtml

Thinking About the Topic

Long ago people thought that women were not as smart or as brave as men. They thought Native Americans were inferior. Sacagawea, who was both a woman and a Native American, became a peacemaker and interpreter for the white men who explored her country. She traveled along with Lewis and Clark, who were following the Missouri River to the Pacific Ocean. These explorers are fun to learn about. Their life was not at all like ours. How did Sacagawea help them? You will find her name spelled two different ways, Sacagawea and Sacajawea.

Directions

Read about Sacagawea. Then get three pieces of paper. Choose question 1 and any other two questions below. Write each question at the top of a piece of paper. Take notes on the questions in complete sentences. Write a conclusion for each question. This conclusion will be the topic sentence of your paragraph, and the notes will be the paragraph.

1. Describe Sacagawea's early life. Where did she live? What was her life like?

2. Who were Lewis and Clark, and what was their mission?

3. Why was Sacagawea with Lewis and Clark? How did she help?

4. Why is Sacagawea an American hero?

5. How and why was Sacagawea chosen to appear on the American dollar coin?

Books

Keywords: *Sacagawea; Sacajawea; Lewis and Clark Expedition.*

Alter, Judy. *Sacagawea: Native American Interpreter*. Chanhasen, MN: Childs World, 2002.

Avery, Susan, and Linda Skinner. *Extraordinary American Indians*. Chicago: Children's Press, 1997.

Marcovitz, Hal. *Sacagawea: Guide for the Lewis and Clark Expedition*. Philadelphia: Chelsea House, 2001.

Moss, Joyce, and George Wilson. *Profiles in American History*. Farmington Hills, MI: Gale, 1995.

Rowland, Della. *Story of Sacajawea, Guide to Lewis and Clark*. New York: Yearling, 1996.

Sanford, William R. *Sacagawea: Native American Hero*. Berkeley Heights, NJ: Enslow, 1997.

Witteman, Barbara. *Sacagawea: A Photo-Illustrated Biography*. Mankato, MN: Bridgestone, 2002.

Internet

PBS	http://www.pbs.org/weta/thewest/people/s_z/sacagawea.htm	Biography.
United States Mint	http://www.usmint.gov/mint_programs/golden_dollar_coin/index.cfm?action=about_sacagawea	Learn why Sacagawea was chosen to be on the gold dollar.
Important Millennium Achievers	http://www.imahero.com/herohistory/sacagawea_herohistory.htm	More detailed biography.
Go West with Lewis and Clark	http://www.nationalgeographic.com/features/97/west/	Interactive site by National Geographic. Try it and find out what it was like to go on the expedition with Lewis, Clark, and Sacagawea.

Other Resources

Interactive expedition. You make the decisions on where to go http://www.pbs.org/lewisandclark/into/index.html

Lewis & Clark: The Journey of the Corps of Discovery (video). Alexandria, VA: PBS Home Video, 1997.

For the Teacher

Classroom resources on the Lewis and Clark expedition, from PBS: http://www.pbs.org/lewisandclark/

Lesson plans for a play about Sacagawea: http://www.teachervision.com/lesson-plans/lesson-3843.html

Teacher's Guide to Sacagawea's Journey: http://www.phillyburbs.com/sacagawea/guide.shtml

---

Joke

Two cowboys came around the bend and saw an Indian with his head leaning against the ground. When he saw the men, the Indian said, "Two men, large horses, one wagon."

One of the cowboys said in amazement, " You can tell all that from listening to the ground?"

"No," the Indian said. "They just ran over me."

SEAHORSE

> ## Something Extra
>
> Print and color the seahorse shape:
> http://www.abcteach.com/AnimalShapes/seahorse.htm
>
> Try creating an origami seahorse: www.ulster.net/~spider/seahrs1.htm

Thinking About the Topic

HEADLINES: Male Seahorse Gives Birth to Over 100 Babies!

Imagine! A hundred babies at one time! It is a good thing baby seahorses do not drink from bottles or need diaper changes. The male seahorse has the babies. What an unusual animal! The seahorse wears its skeleton on the outside. This report should be fun. Be sure to prepare a nice cover for your report. Use the seahorse drawing at http://www.abcteach.com/AnimalShapes/seahorsebooklet.htm. If you decide to raise seahorses, be prepared to be patient. Follow the directions *exactly*.

Directions

There are several good books and Web pages where you can find out about this unusual animal. Using three resources, answer question 1 and two other questions below. Write each question at the top of a separate page. Take notes on the pages you create. Your notes should be in complete sentences. Each question will become a paragraph in your report. After you have found the answers, draw a conclusion about the information. (For example, the conclusion for question 4 might be: "The seahorse lives _____.") Your conclusion will be the topic sentence for the paragraph. Use your notes for the details of each paragraph.

1. Describe the seahorse.

2. What is the life cycle of the seahorse?

3. Describe the unusual birth of the seahorse.

4. What is the habitat of the seahorse?

5. How does the seahorse protect itself from predators?

6. If you had a seahorse for a pet, how would you care for it?

Books

Keywords: *Sea Horses; Sea Life; Gasterosteiformes.*

Freedman, Russell. *Animal Fathers*. New York: Holiday House, 1976.

Morris, Robert Ada. *Seahorse*. Science I Can Read Book. New York: Harper & Row, 1972.

New Book of Popular Science. Danbury, CT: Grolier, 2000.

Rizzatti, Lorella. *Seahorse*: Portable Pets. New York: Harry N. Abrams; 2000.

Walker, Sally M. *Seahorse Reef: A Story of the South Pacific*. Norwalk, CT: Soundprints, 2001.

Internet

Seahorse Park	http://www.poost.nl/seahorse/index.html	Easy to read, good links.
Nova's Seahorse site.	http://www.pbs.org/wgbh/nova/seahorse	Links, basic information, descriptions, photographs.
Ocean Oasis Field Guide to the seahorse.	http://www.oceanoasis.org/fieldguide/hipp-ing.html	Facts and figures. Conservation status links to a study about seahorses at Magill University in Canada.
Beyond Imagination	http://www.aqua.org/seahorses/	Great site. Very well organized and pretty. Enjoy it!

Other Resources

Kingdom of the Seahorse (video). South Burlington, VT: WGBH Boston, 1997.

Disney's The Little Mermaid: Stormy the Wild Seahorse (video). Ariel's Undersea Adventures. Burbank, CA: Walt Disney Home Video, 1993.

Online audio and video clips at Seahorse Park: www.poost.nl/seahorse/picts/media/zp7.qt

For the Teacher

Project Seahorse. Magill University students report on their study of the seahorse. Excellent information for teachers: http://www.seahorse.mcgill.ca/intro.htm

A site about breeding seahorses. Could your class care for seahorses?: http://www.seahorses.de/

Read aloud the stories of divers researching seahorses: http://www.seahorsetales.com/

Joke

Q: What kind of horse can swim underwater without coming up for air?

A: A seahorse !

SNAKES

Something Extra

Play the snake game online: http://www.nokia.com/snake/game.html

Thinking About the Topic

No legs, no arms, but look at that snake go! Some creep so slowly you barely see them move. Others zip by at 20 miles per hour! Some slither. And the sidewinder has a stroll all its own. Some snakes kill their prey with a poisonous bite. Some coil around the victim, slowly squeezing the air out of it. Some swallow their meal alive. Some snakes even eat other snakes. Ooh! Some of us are afraid of snakes even if they aren't poisonous. Maybe that is a good reason to learn more about them.

Directions

Write about snakes as a species or choose a particular snake such as a cobra, python, rattlesnake, or garden snake. Read about your snake. Pick question 1 and any other two questions below. Write each question at the top of a piece of paper. Answer the question in complete sentences. Draw a conclusion from your findings. Each conclusion will be your topic sentence for the paragraph. The notes you take will become details.

1. Describe your snake. How does it look? How does it move?

2. What does a snake eat? Describe its food.

3. Where does the snake live? Does it hibernate?

4. How have snakes helped humans? What problems have they caused?

5. Which snakes are poisonous? How can you tell?

6. Do snakes make good pets? Why or why not?

Books

Keywords: *Snakes; Rattlesnake* (or other breed)*; Texas* (or your state) *snakes; Reptiles.*

Barth, Kelly. *Snakes*. San Diego: Lucent, 2001.

Gish, Melissa. *Snakes*. Mankato, MN: Creative Education, 1998.

Markle, Sandra. *Outside and Inside Snakes*. New York: Atheneum, 1995.

Stille, Darlene R. *Snakes*. Minneapolis, MN: Compass Point Books, 2001.

World Book Student Discovery Encyclopedia. Chicago: World Book, 2000.

Internet

Picture Gallery of Non-Venomous Snakes	http://www.petcommunity.org/Sites/Mike/Pix/snakes.htm	Great photographs of snakes.
University of Massachusetts	http://www.umass.edu/umext/nrec/snake_pit/index.html	Identification guide. Even if you don't live in Massachusetts, your snake might!
American International Rattlesnake Museum	http://www.rattlesnakes.com/core.html	How do rattles grow? And other interesting facts.
Pelotes Island Nature Preserve	http://pelotes.jea.com/vensnake.htm	Learn about snake venom.

Other Resources

Hear a rattlesnake rattle: http://www.wf.net/~snake/rattlesn.htm.

Interactive King Cobra, from National Geographic: http://www.educationplanet.com/. (Search).

National Geographic and other organizations have published great snake videos that are available at school or at your video store. Start by asking your school librarian.

For the Teacher

Many states have snake sites. Try an internet search for snakes and your state name.

A variety of snake crafts: http://familycrafts.about.com/cs/snakecrafts/

Herps lesson plans, from the Smithsonian: http://educate.si.edu/lessons/siyc/herps/start.html

---

Try saying this three times quickly!
Slithering snakes slide slowly lest starving seagulls see them.

SNEAKERS

Something Extra

Win a $500 savings bond if you have the smelliest sneakers, in the annual International Rotten Sneaker Contest, at http://www.odor-eaters.com/rsc.shtml

Organize a class or grade level project. Collect old sneakers and recycle them. (Contact local shoe companies and sporting goods stores for a recycler.)

Thinking About the Topic

From canvas in 1916 to the laceless upper in 2000, sneakers have been the shoes of choice for kids. In 2000, people in the United States spent more than $15 billion on sneakers. Learn lots and have fun. Who *EVER* thought they would research their shoes? What fun! How fashionable!

Directions

Select question 1 and two others below. Write one question at the top of each page. Look in several sources for the answers to your questions. Each question will become a paragraph in your report. Draw a conclusion from the answers you find. The conclusion will be your topic sentence. For example, the conslusion for question 1 might be "Kids have been wearing sneakers for almost 100 years."

1. What is the history of sneakers? Where did they begin? What were the earliest sneakers made of?

2. In 1916, a rubber company introduced a simple sneaker. Tell about it.

3. What were some of the inventions and changes in sneakers during the 1990s?

4. Discuss the parts of a sneaker. You might label a diagram for your report.

5. What are some of the special features of today's sneakers for kids?

Books

Keywords: *Sneakers; Athletic shoes; Inventions; Fashion.*

Woods, Samuel G. *Sneakers: From Start to Finish.* Woodbridge, CT: Blackbirch, 1999.

Young, Robert. *Sneakers: The Shoes We Choose.* Minneapolis, MN: Dillon Press, 1991.

Try an encyclopedia or books on inventions, whatever is available in your library. Ask the librarian for help.

Internet

Sneaker Websites	http://www.nationalgeographic.com/ngforkids/articles	Good information and links to the Web. See March 2002.
Charlie's Sneaker Pages	http://www.sneakers.pair.com/	Photos and info about all kinds of sneakers. Be sure to go all the way down the page. Lots of history there.
Nike's Re-Use a Shoe	http://nikebiz.com/environ/reuse.shtml	Info about recycling.
Slam Dunk Science	http://www.scire.com/sds/sdsmenu.html	Sports shoes.
The History of Your Shoes	http://inventors.about.com/library/inventors/blshoe.htm	Good links that may cover several of your questions. From About.com.
Sneakers	http://www.sneakers.com/	The world's first athletic shoe search.

Other Resources

"The All*Stars of Footware." *National Geographic Kids* (March 2002). Ask the librarian to get this great article for you. It will really help you a lot.

They're Not Just Gym Shoes: http://www.npr.org/ramfiles/me/19980928.me.11.ram. A National Public Radio audio recording.

Create a timeline of sneakers. Maybe you can track how popular they were or how much was spent on them over the years. List some of the major changes.

"Old Sneakers Never Die": http://www.smithsonianmag.si.edu/smithsonian/issues01/nov01/object.html. Excellent article from *Smithsonian Magazine*.

For the Teacher

Conduct a sneaker traction test. Have the class chart the results by brand and type.

Great art project: Make a plaster sculpture of students' old sneakers.

Read-aloud: Sobol, Donald J. *Encyclopedia Brown and the Case of the Disgusting Sneakers.* New York: Morrow, 1990.

Read-aloud: Bunting, Eve. *Nasty, Stinky Sneakers.* New York: HarperCollins, 1994.

Sneaker Hunt: http://pe.central.vt.edu/lessonideas/ViewLesson.asp?ID=1783. Good rainy day activity.

Peters, Julie Anne. *The Stinky Sneakers Contest.* Boston: Little, Brown. 1992. Fun read-aloud.

Conduct your own class stinky sneaker contest. Send in the stinkiest to International Rotten Sneaker Contest at http://www.odor-eaters.com/rsc.shtml. The winning student will receive a $500 savings bond.

Joke

Q: What orbits around the Planet Reebok?

A: The Reebok Satellite cross-trainer, of course!

SPACE EXPLORATION

Something Extra

Build a bubble-powered rocket: http://spaceplace.jpl.nasa.gov/rocket.htm

Thinking About the Topic

Once upon a time in people's imaginations, the moon was a face, watching us. The stars were heroes, like Orion and Hercules. The sun was a fiery chariot driven across the sky. As people learned more about the heavens, they realized how much more they still did not know. After they finished exploring the earth, they raised their sights and began to explore the sky. We even believed that people could walk on the moon!

Directions

When you are ready, select question 1 and two others below. Write one question at the top of each page. Look in several sources for the answers to your questions. Each question will become a paragraph in your report

1.   What do we mean by *space exploration*?

2.   Name some of the ways people have explored space.

3.   What are some of the difficulties of living in outer space? How do we overcome them?

4.   Describe the methods of launching spacecraft. What about landing them?

5.   How has space exploration benefited us? Name several inventions that exist because of space exploration.

Books

Keywords: *Space exploration; Space travel; Apollo 13; Lunar exploration; Space station.*

Berger, Melvin, and Gilda Berger. *Can You Hear a Shout in Space?* New York: Scholastic Reference, 2000.

Dorling Kindersley Science Encyclopedia. New York: Dorling Kindersley, 1993.

Engelbert, Phillis. *Astronomy and Space: From the Big Bang to the Big Crunch.* Detroit: UXL, 1997.

Gifford, Clive. *Kingfisher Facts and Records Book of Space.* New York: Larousse Kingfisher Chambers, 2001.

Loves, June. *Spacecraft*. Broomall, PA: Chelsea House, 2001.

Raintree Steck-Vaughn Illustrated Science Encyclopedia. Austin, TX: Raintree Steck-Vaughn, 1997.

Rinard, Judith E. *The Book of Flight: The Smithsonian Institution's National Air and Space Museum*. Toronto: Firefly Books, 2001.

Internet

National Aeronautics & Space Administration	http://kids.msfc.nasa.gov/	The solar system, the space station, exploration of the moon, satellites: NASA tells you all about it.
Space Telescope Science Institute	http://hubblesite.org/gallery/	View photographs from the Hubble Telescope and read explanations of what you see.
Jet Propulsion Laboratory	http://www.jpl.nasa.gov/kids/kids_index.html	"Laugh and Learn." A fun way to learn about space exploration.
How Stuff Works	http://www.howstuffworks.com/space-station.htm	How the space station works.

Other Resources

Live pictures of the Space Station Processing Facility, updated every 90 seconds: http://science.ksc.nasa.gov/payload/missions/station/sspf-video.html

NASA video gallery includes a music video, *Emotion of Space:* http://www.nasa.gov/gallery/video/

Video clips of space launches and landings: http://www.unitedspacealliance.com/live/archive/

For the Teacher

Web-based activities for classroom use, from the Space Telescope Science Institute: http://amazing-space.stsci.edu/

Space Science Resource Directory, from NASA: http://teachspacescience.org/cgi-bin/ssrtop.plex

Space colony design contest for grades six and up: http://www.nas.nasa.gov/NAS/SpaceSettlement/designer/

Joke

Kay: I heard the astronauts found some bones on the moon.

John: I guess the cow didn't make it back.

STREGA NONA

Something Extra

Make a huge pot of spaghetti for your class and serve it when you make your report. Be sure to get permission from your teacher.

Teach your class to spell spaghetti.

Thinking About the Topic

Strega Nona (Grandma Witch), Big Anthony, and Bambalona are favorite book characters for children. Tomie dePaola made them famous in his *Strega Nona* books. Writing about a character can be fun because you get to write about what you like and do not like. Treat the character like a person. But be sure you explain that this is a character in books by Tomie dePaola.

Directions

To write about Strega Nona, Big Anthony, or Bambolina, you should read several books in the series. When you are ready, select question 1 and two others below. Look in several sources for the answers to your questions. Each question will become a paragraph in your report. Draw a conclusion from the answers you find. The conclusion will be your topic sentence. For example, the conclusion to question 1 might be, "Strega Nona is a fictional grandma who lives in a village in Italy." Add to your paragraph by using your notes for the details.

1. Who is Strega Nona, and where does she live? What is she like?

2. What can Strega Nona do that makes the people in the town love her? Give examples.

3. What did Strega Nona warn Big Anthony not to do? Why do you think she warned him?

4. Describe Strega Nona's magic pot. Why does Big Anthony want to learn the magic?

5. What is it about Strega Nona that you love? Why do you think these books are popular?

Books

Keywords: *Strega Nona; dePaola, Tomie; Children's authors.*

There are several books in the Strega Nona series. You will find them at your library. Read at least two or three. Then read something about the author. The author will help you understand the character better.

DePaola, Tomie. *Strega Nona.* Englewood Cliffs, NJ: Prentice Hall, 1975. (And the other books about Strega Nona).

Elleman, Barbara. *Tomie dePaola: His Art and His Stories.* New York: Putnam, 1999.

"Tomie dePaola." In *Biography for Beginners*. Detroit: Omnigraphics, 1998.

"Tomie dePaola." In *Something About the Author, Volume 15*. Detroit: Gale, 1979.

"Tomie dePaola." In *Talking with Artists, Volume I.* Edited by Pat Cummings.New York: Macmillan, 1992.

Internet

Strega Nona Story	http://www.bingley.com/1975streganona.html	Bibliography.
Book Reviews by Kids	http://www.spaghettibookclub.org/	Search by title for Strega Nona. See what other kids have said about these books.
A Summary of Strega Nona	http://www.viva-books.com/strega.htm	Summary of the books by a book store.
Publishers Page about Tomie dePaola	http://www.eduplace.com/kids/hmr/mtai/depaola.html	The publisher writes about the author.
Professional reviews of *Strega Nona*	http://hallkidsfamily.com/multigenerational/66.shtml	See what professional writers have said about *Strega Nona*.

Other Resources

Online video of the book *Strega Nona:* video.dpi.state.nc.us/Tekdata/StregaNonna.html

DePaola, Tomie. *Strega Nona and Other Stories* (video). Weston, CT: Children's Circle, 1989. (Most libraries have this video.)

Listen to a Tomie dePaola radio interview online at www.nhpr.org/content/fullmonty_view.php/415/

For the Teacher

Strega Nona Language Arts Lesson: faldo.atmos.uiuc.edu/CLA/LESSONS/106.html

Have a Strega Nona Day with your class: www.mrsburns.com/streg001.htm

Art projects using spaghetti (*Making Esther*): doodleshop.com/pages/kidstudio.html

---

Look It Up

Find out about the real area of Italy where Strega Nona lived, Calabria. Search online at http://www.initaly.com/regions/calabria/calabria.htm.

Impress your classmates. Include a map of the area with your report.

Are the people in Calabria like Strega Nona? Does the town look like the drawings in the books you read? Why or why not?

SOJOURNER TRUTH

Something Extra

Print out and color a picture of Sojourner Truth:
http://library.thinkquest.org/10320/Struth.htm

Use your drawing on the cover of your report.

Thinking About the Topic

Do this! Do that! Work harder! Work faster! You belong to me! How would you like to be a slave and have to do what you were told or be beaten? Sojourner Truth was born a slave and worked hard for years. Learn about her life as a slave and about her fight for freedom and women's rights.

Directions

Read about Sojourner Truth. Choose question 1 and any other two questions below. Write each question at the top of a piece of paper. Answer each question in complete sentences. Write a conclusion for each question. This conclusion will be your topic sentence for the paragraph. Add the details to fill out your paragraph.

1. Describe Sojourner Truth's early life. When did she live?

2. Why did Sojourner Truth decide to escape from slavery? What happened when her former owner found her?

3. Tell how Sojourner Truth got her name.

4. How did she take care of herself after she was free?

5. How did she help other people? Why is she famous?

Books

Keywords: *Truth, Sojourner; African American biography; African American History.*

Hacker, Carlotta. *Great African Americans in History.* New York: Crabtree, 1997.

Jaffe, Elizabeth Dana. *Sojourner Truth.* Minneapolis, MN: Compass Point Books, 2000.

Knight, Judson. *African American Biography.* Farmington Hills, MI: UXL, 1999.

Leebrick, Kristal. *Sojourner Truth.* Mankato, MN: Bridgestone Books, 2002.

Lutz, Norma Jean. *Sojourner Truth: Abolitionist, Suffragist, and Preacher.* Broomall, PA: Chelsea House, 2001.

Moss, Joyce, and George Wilson. *Profiles in American History.* Farmington Hills, MI: Gale, 1995.

Internet

Sojourner Truth Memorial Statue Project	http://www.noho.com/sojourner/	History and quotes.
Sojourner Truth Institute	http://www.sojournertruth.org/Art/Gallery1.htm	Pictures of Sojourner Truth, her gravesite, and ideas inspired by her.
University of Pennsylvania	http://digital.library.upenn.edu/women/truth/1850/1850.html	Sojourner Truth's own story as told to Olive Gilbert.
Women in History	http://www.lkwdpl.org/wihohio/trut-soj.htm	Biography.

Other Resources

Video clips to show the class, with follow-up questions: http://www.americanwriters.org/classroom/videolesson/vlp07_truth.asp

Three-minute preview of a video about Sojourner Truth: http://webcast.mediaondemand.com/library_video/20000901/06_sojourner_truth_300.ram

Sojourner Truth. The Black Americans of Achievement Video Collection. Wynnewood, PA: Schlessinger Media, 1992.

Spangler, Lynn C. *Life and Legend of Sojourner Truth.* Princeton, NJ: Films for the Humanities and Sciences, 2001.

For the Teacher

Lesson plans: http://arta.msn.com/schoolhouse/

African American lesson plans, including Sojourner Truth, the Underground Railroad, and *African American Reports*: http://www.proteacher.com/090155.shtml

American Writers: Sojourner Truth: http://www.americanwriters.org/classroom/videolesson/vlp07_truth.asp. Video clips and lesson plans—excellent for upper grades.

Quote from Sojourner Truth

"If the first woman God ever made was strong enough to turn the world upside down all alone, these women together ought to be able to turn it back, and get it right side up again."

HARRIET TUBMAN

> ## Something Extra
>
> Crossword puzzles, quiz, and timeline created by a second-grade class: http://www2.lhric.org/pocantico/tubman/tubman.html. Your class could do this.

Thinking About the Topic

Almost 150 years ago, Harriet Tubman escaped from slavery. When she was free, she risked her life helping others. They escaped to freedom on the Underground Railroad. It sounds like a subway train, but it was not. When the Underground Railroad started, there were no subways. The Railroad was a group of people who helped slaves in the South escape to the North. They risked prison to do what they believed in. Once the slaves were freed, Harriet Tubman devoted her life to helping former slaves. They needed to learn how to take care of themselves. So she helped them learn.

Directions

Using several resources, answer question 1 and two other questions below. Write each question at the top of a separate page. Take notes on the pages you create. Your notes should be written in complete sentences. Each question will become a paragraph in your report. After you have found the answers, draw a conclusion about your information. Your conclusion will be the topic sentence for the paragraph.

1.   Describe Harriet Tubman's early life.

2.   What was slavery like for Harriet Tubman? Why did she decide to escape?

3.   How did Harriet Tubman help with the Underground Railroad? Why did she do it?

4.   What did she do after the Civil War? Why?

5.   What do you think was the most important thing Ms. Tubman did? Explain.

Books

Keywords: *Tubman, Harriet; Underground Railroad; Slavery—United States.*

Contemporary Black Biography. Farmington Hills, MI: Thomson, 1992-.

Hacker, Carlotta. *Great African Americans in History*. New York: Crabtree, 1997.

Halvorsen, Lisa. *Harriet Tubman*. Farmington Hills, MI: Blackbirch Marketing, 2002.

Knight, Judson. *African American Biography*. Farmington Hills, MI: UXL, 1999.

Lutz, Norma Jean. *Harriet Tubman: Leader of the Underground Railroad*. Broomall, PA: Chelsea House, 2001.

Nielsen, Nancy J. *Harriet Tubman*. Mankato, MN: Bridgestone, 2002.

Rau, Dana Meachen. *Harriet Tubman*. Minneapolis, MN: Compass Point Books, 2000.

Rustad, Martha E. H. *Harriet Tubman*. Mankato, MN: Capstone Press, 2002.

Internet

Harriet Tubman Home	http://www.nyhistory.com/harriettubman/life.htm	Biography. Harriet Tubman's home. Take an online drive on the route Tubman took as conductor of the Underground Railroad.
Spectrum	http://www.incwell.com/Biographies/Tubman.html	Biography.
White House	http://www.whitehouse.gov/kids/timeline/railroad.html	History of the Underground Railroad.
Harriet Tubman	http://www.pbs.org/wgbh/aia/part4/4p1535.html	Information about Tubman's life from PBS. Includes a picture.

Other Resources

Virtual field trip on the Underground Railroad: http://www.nationalgeographic.com/features/99/railroad/

Online interactive game about the Underground Railroad: http://www.coollessons.org/slaveryhistory.htm

Your school or public library probably has a video on famous African Americans. They may even have one on Harriet Tubman. Ask the librarian.

For the Teacher

Teaching activities from the National Archives: http://www.nara.gov/education/teaching/woman/teach.html

Teaching guide on slavery, from PBS: http://www.pbs.org/wgbh/aia/tguide/4index.html

Limerick

There once was a woman named Harriet
Whose idea of slavery was, Bury it!
She transported people
Through forest and steeple
Within her invisible chariot.

TYRANNOSAURUS REX

Something Extra

Build a paper T-rex: http://www.enchantedlearning.com/crafts/Trexcutout.shtml

Thinking About the Topic

Thump! Thump! Thump! With every step it made the earth thunder and shake. The other animals ran to hide! The Tyrannosaurus rex was tall, with eyes on the top of its head. How could they get away? Scientists have found an almost complete Tyrannosaurus rex skeleton that they have named Sue. See what you can learn about Sue. (You can report on any other dinosaur and still use our questions.)

Directions

Write each question at the top of a piece of paper. Answer question 1 and any two other questions below in complete sentences. When you finish a question, write a conclusion. The conclusion will be your topic sentence, and the answer will make up your paragraph.

1. Describe Tyrannosaurus rex.

2. Describe the differences between Tyrannosaurus and other dinosaurs.

3. What was the earth like during Tyrannosaurus rex's time? Include plant life and the other animals.

4. Tell about Tyrannosaurus rex's diet. What did it eat? How did it get food? How did it eat the food?

5. Where and how have Tyrannosaurus rex skeletons been found? What about the dinosaur named Sue?

Books

Keywords: *Tyrannosaurus Rex; Dinosaurs.*

Cohen, Daniel. *Tyrannosaurus Rex.* Mankato, MN: Capstone, 2001.

Gaines, Richard M. *Tyrannosaurus Rex.* Edina, MN: Abdo, 2001.

Marshall, Chris, ed. *Dinosaurs of the World.* Tarrytown, NY: Marshall Cavendish, 1999.

Relf, Patricia. *A Dinosaur Named Sue: The Story of the Colossal Fossil.* New York: Scholastic, 2000.

Rodriguez, K. S. *Tyrannosaurus Rex.* Austin, TX: Raintree Steck-Vaughn, 2000.

Sattler, Helen R. *The New Illustrated Dinosaur Dictionary.* New York: Lothrop, Lee & Shepard, 1990.

Zoehfeld, Kathleen Weidner. *Terrible Tyrannosaurs.* New York: HarperCollins, 2001.

Internet

The Field Museum, Chicago	http://www.fmnh.org/sue/default.htm	All about Sue, the most complete Tyrannosaurus skeleton ever found.
Keith Holmes	http://www.wf.carleton.ca/Museum/rex/p1.htm	Facts and illustrations. Relatives of T-rex.
Columbia Electronic Encyclopedia	http://kids.infoplease.lycos.com/ce6/sci/A0849861.html	Good basic information.

Other Resources

James, Jasper. *Walking with Dinosaurs* (video). Beverly Hills, CA: CBS Fox Video, 2000.

View a video clip of Tyrannosaurus, from BBC: http://www.bbc.co.uk/dinosaurs/fact_files/volcanic/tyrannosaurus.shtml

How about family night movie: *Jurassic Park*, popcorn, and sodas?

Go to your local natural history museum if it has a dinosaur display. Or call the museum curator and ask your questions. Take notes. This is a good resource.

For the Teacher

Lesson plans for specific types of dinosaurs: http://www.sedl.org/scimath/pasopartners/dinosaurs/lesson4.html

PBS broadcast on T-rex for older grades: http://www.pbs.org/wgbh/nova/trex/

Joke

Q: What did the Tyrannosaurus rex have that no other dinosaurs had?

A: Baby Tyrannosauruses!

VIRTUAL REALITY

Something Extra

Make your own video game! Download a free demo by choosing "Play or make games with Creator": http://www.stagecast.com/

Thinking About the Topic

When you play a video game you really get into it, feeling like you are actually there. You move around, copying the things your character does. How much more exciting it could be with virtual reality! The room disappears, the sounds move, you are in another place. Just what is virtual reality, and how does it feel so real? Find out. See if you can discover ways doctors and other professionals may use virtual reality.

Directions

Select question 1 and two others below. Write one question at the top of each page. Look in several sources for the answers to your questions. Each question will become a paragraph in your report. Draw a conclusion from the answers you find. The conclusion will be your topic sentence. Your notes will be the paragraph details.

1.   What is virtual reality? What senses does virtual reality stimulate?

2.   What special equipment do you need for virtual reality? What do these pieces do?

3.   Would video games be more exciting with VR? Why?

4.   Describe some useful purposes for virtual reality (besides games).

5.   Report on possibilities for using virtual reality in the future.

Books

Keywords: *Virtual Reality; Human-Computer Interaction; Computer Simulation; Video games.*

Baker, Christopher W. *Virtual Reality: Experiencing Illusion.* Brookfield, CT: Millbrook Press, 2000.

Jefferis, David. *Cyberspace; Virtual Reality and the World Wide Web.* New York: Crabtree, 1999.

World Book Encyclopedia. Chicago: World Book, 2002.

Internet

How Stuff Works	http://www.howstuffworks.com/3dgraphics.htm	Explains why 3-D graphics look so real.
How Stuff Works	http://www.howstuffworks.com/augmented-reality.htm	Augmented reality, or a blending of the real with the computer enhancement.
ThinkQuest	http://library.thinkquest.org/J0110373/vrtours/vrtour.html	Students create a virtual tour of their school and tell you how to do it.
Virtual Reality Lab at University of Michigan	http://www-vrl.umich.edu/index.html	Neat site. I love the football trainer. Take your time. You might write to the students who compose this site and ask questions.

Other Resources

Visit *Palaces in Thailand with Virtual Reality:* http://www.palaces.thai.net/

See some of the greatest places in the world, courtesy of the Science Museum of Minnesota: http://www.sci.mus.mn.us/greatestplaces/medias/media_html/qtvr.html#falls

You would really benefit from interviewing someone who knows about virtual reality. See if there is a local source. Have your teacher or librarian help you find someone.

For the Teacher

Electronic School, the school technology authority: http://www.electronic-school.com/index.html

Explore the world of virtual reality polyhedral: http://www.theteacherscorner.net/math/geometry/

Check ERIC for the latest on virtual reality: http://www.askeric.org/Search/topicsA-Z.shtml

---

Joke

Alix: I've got something that will let you see through walls.

Blair: Wonderful! What is it?

Alix: A window.

WHALES

Something Extra

Make a whale mobile:
http://www.enchantedlearning.com/crafts/Whalemobile.shtml

Thinking About the Topic

Blue whales are the biggest creatures on earth, yet they eat one of the smallest creatures. Dolphins, a relative of the whale, like to play with passing boats. Narwhals look like sea unicorns. Cetaceans (whales and dolphins) look like fish. Are they? They can actually talk to each other. Learn more about these huge, fascinating creatures of the deep.

Directions

Write about whales in general or choose a particular kind of whale. Some types of whales are killer whales, narwhals, blue whales, and humpback whales. Answer question 1 and any two other questions below in complete sentences. Write each question at the top of a piece of paper. When you finish a question, write a conclusion. The conclusion will be your topic sentence, and the details will make your paragraph.

1. Describe the whale. What family is it in? Why is this unique?

2. Describe a whale's life. How does it breathe? What does it eat? Where does it live?

3. How do whales raise their young?

4. How do whales communicate with each other? Describe their song.

5. Are whales endangered species? Why? What is being done to save the whales?

Books

Keywords: *Whales; Humpback Whale; Killer Whale; Orca; Bottlenose Dolphin.*

Carwardine, Mark, ed. *Whales, Dolphins and Porpoises.* Alexandria, VA: Time-Life Books, 1998.

Fenton, Julie A. *Killer Whales and Other Toothed Whales.* World Books' Animals of the World. Chicago: World Book, 2001.

Holmes, Kevin J. *Whales.* Mankato, MN: Capstone, 1998.

Petty, Kate. *Whales Can Sing.* Brookfield, CT: Copper Beech Books, 1998.

World Book Student Discovery Encyclopedia. Chicago: World Book, 2002.

Internet

Enchanted Learning	http://www.zoomwhales.com/ subjects/whales/allabout/	Information about whales written especially for kids.
Gray Whales with Winston	http://www.geocities.com/ RainForest/Jungle/1953/index.html	A guide to gray whales, including a kids' corner with games.
National Oceanographic Administration	http://www.pmel.noaa.gov/vents/ acoustics/whales/bioacoustics.html	Choose spectograms for sounds of the blue whale, minke whale, and humpback whale. Also has distribution maps.
Save the Whales	http://www.savethewhales.org	Drawings and descriptions of each type of whale and dolphin.
Whales in Danger Information Service	http://whales.magna.com.au/ DISCOVER/gallery/index.html	Great photographs!

Other Resources

Hear the sounds of whales, from Australia: http://dkd.net/whales/wsounds.html

Your school or public library should have National Geographic or other videos about the whale. Check them out.

For the Teacher

Lesson plans from the Royal Ontario Museum: http://www.rom.on.ca/wwatch/teachers-kit/ lesson_plans.html

Ocean Planet, from the Smithsonian, for older students: http://educate.si.edu/lessons/currkits/ ocean/main.html

Several lesson plans about whales for all elementary grades: http://curry.edschool.virginia. edu/go/Whales/LessonPlans.HTML

Joke

Q: Why did the whale cross the ocean?

A: To get to the other tide!

LIVING IN A WHEELCHAIR

Something Extra
Borrow a wheelchair and spend one day in it. Find out what it is really like for children who "live in a wheelchair." What did you have to do differently?

Thinking About the Topic

Have you ever thought about what it would be like to be in a wheelchair all of the time? What would you have to learn that other children do not? What special equipment would you need? What could you do that other children could not? This is a good topic; especially if you have a friend or someone else you know who is in a wheelchair. You might even find out about sporting events played in a wheelchair.

Directions

When you are ready, select question 1 and two others below. Write one question at the top of each page. Look in several sources for the answers to your questions. Each question will become a paragraph in your report. Draw a conclusion from the answers you find. The conclusion will be your topic sentence. The details you find will complete the paragraph.

1.   What kind of wheelchairs are available? Why would a child need to "live" in one?

2.   How is a child who lives in a wheelchair the same as other children? How is he or she different?

3.   What are ways you can try to improve life for a friend in a wheelchair?

4.   What accommodations must be made at home and school for a child in a wheelchair?

5.   Being in a wheelchair is only one way children can be different. Research and write about others.

6.   Find out and write about wheelchair sports or wheelchair olympics.

Books

Keywords: *Wheelchair; Physically Handicapped;* add *Juvenile Literature.*

Apel, Melanie Ann. *Let's Talk About Being in a Wheelchair.* New York: PowerKids Press, 2002.

Heelan, James Riggio. *Rolling Along: The Story of Taylor and His Wheelchair.* Atlanta, GA: Peachtree, 2000.

Moran, George. *Imagine Me on a Sit-Ski!* Morton Grove, I: A. Whitman, 1995.

Ask the librarian to help you find other books that will help with this report.

Internet

See Me, Not My Chair	http://www.nald.ca/STORY/archive/1996/story17.htm	An excellent article about how a young man feels about his life in a wheelchair.
Wheelchair Sports Association	http://www.nswwsa.org.au/	Look at the different sports. Read some of the stories.
ADA information	http://www.panynj.gov/aviation/ladaovermain.htm	What are the rules for space and furnishings for physically challenged people?

Other Resources

This is a good topic for an interview. If you know someone who is in a wheelchair, see if he or she will answer a few questions you may have. Make sure you are ready to take notes and ask specific questions. Be very professional. Make sure your questions are considerate. Remember you are doing research. Have your teacher review your questions before your interview. **Hint**: A thank you note to the person you interview is always appreciated.

Anna's Dream. 2002. PAX made-for-TV film of a young girl living in a wheelchair.

Walking on Air (video). WonderWorks Family Movie. Los Angeles: Public Media Video, 1986.

For the Teacher

This topic is one that can help students look at one another's differences. Have a class discussion about all the ways we feel different from each other. All children feel different. Maybe they can talk about that. Also talk about ways we are the same.

Consider inviting a guest speaker to your class, perhaps a high school student who lives in a wheelchair or the school counselor. Let the students ask questions.

Search This Site

Find statistics on the following site for your report: http://www.apta.com/stats/vehicles/. Do you have a bus system in your city? Or a subway? How many people in wheelchairs are using public transportation? Is it increasing or decreasing?

WHO AM I?
WHO WERE MY ANCESTORS?

> ## Something Extra
>
> Create a family genealogy chart going back to your grandparents. If you can, add pictures to your chart: http://www.libofmich.lib.mi.us/binary/pedigreechart.pdf
>
> *Search your Ancestors*: http://www.everton.com/index.php

Thinking About the Topic

Have you ever thought about your family? Where were your parents born? Where did your grandparents and great-grandparents grow up? This project will help you do a little digging into family history. You may need to make a few calls and get a little family help. But it is YOUR project. Have fun!

Directions

Yes, you are looking into your own family history. But you still need books and other resources to help you learn the right way to do this. A great achievement would be a family genealogy chart to share with your class and family. A family history has stories. Relate a story that everyone in the family knows from the oldest generation you can interview.

- **Everyone answers this basic question:** What is a family history? How do you gather information to create one?

- **Ask parents, grandparents, and great-grandparents:**

  – Where were you born?

  – How many brothers and sisters do you have? Tell me about your cousins and aunts and uncles.

  – What are your best memories of your family when you were growing up?

  – Did you go to family reunions when you were young? Who was there? What did you do?

  – What do you remember most about your own parents?

  – How was your life when you were young different from mine now??

Books

Keywords: *Genealogy—Juvenile literature; Family history.*

Perl, Lila. *The Great Ancestor Hunt: The Fun of Finding Out Who You Are.* New York: Clarion, 1989.

Sweeney, Joan. *Me and My Family Tree.* New York: Crown, 1999.

Taylor, Maureen Alice. *Through the Eyes of Your Ancestors.* Boston: Houghton Mifflin, 1999.

Internet

What Is Genealogy	http://www.geocities.com/EnchantedForest/5283/genekids.htm	"Getting Started"—for beginners.
Genealogy Instructions for Kids, Teenagers, and Beginners.	http://home.earthlink.net/~howardorjeff/instruct.htm#forms	Good links on this page. Be sure to look at the definitions.
World Gen Web	http://www.rootsweb.com/~wgwkids/	For kids to search family history.

Other Resources

Interview parents and grandparents. Ask about *their* parents. Get as much information as you can for your genealogy chart. Have your parents help you get names and dates into the right place. Use a tape recorder when you talk with your family. Take your camera when you do interviews. A grandparent who lives out of town can be interviewed by phone or e-mail.

Part of your report can be your own story about your family members. Choose two to write about.

For the Teacher

This is a great opportunity to help students understand their own history. Maybe a class project drawing two-generation genealogy charts would be fun.

Port of Entry: Immigration, from the Library of Congress: http://lcweb2.loc.gov/ammem/ndlpedu/activity/port/teacher.html

---

The Van Gogh Family Tree

The brother who worked at a convenience store: Stopn Gogh

His magician uncle: Wherediddy Gogh

The son who made all As in school: Wayto Gogh

A sister who loved disco: Go Gogh

One of the Beatles: Ring Gogh

The uncle who loved to play games: Bing Gogh

THE WRIGHT BROTHERS

> ## Something Extra
> Build a scale model of the 1900 Kite model Wright aircraft:
> http://wright.grc.nasa.gov/WWW/Wright/ROGER/1900model.htm

Thinking About the Topic

When Orville Wright and Wilbur Wright were boys, airplanes had not even been invented. Even bicycles were pretty new. The Wright brothers rode bikes, but they dreamed of flying. When they grew older, the Wright brothers ran a bicycle shop during the warmer months to earn enough money to design their airplane in the winter. Find pictures for your report.

Directions

Select question 1 and two others below. Write one question at the top of each page. Look in several sources for the answers to your questions. Each question will become a paragraph in your report. Draw a conclusion from the answers you find. The conclusion will be your topic sentence. The details you find will complete the paragraph.

1. Tell about Orville Wright and Wilbur Wright's early life. Where did they grow up?

2. How did the Wright brothers learn about flight?

3. Describe the difference between the glider and the Flyer I. Why was Flyer I such a big advancement?

4. Tell about the first flight.

5. Discuss how the Wright brothers' invention changed the world.

Books

Keywords: *Wright, Orville; Wright, Wilbur; Aeronautics History; Kitty Hawk, N.C.; Airplanes.*

Joseph, Paul. *Wright Brothers.* Minneapolis, MN: Abdo & Daughters, 1997.

Old, Wendie C. *The Wright Brothers: Inventors of the Airplane.* Berkeley Heights, NJ: Enslow, 2000.

Shea, George. *First Flight: The Story of Tom Tate and the Wright Brothers.* New York: HarperCollins, 1997.

Sproule, Anna. *The Wright Brothers: The Birth of Modern Aviation.* Woodbridge, CT: Blackbirch Press, 1999.

World Book Encyclopedia. Chicago: World Book, 2002.

Internet

Wright Brothers Aeroplane Company and Museum	http://www.first-to-fly.com/	The Wright brothers' story, inventions, and experiments for you, in great detail. Great site!
Outer Banks	http://www.outerbanks.com/wrightbrothers/wrightlc.htm	Photographs of Kitty Hawk and the airplane prototypes.
Orville Wright	http://aeroweb.brooklyn.cuny.edu/history/wright/first.htm	Orville Wright's own story of the first flight.
First Flight Society	http://www.firstflight.org/	Includes pictures from the first flight.

Other Resources

Look for the links along the side of the page to listen to music from the Wright brothers' era: http://www.first-to-fly.com/Adventure/Workshop/box.htm

Simulations of the first flight: http://firstflight.open.ac.uk/

Sabin, Louis. *Wilbur and Orville Wright: The Flight to Adventure* (sound recording). Mahwah, NJ: Troll, 1983.

For the Teacher

A variety of lesson plans from NASA: http://wright.grc.nasa.gov/WWW/Wright/lesson.htm

---

Joke

Orville: Wanna fly?

Wilbur: Sure.

Orville: Just a sec. I'll catch one for you.

ZOOS

> ## Something Extra
>
> Create your own animals by switching around animal parts:
> http://www.switcheroozoo.com/
>
> Talk your parents into a family outing to visit the zoo. Take pictures for your report

Thinking About the Topic

Which animal can use a nose to pick up a toy? Which has a neck as long as a leg? Which can peel a banana with its hands? What animal eats from the tops of trees while standing on the ground? You know! Of course you do. Everyone knows about elephants, giraffes, and monkeys. How do you know about these strange creatures from Africa and South America? Why, you saw them in the zoo!

Directions

When you are ready, select question 1 and two others below. Write one question at the top of each page. Look in several sources for the answers to your questions. Each question will become a paragraph in your report. Draw a conclusion from the answers you find. The conclusion will be your topic sentence. The details you find will complete the paragraph.

1. Describe an early zoo. What was it like? What kinds of animals were in early zoos?

2. Why were zoos first started?

3. Why do we have zoos today? Report on at least three reasons and explain them.

4. What are some special needs of animals that live in the zoo? Write about two types of animals with special needs (housing, food, space, etc.).

5. Name some of the people who work in the zoo. What education do they need? What are their jobs?

Books

Keywords: *Zoos; Wildlife Reserves; Wildlife Conservation; Zoologist; Zoo Animals.*

Duden, Jane. *Animal Handlers & Trainers.* New York: Crestwood House, 1989.

New Book of Popular Science. Danbury, CT: Grolier, 2000.

Powell, Jillian. *Animal Rights.* Talking About series. Austin, TX: Raintree Steck-Vaughn, 2000

Raintree Steck-Vaughn Illustrated Science Encyclopedia. Austin, TX: Raintree Steck-Vaughn, 1997.

Rinard, Judith E. *What Happens at the Zoo.* Washington, DC: National Geographic Society, 1984.

Internet

Lincoln Park Zoo	http://www.lpzoo.com/tour/tour.html	Take a virtual tour of the Lincoln Park Zoo and meet the animals.
San Diego Zoo	http://www.sandiegozoo.org/wildideas/kids/index.html	Animal stories, working in a zoo, crafts and science experiments.
Dallas Aquarium and Zoo	http://www.dwazoo.com/	Webcams and conservation information.
ZooBooks	http://www.zoobooks.com/gatewayPages/gateway1Kids.html	Learn about your favorite animals and play interactive games.
Zoo articles from National Geographic	http://news.nationalgeographic.com/news/2002/08/0827_020827_TVzoos.html	Read the article and link to the URLs provided.

Other Resources

View animal babies and other interesting animals from a Webcam at the National Zoo: http://natzoo.si.edu/Webcams/webcams.htm

Virtual tour of the Denver Zoo: http://www.denverzoo.org/vr/virtualReality.htm

For the Teacher

Web toolboxes for educators: http://www.ed.sc.edu/caw/toolboxzoo.html

Science lesson plans for grades one through eight: http://www.csun.edu/~vceed009/lesson.html

Lesson plans from *ZooBooks:* http://www.zoobooks.com/links/lessonplans.html

Read-aloud: Altman, Joyce, and Sue Goldberg. *Dear Bronx Zoo.* New York: Macmillan, 1990.

Joke

Prisoner 1: What are you in for?

Prisoner 2: For feeding kangaroos.

Prisoner 1: Just for feeding kangaroos?

Prisoner 2: Yes. For feeding kangaroos. I was feeding them to the lions in the zoo.

Bibliography

Aaseng, Nathan. *The Unsung Heroes*. Minneapolis, MN: Lerner, 1989.

Abbott, John S. C. 1874. *David Crockett: His Life and Adventures*. Electronic Text Center, University of Virginia Library. Available: http://etext.lib.virginia.edu/ebooks/subjects/subjects-young. (Accessed June 16, 2003).

Acuff, Dan S. *What Kids Buy and Why: The Psychology of Marketing to Kids*. New York: Simon & Schuster, 1997.

Adler David A. *A Picture Book of Davy Crockett*. New York: Holiday House, 1998.

AIDS. Teen Health video series. Wynnewood, PA: Schlessinger Media, 2002.

All About Dinosaurs. Schlessinger Science Library for Children series. Bala Cynwyd, PA: Library Video, 1999.

All About Food Chains. Animal Life for Children video series. Wynnewood, PA: Schlessinger Media, 1999.

Allaby, Michael. *Tornadoes and Other Dramatic Weather Systems*. New York: Dorling Kindersley, 2001.

Allen, Thomas B. *Animals of Africa*. New York: Hugh Lauter Levin Associates, 1997.

Alter, Judy. *Sacagawea: Native American Interpreter*. Chanhassen, MN: Childs World, 2002.

Altman, Joyce, and Sue Goldberg. *Dear Bronx Zoo*. New York: Macmillan, 1990.

Amazing Animal: Amazing Endangered Animals (video). New York: DK Vision, 1997.

Amazing Grace: The Story of a Song with Bill Moyers (video). Princeton, NJ: Films for the Humanities and Sciences, 1994.

Amazing Monkeys and Apes (video). New York: DK Vision, 1997.

American Citizenship. American Government for Children video series. Wynnewood, PA: Schlessinger Media, 2002.

American Tall Tales: Davy Crockett (video). Allen, TX: Lyrick Studios, 1991.

Andersen, Hans Christian. *The Complete Hans Christian Andersen Fairy Tales*. Westminster, MD: Random House, 1993.

Ants. Bug City video series. Wynnewood, PA: Schlessinger Media, 1998.

Antz (video). Universal City, CA: Dreamworks, 1999.

Apel, Melanie Ann. *Let's Talk About Being in a Wheelchair*. New York: Power Kids, 2002.

Ardley, Neil. *Music*. London: Dorling Kindersley, 2000.

Arthur's Baby (video). New York: Random House, 1997.

Arthur's Famous Friends (video). New York: Random House Home Video, Sony Wonder, 2000.

Aurora: Rivers of Light in the Sky (video). Anchorage, AK: SkyRiver Films, 1994

Author Talk: Conversations with Judy Blume, Bruce Brooks, Karen Cushman, Russell Freedman, Lee Bennett Hopkins, James Howe, Johanna Hurwitz, E. L. Konigsburg, Lois Lowry, Gary Paulsen, and Laurence Yep. Edited by Marcus Leonard. Riverside, NJ: Simon & Schuster, 2000.

Avery, Susan, and Linda Skinner. *Extraordinary American Indians.* Chicago: Children's Press, 1992.

Ayer, Eleanor. *Homeless Children.* Lucent Overview Series. San Diego: Lucent, 1997.

Bailey, Donna. *Fishing.* Austin, TX: Steck-Vaughn, 1991.

Bailey, John. *Young Fishing Enthusiasts.* New York: DK Publishing, 1999.

Bair, Diane. *Bat Watching.* Mankato, MN: Capstone, 2000.

Baker, Christopher W. *Virtual Reality: Experiencing Illusion.* Brookfield, CT: Millbrook Press, 2000.

"Ballad of Davy Crockett." *Music of Disney: A Legacy in Song.* (sound recording). Burbank, CA: Walt Disney Records, 1992.

Barnes, Emilie. *A Little Book of Manners.* Eugene, OR: Harvest House, 1998.

Barnes, Rachel. *Abstract Expressionists.* Crystal Lake, IL: Heinemann, 2002.

Barney's Best Manners (video). Allen, TX: Barney Home Video, 1993.

Barth, Kelly. *Snakes.* San Diego: Lucent, 2001.

Bat Adventures. Audubon's Animal Adventure Series. Wynnewood, PA: Library Video Co.

Bausum, Ann. *Our Country's Presidents.* Washington, DC: National Geographic Society, 2001.

Becker, John E. *Bald Eagle.* San Diego: Kidhaven, 2002.

Bees. Bug City Video Series. Wynnewood, PA: Schlessinger Media, 1998.

Benton, Michael. *Dinosaurs.* New York: Kingfisher, 1998.

Belle of Amherst (video). New York: Kino, 1994.

Berenstain, Stan. *The Big Honey Hunt.* New York: Random House, 1962.

Berenstain, Stan, and Jan Berenstain. *The Berenstain Bears' Trouble with Money.* New York: Random House, 1983.

Berg, Julie. *The Berenstains.* Young at Heart. Edina, MN: Abdo, 1993.

Berger, Melvin. *Germs Make Me Sick.* New York: Harper & Row, 1995.

———. *Germs Make Me Sick* (sound recording). New York: HarperCollins, 1987.

Berger, Melvin, and Gilda Berger. *Can You Hear a Shout in Space?* New York: Scholastic Reference, 2000.

———. *Do Tornadoes Really Twist? Questions and Answers About Tornadoes and Hurricanes.* New York: Scholastic, 2000.

Berry, Joy. *What to Do When Mom or Dad Says . . . "Don't Slurp Your Food."* Danbury, CT: Grolier, 1984.

Big Cats of Kalahari: Animals of Africa (video). Woodland Hills, CA: Celebrity Home Entertainment, 1991.

Biography for Beginners. Detroit: Omnigraphics, 1995– .

Biography Today: Profiles of Interest to Young People. Detroit: Omnigraphics, 1992– .

Biography Today Author Series. Detroit: Omnigraphics, 1996–.

Blue, Rose. *History of Gospel Music.* Broomall, PA: Chelsea House, 2001.

Boekhoff, P. M. *Benjamin Franklin.* San Diego: KidHaven, 2002.

Boekhoff, P. M., and Stuart A. Kallen. *Benjamin Franklin.* Inventors and Creators Series. Farmington Hills, MI: KidHaven, 2002.

Bohannon, Lisa Frederkisen. *Failure Is Impossible: The Story of Susan B. Anthony.* Greensboro, NC: Morgan Reynolds, 2001.

Bolton, Linda. *Surrealists.* Crystal Lake, IL: Heinemann, 2002.

Bowers, Vivien. *Crime Science: How Investigators Use Science to Track Down the Bad Guys.* Buffalo, NY: Firefly, 2001.

Bowler, Sarah. *Abraham Lincoln: Our Sixteenth President.* Chanhassen, MN: Child's World, 2001.

Boys Who Rocked the World: From King Tut to Tiger Woods. Hillsboro, OR.: Beyond Words, 2001

Brady, Maxine. *The Monopoly Book: Strategy and Tactics of the World's Most Popular Game.* New York: D. McKay, 1976.

Braun, Lilian Jackson. *The Cat Who* . . . . Various publishers and titles, 1966– .

Bredeson, Carmen. *Presidential Medal of Freedom Winners.* Springfield, NJ: Enslow, 1996.

———. *Ten Great American Composers.* Berkeley Heights, NJ: Enslow, 2002.

Bridges (video). David Macaulay. South Burlington, VT: WGBS Boston Video, 2000.

Bridges, Jeff. *Cooking Up an End to Childhood Hunger in America.* New York: Time, 2001.

Brimner, Larry Dane. *E-Mail.* New York: Children's Press, 1997.

Brittain, Liana. *Genealogy for Children: A Resource for Teachers, Parents and Grandparents.* Almonte, ONT: Educational Support Personnel, 1997.

Brody, Seymour. *Jewish Heroes & Heroines of America: 150 True Stories of American Jewish Heroism.* Hollywood, FL: Lifetime Books, c1996.

Bug's Life (video). Burbank, CA: Walt Disney Home Video, 1998.

Bunch, Bryan, ed. *Diseases.* Danbury, CT: Grolier, 1997.

Bunting, Eve. *Fly Away Home.* New York: Clarion Books, 1991.

———. *Nasty, Stinky Sneakers.* New York: HarperCollins, 1994.

Burkholder, Kelly. *Poetry.* Vero Beach, FL: Rourke Press, 2001.

Butterflies and Moths. Bug City video series. Wynnewood, PA: Schlessinger Media, 1998.

Buy Me That 3! A Kid's Guide to Food Advertising (video). Chicago: Films Incorporated Video, 1992.

Caffey, Donna. *Yikes, Lice.* Morton Grove, IL: Albert Whitman, 1998.

Cannon, Janell. *Stellaluna.* San Diego: Harcourt Brace Jovanovich, 1993.

Cart, Michael. *In the Stacks: Short Stories about Libraries and Librarians.* Woodstock, NY: Overlook Press, 2002

Carwardine, Mark, ed. *Whales, Dolphins and Porpoises.* Alexandria, VA: Time-Life Books, 1998.

Cerullo, Mary. *The Octopus: Phantom of the Sea.* New York: Cobblehill, 1997.

Challoner, Jack. *Hurricane and Tornado.* London: Dorling Kindersley, 2000.

Chandler, Gary, and Kevin Graham. *Alternative Energy Sources.* New York: Twenty-First Century Books, 1996.

Chemerka, William R. *Davy Crockett Almanac and Book of Lists.* Austin, TX: Eakin, 2000.

Chicken Fat: Youth Fitness Video (video). Long Branch, NJ: Kimbo Educational, 1996.

Classic Disney: 60 Years of Musical Magic (sound recording). Burbank, CA: Walt Disney Records, 1997.

Claybourne, Anna. *Tornadoes.* Reading About series. Brookfield, CT: Copper Beech, 2000.

Cleary, Beverly. *Dear Mr. Henshaw.* New York: Morrow, 1983.

Cleave, Andrew. *Big Cats: A Portrait of the Animal World.* Portraits of the Animal World. New York: Todtri Productions, 1998.

Coerr, Eleanor. *Sadako and the Thousand Paper Cranes.* New York: Putnam, 1977.

Cohen, Daniel. *Tyrannosaurus Rex.* Mankato, MN: Capstone, 2001.

Cole, Joanna. *Magic School Bus and the Electric Field Trip.* New York: Scholastic, 1997.

———. *Magic School Bus inside a Beehive.* New York: Scholastic. 1996

Cole, Joanna, and Bruce Degen. *Magic School Bus: Gets Eaten* (video). New York: KidVision, 1995.

Collier, Bryan. *Uptown.* New York: Henry Holt, 2000.

Collins, Paul. *Judo.* Philadelphia: Chelsea House, 2001.

Colombo, Luann. *Gross but True Germs.* New York: Little Simon, 1997.

Coming to America (video). Hollywood, CA: Paramount, 1990.

Communities Across America Today. Washington, DC: National Geographic Society, 2001.

Contemporary Black Biography. Detroit: Gale, 1992– .

Contemporary Musicians. Detroit: Gale, 1989– .

Cooper, Kay. *Where Did You Get Those Eyes? A Guide to Discovering Your Family History.* New York: Walker, 1988.

Copeland, Lennie. *The Lice-Buster Book: What to Do When Your Child Comes Home with Head Lice!* Boston: Warner Home Video, 1996.

Corcoran, John, and Emil Farkas. *Original Martial Arts Encyclopedia.* Los Angeles: Pro-action, 1993.

Costain, Meredith. *Welcome to Japan.* Broomall, PA: Chelsea House, 2001.

———. *Welcome to Mexico.* Broomall, PA: Chelsea House, 2001.

Cott, Nancy F. *Young Oxford History of Women in the United States.* New York: Oxford, 1994.

Creepy, Crawly Creatures in Your Back Yard (video). Washington, DC: National Geographic Society, 2001.

Crichton, Michael, and David Koepp. *Jurassic Park* (video). Universal City, CA: MCA Home Video, 1994.

Criswell, Sarah Dixon. *Homelessness.* San Diego: Lucent, 1998.

Croswell, Ken. *See the Stars: Your First Guide to the Night Sky.* Honesdale, PA.: Boyds Mill Press, 2000.

Cummings, Pat, ed. *Talking with Artists: Volume I.* New York: Macmillan, 1992.

D'Aulaire, Ingri, and Edgar Parin D'Aulaire. *Abraham Lincoln.* Garden City, NY: Doubleday, 1957.

Davy Crockett: King of the Wild Frontier (video). (Starring Fess Parker). Burbank, CA: Walt Disney Home Video, 1955.

Deane, Peter M. G. *Coping with Allergies.* New York: Rose, 1999.

DePaola, Tomie. *Strega Nona*. East Rutherford, NJ: Putnam, 1975.

———. *Strega Nona and Other Stories* (video). Weston, CT: Children's Circle, 1989.

Diagram Group. *Junior Science on File*. New York: Facts on File, 2002.

Dickinson, Emily. *Emily Dickinson: Poetry for Young People,* Poetry for Young People, New York: Sterling, 1994.

———. *I'm Nobody! Who Are You?: Poems of Emily Dickinson for Children*. Owings Mills, MD: Stemmer House, 1978.

———. *Poems for Youth*. Boston: Little, Brown, 1996.

Dickinson, Terence. *Exploring the Night Sky: The Equinox Astronomy Guide for Beginners*. Willowdale, ONT: Firefly Books, 2001.

Discovery Channel. *Ultimate Guide: Big Cats* (video). London: BMG Video, 1998.

———. *Ultimate Guide: Octopus* (video). Santa Monica, CA: Discovery Channel Video, 2001.

Disney's The Little Mermaid: Stormy the Wild Seahorse (video). Ariel's Undersea Adventures. Burbank, CA: Walt Disney Home Video, 1993.

Dixon, Franklin W. *The Hardy Boys Detective Handbook*. New York: Grossett & Dunlap, 1972.

DK Science Encyclopedia. New York: Dorling Kindersley, 1998.

Dommemuth-Costa, Carol. *Emily Dickinson: Singular Poet*. Minneapolis, MN: Lerner, 1998.

Donald, Rhonda Lucas. *Recycling*. New York: Children's Press, 2001.

Dora the Explorer: Dora's Backpack Adventure (video). Hollywood, CA: Paramount, 2002.

Dorling Kindersley Science Encyclopedia. New York: Dorling Kindersley, 1993.

Drinkard, G. Lawson. *Fishing in a Brook: Angling Activities for Kids*. Salt Lake City, UT: Gibbs Smith: 2000.

Duden, Jane. *Animal Handlers & Trainers*. New York: Crestwood House, 1989.

DuPrau, Jeanne. *Cloning*. San Diego: Lucent, 2000.

Earle, Anne. *Zipping, Zapping, Zooming Bats*. Let's Read and Find Out Science. New York: HarperCollins, 1995.

Edelson, Edward. *Allergies*. Broomall, PA: Chelsea House, 1999.

Edwards, Judith. *Jamestown, John Smith and Pocahontas in American History*. Berkeley Heights, NJ: Enslow, 2002.

Electricity. The Way Things Work video series. Wynnewood, PA: Schlessinger Media, 2002.

Elleman, Barbara. *Tomie dePaola: His Art and His Stories*. New York: Putnam, 1999.

Emmer, Rae. *Community Service*. New York: PowerKids Press, 2001.

Encyclopedia of Family Health. New York: Marshall Cavendish, 1998.

Encyclopedia of Health. New York: Marshall Cavendish, 2002.

Endangered and Extinct Animals (video). Wynnewood, PA: Schlessinger Media, 1999.

Endangered Animals. Danbury, CT: Grolier Educational, 2002.

Endangered Species. Critical Thinking about Environmental Issues. Farmington Hills, MI: Greenhaven Press, 2002.

Engelbert, Phillis. *Astronomy and Space: From the Big Bang to the Big Crunch*. Detroit: UXL, 1997.

———— *Technology in Action: Science Applied to Everyday Life*. Detroit: UXL, 1999.

Epstein, Dan. *The 70's* Twentieth Century Pop Culture Series. Philadelphia: Chelsea House, 2000.

————. *The 80's.* Twentieth Century Pop Culture Series. Philadelphia: Chelsea House, 2000.

Family Tree (video). Burbank, CA: Warner Home Video, 2000.

Family Trees Quick & Easy 5.0 (CD-ROM). Pleasanton, CA: Individual Software, 2002.

Featherstone, Jane. *Energy*. Austin, TX: Raintree Steck-Vaughn, 1999.

Fletcher, Ralph. *Poetry Matters: Writing a Poem from the Inside Out*. New York: HarperCollins, 2002

Fletcher, William. *Recording Your Family History: A Guide to Preserving Oral History*. New York: Dodd, Mead, 1986

Food for Thought (video). Washington, DC: National Geographic Society, 1998.

Fowler, Allan. *Really Big Cats*. New York: Children's Press, 1998.

Fraser, Lindsey. *Conversations with J. K. Rowling*. New York: Scholastic, 2001.

Freedman, Russell. *Animal Fathers*. New York: Holiday House, 1976.

Freville, Nicholas. *Nigeria*. Broomall, PA: Chelsea House, 2000.

Friends for Life: Living with AIDS (video). Burbank, CA: Walt Disney Home Studio, 2002.

Fritz, Jean. *The Double Life of Pocahontas*. North Bellmore, NY: Marshall Cavendish, 1991.

Frost, Helen. *Birds*. Mankato, MN: Capstone, 2001.

————. *Rabbits*. Mankato, MN: Capstone, 2001.

Fuhr, Ute et al. *Bees*. A First Discovery Book. New York: Scholastic, 1997.

Fuller, Millard. *More Than Houses: How Habitat for Humanity Is Transforming Lives and Neighborhoods*. Nashville, TN: Word Pub, 2000.

Furgang, Kathy. *Let's Take a Field Trip to an Ant Colony*. New York: PowerKids Press, 2000.

Gaines, Richard M. *Tyrannosaurus Rex*. Edina, MN: Abdo, 2001.

Gale Encyclopedia of Childhood and Adolescence. Detroit: Gale, 1998.

Gale Encyclopedia of Medicine. Farmington Hills, MI: Gale, 2001.

Gall, Timothy L., and Susan B. Gall, ed. *Junior Worldmark Encyclopedia of the Nations.*, 3rd ed. Detroit: UXL, 2001.

Ganeri, Anita. *Journey Through India*. Topeka, KS: BT Bound, 1999.

George, Jean Craighead. *How to Talk to your Dog*. New York: HarperCollins, 2000.

George Washington Carver. Inventors of the World video series. Wynnewood, PA: Schlessinger Media, 2002.

Gerholdt, James E. *Bald Eagles*. Edina, MN: Abdo, 1997.

Gibbons, Gail. *Bats*. New York: Holiday House, 2000.

————. *Honey Makers*. Scranton, PA: HarperCollins, 2000.

————. *Monarch Butterfly*. Topeka, KS: BT Bound, 1999.

————. *Soaring with the Wind: The Bald Eagle*. New York: Morrow, 1998.

Giblin, James. *From Hand to Mouth, or How We Invented Knives, Forks, Spoons and Chopsticks*. New York: Crowell, 1987.

Gifford, Clive. *Kingfisher Facts and Records Book of Space.* New York: Larousse Kingfisher Chambers, 2001.

Gilbert, Adrian. *The Eighties.* Look at Life in. Austin, TX: Raintree Steck-Vaughn, 2000.

Gillespie, John T. *The Newbery Companion: Booktalk and Related Materials for Newbery Medal and Honor Books (Newbery Companion).* Englewood, CO: Libraries Unlimited, 2001.

Gish, Melissa. *Snakes.* Mankato, MN: Creative Education, 1998.

Goober Peas. *Civil War Songbook.* Riverside, CA: WEM Records, 1999.

Gordon, Lois G. *American Chronicle.* New York: Columbia University Press, 1995.

Gorman, Ed. *The Fine Art of Murder: The Mystery Readers Indispensable Companion.* New York: Galahad, 1995.

Gourley, Catherine. *Wheels of Time: A Biography of Henry Ford.* Brookfield, CT: Millbrook, 1997.

Grabowski, John F. *Abraham Lincoln: Civil War President.* Broomall, PA: Chelsea House, 2001.

Graff, Stewart, and Polly Anne Graff. *Helen Keller: Crusader for the Blind & Deaf.* New York: Young Yearling, 1991.

Graham, Ian. *Energy Forever: Geothermal and Bioenergy.* Austin, TX: Raintree Steck-Vaughn, 1999.

Grant, Bruce. *A Furious Hunger: America in the 21st Century.* Carlton, VIC: Melbourne University Press, 1999.

Grant, R. G. *The Seventies.* Look at Life in. Austin, TX: Raintree Steck-Vaughn, 2000.

Gray, J. E. B. *Tales From India.* Carey, NC: Oxford University Children's Press, 2001.

Green Card (video). Burbank, CA: Touchstone, 1991.

Gregson, Susan R. *Benjamin Franklin.* Mankato, MN: Bridgestone, 2001.

Gresko, Marcia. *Letters Home from Japan.* Farmington Hills, MI: Blackbirch Marketing, 2000.

Grolier Library of International Biographies. Danbury, CT: Grolier, 2000.

Grolier Library of North American Biographies. Danbury, CT: Grolier Educational Corporation, 1994.

Growing Up (video). Burbank, CA: Walt Disney Home Video, 1995.

Guber, Selina S. *Marketing To and Through Kids.* New York: McGraw-Hill, 1993.

Gutman, Bill. *Becoming Your Bird's Best Friend.* Brookfield, CN: Millbrook Press, 1996.

Gutman, Dan. *The Kid Who Ran for President* (sound recording). Prince Frederick, MD: Recorded Books, 2001.

Hacker, Carlotta. *Great African Americans in History.* New York: Crabtree, 1997.

Haduch, Bill. *Food Rules! The Stuff You Munch, Its Crunch, Its Punch, and Why You Sometimes Lose Your Lunch.* New York: Dutton, 2001.

Halvorsen, Lisa. *Harriet Tubman.* Farmington Hills, MI: Blackbirch Marketing, 2002.

Hansen, Ann Larken. *Cats.* Minneapolis, MN: Abdo & Daughters, 1997.

Harrison, Carol. *Dinosaurs Everywhere!* New York: Scholastic, 1998.

Harrison, Virginia. *The World of Bats.* Milwaukee, WI: G. Stevens, 1989.

Harry Potter and the Sorcerer's Stone (video). Burbank, CA: Warner Home Video, 2002.

Hartley, Karen, and Chris MacRo. *Ant.* Des Plaines, IL: Heinemann, 1998.

———. *Bee.* Des Plaines, IL: Heinemann, 1998.

Hartzog, John. *Everyday Science Experiments in the Backyard.* New York: Rosen, 2000.

Hausman, Herald. *How Chipmunk Got Tiny Feet.* New York: HarperCollins, 1995.

Haycroft, Howard. *The Art of the Mystery Story.* Cheshire, CT: Biblo-Moser, 1975.

Hayes, Cheri. *There's a Louse in My House: A Kid's Story About Head Lice.* New York: Jayjo, 2001.

Head, Honor. *Guinea Pig.* Austin, TX: Raintree/Steck, 2001.

———. *Hamsters and Gerbils.* Austin, TX: Raintree/Steck, 2000.

———. *Rats and Mice.* Austin, TX: Steck-Vaughn, 2000.

Head Lice to Dead Lice: Safe Solutions for Frantic Families (video). Weston, MA: Sawyer Mac Productions, 1997.

Heelan, Jamee Riggio. *Rolling Along: The Story of Taylor and His Wheelchair.* Atlanta, GA: Peachtree, 2000.

Hegel, Claudette. *Newbery and Caldecott Trivia and More for Every Day of the Year.* Englewood, CO: Libraries Unlimited, 2000.

Henry Ford. Inventors of the World video series. Wynnewood, PA: Schlessinger Media, 2001.

Herbert, Rosemary. *The Oxford Companion to Crime and Mystery Writing.* New York: Oxford University Press, 1999.

Hermes, Jules. *The Children of India.* Minneapolis, MN: Carolrhoda, 1993.

Hettinga, Donald R. *The Brothers Grimm: Two Lives, One Legacy.* New York: Clarion Books, c2001.

Hill, Lee Sullivan. *Bridges Connect.* Minneapolis, MN: Carolrhoda, 1997.

———. *Libraries Take Us Far.* Minneapolis, MN: Carolrhoda, 1998.

Hip Hop Animal Rock (video). Wilmington, NC: Educational Records Center, 2000.

Hirschi, Ron. *Octopuses.* Minneapolis, MN: Carolrhoda, 2000.

Holler, Anne. *Pocahontas: Powhatan Peacemaker.* Broomall, PA: Chelsea House, 1992.

Holmes, Kevin J. *Bees.* Mankato, MN: Bridgestone, 1998.

———. *Whales.* Mankato, MN: Capstone, 1998.

Hoose, Phillip. *It's Our World, Too!: Stories of Young People Who Are Making a Difference* Gordonsville, VA: Farrar, Straus & Giroux, 2002.

Hopkins, Lee Bennett. *Pass the Poetry, Please!* New York: HarperCollins, 1998.

Hoving, Walter. *Tiffany's Table Manners for Teenagers.* New York: Random House, 1989

Hurricanes and Tornadoes. Weather Fundamentals video series. Wynnewood, PA: Schlessinger Media, 1998.

Hurwitz, Jane. *Coping in a Blended Family.* New York: Rosen, 1997.

Hurwitz, Joanna. *Helen Keller: Courage in the Dark.* New York: Random House, 1997.

I Was Dreaming of To Come to America: Memories of Ellis Island Oral History Project. Glenview Lake, IL: Scott Foresman, 1997.

Immigration. American History for Children Video Series. Wynnewood, PA: Schlessinger Media, 1996.

Immune System. Human Body in Action video series. Wynnewood, PA: Schlessinger Media, 2001.

India. Children of the World. Milwaukee, WI: G. Stevens, 1988.

It's Just Good Manners (video). Atlanta, GA: Mind Your Manners Pub, 1995.

Izenberg, Neil. *Human Diseases and Conditions.* New York: C. Scribner's Sons, 2000.

Jackie Chan Adventures; The Power Within (video). Culver City, CA: Columbia Tristar, 2001.

Jaffe, Elizabeth Dana. *Sojourner Truth.* Minneapolis, MN: Compass Point Books. 2000.

James, Jasper. *Walking with Dinosaurs* (video). Beverly Hills, CA: CBS Fox Video, 2000.

Janeczko, Paul B. *How to Write Poetry.* New York: Scholastic Reference, 1999.

————. *The Place My Words Are Looking For: What Poets Say About and Through Their Work.* New York: Bradbury Press, 1990.

Japanese-American Heritage. American Cultures for Children video series. Wynnewood, PA: Schlessinger Media, 1997.

Jefferis, David. *Cyberspace, Virtual Reality and the World Wide Web.* New York: Crabtree, 1999.

Jeffries, Michael and Gary A. Lewis. *Inventors and Inventions.* Facts America Series. New York: Smithmark, 1992.

Jeunesse, Gallimard, and James Prunier. *Monkeys and Apes.* New York: Scholastic, 1999

Johmann, Carol. *Bridges: Amazing Structures to Design, Build & Test.* Charlotte. VT: Williamson Publishing, 1999.

Johnson, Julie. *Bullies and Gangs.* Brookfield, CT: Copper Beech Books 1998.

Johnston, Marianne. *Let's Visit the Library.* New York: Rosen, 2000.

Joseph, Paul. *Wright Brothers.* Minneapolis, MN: Abdo & Daughters, 1997.

Jumanji (video). Burbank, CA: Columbia TriStar, 1996.

Junior Science on File (looseleaf). New York: Facts on File, 1991– .

Jurassic Park (video). Universal City, CA: MCA Universal. 1994.

Kallen, Stuart A. *Benjamin Franklin.* Adina, MN: Abdo & Daughters, 1996.

————. *Life in Tokyo.* Farmington Hills, MI: Lucent, 2000.

Kalman, Bobbie. *India: The Culture.* The Lands, Peoples, and Cultures. New York: Crabtree, 2001.

Kane, Joseph. *Famous First Facts: A Record of First Happenings, Discoveries, and Inventions in American History.* New York: H. W. Wilson, 1997.

Keller, Helen. *The Story of My Life.* Garden City, NY: Doubleday, 1905.

Kellogg, Steven. *Sally Ann Thunder Ann Whirlwind Crockett: A Tall Tale.* New York: Morrow, 1995.

Kent, Zachary. *Andrew Carnegie: Steel King and Friend to Libraries.* Springfield, NJ: Enslow, 1999.

Kids Are Consumers. Kids Make a Difference. Washington, DC: National Geographic Society, 2001.

Kingdom of the Seahorse (video). South Burlington, VT: WGBH Boston, 1997.

Kingman, Lee. *Newbery and Caldecott Medal Books, 1966–1975.* Boston: Horn Book, 1977.

————. *Newbery and Caldecott Medal Books, 1976–1985.* Boston: Horn Book, 1986.

Kite, Patricia. *Down in the Sea: The Octopus.* Morton Grove, IL: Albert Whitman, 1993.

Kittredge, Mary. *Common Cold.* Broomall, PA: Chelsea House, 2000.

Knight, Judson. *African American Biography*. Farmington Hills, MI: UXL, 1999.

Knotts, Bob. *Martial Arts*. New York, Children's Press, 2000.

Kovaks, Deborah. *Meet the Authors and Illustrators*. Topeka, KS: BT Bound, 2001.

Kowal, L.A. *The Proper Pig's Guide to Mealtime Manners*. Chandler, AZ: Five Star, 1996.

Kramer, Barbara. *George Washington Carver: Scientist and Inventor*. Berkeley Heights, NJ: Enslow, 2002.

Krull, Kathleen. *Lives of the Artists: Masterpieces, Messes (and What the Neighbors Thought)*. San Diego: Harcourt Brace, 1995.

Kunitz, Stanley J. *The Junior Book of Authors*. New York: H. W. Wilson, 1951– .

Laderer, Mandy. *Fit-Kids: Getting Kids "Hooked" on Fitness Fun!* Hicksville, NY: Allure, 1994.

Lambert, Kathy Kristensen. *Martin Luther King, Jr.: Civil Rights Leader*. Broomall, PA: Chelsea House, 1993.

Landau, Elaine. *India*. True Books. Danbury, CT: Children's Press, 2000.

Lands and Peoples. Danbury, CT: Grolier, 2001.

Lauber, Patricia. *The Octopus Is Amazing*. New York: Crowell, 1990.

———. *Who Eats What?: Food Chains and Food Webs*. New York: HarperCollins, 2001.

Lauw, Darlene. *Electricity*. New York: Crabtree, 2002.

Lawlor, Veronica. *I Was Dreaming to Come to America: Memories from the Ellis Island Oral History Project*. New York: Viking, 1995.

Lawson, Robert. *Ben and Me* (video). Burbank, CA: Disney Home Video, 1991.

Leebrick, Kristal. *Sojourner Truth*. Mankato, MN: Bridgestone Books, 2002.

Leedy, Loreen. *The Edible Pyramid: Good Eating Every Day*. New York: Holiday House, 1994.

Leeson, Tom. *Giant Panda*. Woodbridge, CT: Blackbirch, 2000.

Legg, Gerald. *From Caterpillar to Butterfly*. Lifecycles. Danbury, CT: Franklin Watts, 1998.

Lemke, Bob, ed. *Standard Catalog of Baseball Cards*. Iola, WI: Krause, 1988 -.

LeShan, Eda. *What's Going to Happen to Me?: When Parents Separate or Divorce*. New York: Four Winds, 1978.

Lessem, Don. *Dinosaurs to Dodos: An Encyclopedia of Extinct Animals*. New York: Scholastic, 1999.

Lewis, Barbara. *Kids Guide to Service Projects: Over Service 500 Ideas for Young People Who Want to Make a Difference*. Minneapolis, MN: Free Spirit, 1995.

Lewis & Clark: The Journey of the Corps of Discovery (video). Alexandria, VA: PBS Home Video, 1997.

Licemeister: An instructional video. Available at www.headlice.org/catalog/index.htm#lmkit.

Littlefield, Holly. *Colors of India*. Colors of the World. Minneapolis, MN: Lerner, 2000.

Llewellyn, Claire. *Chimps Use Tools*. Brookfield, ON: Copper Beech Books, 1999.

Lommel, Cookie. *History of Rap Music*. Broomall, PA: Chelsea House, 2001.

Louis, Nancy. *Heroes of the Day: The War on Terrorism*. Edina, MN: Abdo, 2002.

Love, Ann, and Jane Drake. *Fishing*. Illustrated by Pat Cupples. Toronto: Kids Can Press, 1999.

Loves, June. *Airplanes*. Broomall, PA: Chelsea House, 2001.

———. *Cars*. Broomall, PA: Chelsea House, 2002.

———. *Spacecraft*. Broomall, PA: Chelsea House, 2001.

Lowery, Linda. *Pablo Picasso*. Minneapolis, MN: Carolrhoda, 1999.

Lumpkin, Susan. *Big Cats*. New York: Facts on File, 1993.

Lutz, Norma Jean. *Harriet Tubman: Leader of the Underground Railroad*. Broomall, PA: Chelsea House, 2001.

———. *Sojourner Truth: Abolitionist, Suffragist, and Preacher*. Broomall, PA: Chelsea House, 2001.

Lynn, Sara, and Diane James. *What We Eat: A First Look at Food*. Chicago: World Book/Two-Can, 2000.

Lyons, Mary E. *Feed the Children First: Irish Memories of the Great Hunger*. New York: Atheneum Books for Young Readers, 2002.

Ma, Marina. *My Son Yo Yo*. Ann Arbor: University of Michigan Press, 1995.

Ma, Yo Yo. *Along the Silk Road*. Seattle: University of Washington Press, 2002.

Macaulay, David. *The Way Things Work*. London: Dorling Kindersley, 1988.

MacDonald, Patricia A. *Pablo Picasso: Greatest Artist of the 20th Century*. Woodbridge, CT: Blackbirch Marketing, 2001.

Macmillan Encyclopedia of Science. New York: Macmillan Reference, 1997.

Magic School Bus: Butterfly and the Bog Beast (video). New York: KidVision, 1999.

Major Authors and Illustrators for Children and Young Adults. Detroit: Gale, 1993– .

Malam, John. *Henry Ford: An Unauthorized Biography*. Crystal Lake, IL: Heinemann, 2001.

Managing Childhood Asthma (video). Garden Grove, CA: Medcom, 1994.

Marcovitz, Hal. *Sacagawea: Guide for the Lewis and Clark Expedition*. Philadelphia: Chelsea House, 2001.

Markle, Sandra. *Outside and Inside Snakes*. New York: Atheneum, 1995.

Marshall, Chris, ed. *Dinosaurs of the World*. Tarrytown, NY: Marshall Cavendish, 1998.

Marshall, Elizabeth L. *A Student's Guide to the Internet*. Brookfield, CT: Twenty-First Century Books, 2001.

Martin Luther King, Jr.: The Man and the Dream (video). New York: A & E Home Video, 1999.

Marzollo, Jean. *My First Book of Biographies: Great Men and Women Every Child Should Know*. New York: Scholastic, 1994.

Mason, Paul. *Pop Artists*. Crystal Lake, IL: Heinemann, 2002.

Maynard, Thane. *Primates: Apes, Monkeys and Prosimians*. New York: Franklin Watts, 1994.

McCarthy, Pat. *Henry Ford: Building Cars for Everyone*. Berkeley Heights, NH: Enslow, 2002.

McGinty, Alice B. *Staying Healthy: Let's Exercise*. New York: PowerKids Press, 1998.

McLeish, Ewan. *Energy Resources: Our Impact on the Planet*. Austin, TX: Raintree Steck-Vaughn, 2002.

McNeal, James U. *Kids As Customers: A Handbook of Marketing to Children*. New York: Lexington, 1992.

Meet the Authors and Illustrators. Scranton, PA: Scholastic Paperbacks, 1993.

Meltzer, Milton. *Poverty in America*. New York: Morrow, 1987.

Merrick, Patrick. *Lice*. Naturebooks Creepy Crawlers Series. New York: Child's World, 2000.

Metil, Luana, and Jace Townsend. *The Story of Karate from Buddhism to Bruce Lee*. Minneapolis, MN: Lerner, 1995.

Mexican-American Heritage (video). American Cultures for Children Video Series. Wynnewood, PA: Schlessinger Video Productions, 1997.

Micucci, Charles. *Life and Times of the Peanut*. Boston: Houghton Mifflin, 1997.

Miracle Worker (video). Santa Monica, CA: MGM Home Entertainment, 2001.

Mitchell, Mary. *Dear Ms. Demeanor: The Young Person's Etiquette Guide to Handling Any Social Situation with Confidence and Grace*. Chicago: Contemporary, 1994.

Mitton, Jacqueline. *The Scholastic Encyclopedia of Space*. New York: Scholastic Reference, 1999.

Mongillo, John, and Linda Zuirdt-Warshaw. *Encyclopedia of Environmental Science*. Phoenix, AZ: Oryx Press, 2000.

Monkey Business and Other Family Fun (video). Washington, DC: National Geographic Kids, 1996.

Monopoly (computer file). Beverly, MA: Hasbro Interactive, 1999.

Monroe, Judy. *Susan B. Anthony Women's Voting Rights Trial: A Headline Court Case*. Berkeley Heights, NH: Enslow, 2002.

Moran, George. *Imagine Me on a Sit-Ski!* Morton Grove, IL: A. Whitman, 1995.

Morgan, Sally. *Hurricanes*. Read About series. Brookfield, CT. Copper Beech, 2000.

Morris, Neil. *Karate*. Chicago: Heinemann, 2001.

———. *Tae Kwon Do*. Chicago: Heinemann, 2001.

Morris, Robert Ada. Seahorse. Science I Can Read Book. New York: Harper & Row, 1972.

Morris the Moose. (video). Racine, WI: Golden Book Video, 1993.

Moss, Joyce, and George Wilson. Profiles in American History: Significant Events and the People Who Shaped Them. Farmington Hills, MI: Gale, 1994– .

Moupin, Melissa. *The Story of Coca Cola*. Mankato, MN: Smart Apple Media, 2003.

Murphy, Jane. *Stay Tuned: Raising Savvy Kids in the Age of the Couch Potato*. New York: Doubleday, 1996.

Musical Instruments. The Way Things Work video series. Wynnewood, PA: Schlessinger Media, 2002.

Nadeau, Isaac. *Food Chains in a Backyard Habitat*. New York: Rosen, 2002.

Nardo, Don. *Cloning*. San Diego: Lucent, 2001.

———. *Germs*. San Diego: Kidhaven, 2002.

National Pediculosis Association. *All Out Comb Out* (video). Needham, MA: National Pediculosis Association. [n.d.]

New Book of Popular Science. Danbury, CT: Grolier, 2000– (annual).

Newbery and Caldecott Medal Books, 1976–2000: A Comprehensive Guide to the Winners. Chicago: American Library Association, 2001.

Newbery Medal Books, 1922–1955. Boston: Horn Book, 1957.

Newton, David E., Rob Nagel, and Bridget Travers, eds. *UXL Encyclopedia of Science*. Detroit: UXL, 1998.

Nicholson, Lois P. *George Washington Carver*. New York: Chelsea House, 1994.

Nicolson, Cynthia Pratt. *Baa! The Most Interesting Book You'll Ever Read about Genes and Cloning*. Tonawanda, NY: Kids Can Press, 2001.

Nielsen, Nancy J. *Harriet Tubman*. Mankato, MN: Bridgestone, 2002.

Nnoromele, Salome. *Nigeria,* Modern Nations of the World. Farmington Hills, MI: Lucent, 2001.

Nobisso, Josephine. *In English, of Course*. Westhampton Beach, NY: Gingerbread House, 2002.

Oakley, Ruth. *Board and Card Games*. New York: Marshall Cavendish, 1989

Oberle, Lora Polack. *Abraham Lincoln*. Mankato, MN: Bridgestone Books, 2002.

Octopus-octopus (video). Undersea World of Jacques Cousteau. Beverly Hills, CA: Pacific Arts, 1989.

Old, Wendie C. *The Wright Brothers: Inventors of the Airplane*. Berkeley Heights, NJ: Enslow, 2000.

Orbanes, Philip. *The Monopoly Companion: The Player's Guide: The Game from A to Z, Winning Tips, Trivia*. Avon, MA: Adams Media, 1999.

Osborne, Will. *Dinosaurs*. Magic Tree House Research Guide. New York: Random House, 2000.

Otfinoski, Steven. *Speaking Up, Speaking Out: A Kid's Guide to Making Speeches, Oral Reports, and Conversation*. Brookfield, CT: Millbrook Press, 1996.

Our Friend, Martin (video). Los Angeles: 20th Century Fox, 2000.

Oxlade, Chris. *Bridges*. Building Amazing Structures. Crystal Lake, IL: Heinemann Library, 2000.

Packer, Alex J. *How Rude! The Teenagers Guide to Good Manners, Proper Behavior and Not Grossing People Out*. Minneapolis, MN: Free Spirit, 1997.

Parker, David. *Stolen Dreams: Portraits of Working Children*. Minneapolis, MN: Lerner, 1998.

Parker, Janice. *The Science of Structures*. Milwaukee, WI: Gareth Stevens, 2001.

Parker, Steve. *Benjamin Franklin and Electricity*. Broomall, PA: Chelsea House, 1995.

Parks, Aileen Wells. *Davy Crockett: Young Rifleman*. Childhood of Famous Americans Series. New York: Aladdin, 1986.

Parlett, David Sidney. *The Oxford History of Board Games*. New York: Oxford University Press, 1999.

Parris, Ronald G. *Hausa*. New York: Rosen, 1996.

Pascoe, Elaine. *Butterflies and moths*. Woodbridge, CT: Blackbirch Press, 1997.

Patent, Dorothy H. *Eagles of America*. New York: Holiday House. 1995.

Paull, Frankie, and Bob Cary. *Cool Fishin' for Kids Age 5 to 85*. Superior, WI: Savage, 1997.

Penzler, Otto. *The Crown Crime Companion: The Top 100 Mystery Novels of All Time*. New York: Crown, 1995.

Perl, Lila. *The Great Ancestor Hunt: The Fun of Finding Out Who You Are*. New York: Clarion, 1989.

Perrault, Charles. *Perrault's Fairy Tales*. Translated by A. E. Johnson. New York: Dover, 1969.

Peters, Julie Anne. *The Stinky Sneakers Contest*. Boston: Little, Brown, 1992

Petty, Kate. *Whales Can Sing*. Brookfield, CT: Copper Beech Books, 1998.

Pocahontas (video). Burbank, CA: Walt Disney Home Video, 1995.

Polisar, Barry. *Don't Do That! A Child's Guide to Bad Manners, Ridiculous Rules, and Inadequate Etiquette*. Silver Spring, MD: Rainbow Morning, 1994.

Polland, Barbara K. *We Can Work it Out: Conflict Resolution for Children*. Berkeley, CA: Tricycle Press, 2000.

Pollard, Jeanne. *Building Toothpick Bridges*. Math Project Series. Parsippany, NJ: Dale Seymour, 1985.

Post, Elizabeth L. *Emily Post's Teen Etiquette*. New York: HarperPerennial, 1995.

Powell, Jillian. *Animal Rights*. Talking About series. Austin, TX: Raintree Steck-Vaughn, 2000

———. *Talking About Adoption*. Austin, TX: Raintree Steck-Vaughn, 1999.

Power of Speech (video). Princeton, NJ: Films for the Humanities and Sciences, 1994.

Preiss, Byron. *The Art of Leo & Diane Dillon*. New York: Ballantine, 1981.

Prelutsky, Jack. *Pizza the Size of the Sun* (sound recording). Old Greenwich, CT: Listening Library, 1999.

President Abraham Lincoln (video). Irving, TX: Nest Entertainment, 1993.

Presnall, Judith Janda. *The Giant Panda*. Farmington Hills, MI: Lucent, 1998.

Profiles of the Presidents. Minneapolis, MN: Compass Point Books, 2002.

Quip with Yip and Friends (video). Hollywood, CA: Fries Home Video, 1990.

Raatma, Lucia. *Abraham Lincoln*. Minneapolis, MN: Compass Point Books, 2000.

———. *Benjamin Franklin*. Minneapolis, MN: Compass Point Books, 2001.

Raintree Steck-Vaughn Illustrated Science Encyclopedia. Austin, TX: Raintree Steck-Vaughn, 1997– .

Rau, Dana Meachen. *Harriet Tubman*. Minneapolis, MN: Compass Point Books, 2000.

Reilly, Mary Jo, and Leslie Jermyn. *Mexico*. Cultures of the World. New York: Benchmark, 2002.

Relf, Patricia. *A Dinosaur Named Sue: The Story of the Colossal Fossil*. New York: Scholastic, 2000.

Retan, Walter. *The Story of Davy Crockett Frontier Hero*. Famous Lives. Milwaukee, WI: Gareth Stevens, 1997.

Ricciuti, Edward R. *America's Top 10 Bridges*. Woodbridge, CT: Blackbirch, 1998.

Richards, Jon. *Fantastic Cutaway Book of Flight*. Brookfield, CN: Cooper Beech, 1998.

———. *Racing Cars*. Cutaway Series. Brookfield, CT: Copper Beech, 1998.

Richardson, Adele. *Eagle: Birds of Prey*. Mankato, MN.: Capstone, 2002.

Richardson, Hazel. *How to Clone a Sheep*. New York: Franklin Watts, 2001.

Rinard, Judith E. *The Book of Flight: The Smithsonian Institution's National Air and Space Museum*. Toronto: Firefly Books, 2001.

———. *What Happens at the Zoo*. Washington, DC: National Geographic Society, 1984.

Rizzatti, Lorella. *Seahorse*: Portable Pets. New York: Harry N. Abrams, 2000.

Rodriguez, K. S. *Tyrannosaurus Rex*. Austin, TX: Raintree Steck-Vaughn, 2000.

Roehm, Michelle. *Girls Who Rocked the World 2: Heroines from Harriet Tubman to Mia Hamm*. Hillsboro, OR: Beyond Words Publishing, c2000.

Rogers, Fred. *Divorce*. New York: G. P. Putnam, 1996.

Ronney, Anne. *Chilling Out: How to Use the Internet to Make the Most of Your Free Time*. London: Big Fish, 2000.

Rowland, Della. *Story of Sacajawea, Guide to Lewis and Clark*. New York: Yearling, 1996.

Rowling, J. K. *Harry Potter and the Chamber of Secrets*. Farmington Hills, MI: Thorndike, 2000.

————. *Harry Potter and the Goblet of Fire.* Farmington Hills, MI: Thorndike, 2000.

————. *Harry Potter and the Prisoner of Azkaban* Farmington Hills, MI: Thorndike, 2000.

————. *Harry Potter and the Sorcerer's Stone.* Farmington Hills, MI: Thorndike, 1999.

Royston, Angela. *Life Cycle of a Butterfly.* Des Plaines, IL: Heinemann First Library, 2002.

————. *Recycling.* Austin, TX: Raintree Steck-Vaughn, 1998

Rozakis, Laurie. *Homelessnes: Can We Solve the Problem?* Issues of Our Times. New York: Twenty-First Century Books, 1995.

Ruff, Sue, and Don Wilson. *Bats.* New York: Benchmark Books, 2001.

Rustad, Martha E. H. *George Washington Carver.* Mankato, MN: Capstone Press, 2001.

————. *Harriet Tubman.* Mankato, MN: Capstone Press, 2002.

————. *Susan B. Anthony.* Mankato, MN: Capstone Press, 2001.

Rutten, Joshua. *Red Pandas.* Mankato, MN: Child's World, 1998.

Ryan, Margaret. *How To Read and Write Poems.* New York: Franklin Watts, 1991.

Sabin, Louis. *Wilbur and Orville Wright: the Flight to Adventure* (sound recording). Mahwah, NJ: Troll, 1983.

Sacagawea. Great Americans for Children video series. Wynnewood, PA: Schlessinger Media, 2003.

Sanders, Pete. *Bullying.* What Do You Know About Series. Brookfield, CT: Copper Beech Books, 1996.

Sanford, William R. *Sacagawea: Native American Hero.* Berkeley Heights, NJ: Enslow, 1997.

Santrey, Laurence. *Davy Crockett: Young Pioneer.* Mahwah, NJ: Troll, 1983.

Sattler, Helen R. *The New Illustrated Dinosaur Dictionary.* New York: Lothrop, Lee & Shepard, 1990.

Schaaf, Fred. *40 Nights to Knowing the Sky: A Night-by-Night Skywatching Primer.* New York: Henry Holt, 1998.

Schaefer, Lola M. *Butterflies: Pollinators and Nectar Sippers.* Mankato, MN: Bridgestone Books, 2000.

————. *Martin Luther King, Jr.* Mankato, MN: Capstone Press, 1999.

Schlessinger, Yaffa A. *An Interview with My Grandparent.* New York: McGraw-Hill, 1998.

Schmittroth, Linda, Mary R. McCall, and Bridget Travers. *Eureka.* Detroit: UXL, 1995– .

Schwarzenegger, Arnold. *Arnold's Fitness for Kids Ages 11–14: A Guide to Health, Exercise, and Nutrition.* New York: Doubleday, 1993.

————. *Arnold's Fitness for Kids Ages 6–10: A Guide to Health, Exercise, and Nutrition.* New York: Doubleday, 1993.

Scott Standard Postage Stamp Catalog. Sidney, OH: Scott, 1973– .

See How They Grow: Pets (video). New York: Sony, 1995.

Sharmat, Mitchell. *Gregory, the Terrible Eater.* New York: Simon & Schuster, 1980.

Shea, George. *First Flight: The Story of Tom Tate and the Wright Brothers.* New York: HarperCollins, 1997.

Shields, Charles J. *Mythmaker; The Story of J. K. Rowling.* Who Wrote That? Series. Broomall, PA: Chelsea House, 2002.

Sifakis, Carl. *Encyclopedia of American Crime.* 2nd ed. New York: Facts on File, 2001.

Silverstein, Alvin, Virginia Silverstein, and Laura Silverstein Nunn. *Allergies.* New York: Franklin Watts, 1999.

Simon, Seymour. *Big Cats.* Topeka, KS: BT Bound, 1999.

Smith, Charles R. *Perfect Harmony: A Musical Journey with the Boys Choir of Harlem.* Boston: Hyperion, 2002

Smook, Rachel Gaillard. *Stepfamilies: How a New Family Works.* Berkeley Heights, NH: Enslow, 2001.

Sobol, Donald J. *Encyclopedia Brown and the Case of the Disgusting Sneakers.* New York: Morrow, 1990.

Sojourner Truth. The Black Americans of Achievement Video Collection. Wynnewood, PA: Schlessinger Media, 1992.

Something About the Author. Detroit: Gale, 1971– .

Something About The Author: Autobiography Series. Detroit: Gale Research, 1986– .

Sound of Hope (sound recording). New York: Eastwest Records, 1994.

Spangler, Lynn C. *Life and Legend of Sojourner Truth.* Princeton, NJ: Films for the Humanities and Sciences, 2001.

Spinelli, Jerry. *The Library Card.* Scranton, PA: Scholastic, 1998.

Sproule, Anna. *The Wright Brothers: The Birth of Modern Aviation.* Woodbridge, CN: Blackbirch Press, 1999.

St. George, Judith. *The Brooklyn Bridge: They Said It Couldn't Be Built.* New York: Putnam, 1982.

Stearman, Kaye. *Why Do People Live on the Streets.* Exploring Tough Issues. Austin, TX: Raintree Steck-Vaughn, 2001.

Steffens, Bradley. *The Importance of Emily Dickinson.* Importance Of. San Diego, CA: Lucents, 1998.

Stefoff, Rebecca. *Japan.* Broomall, PA: Chelsea House, 1998.

Stevenson, Joycelynn. *The Magic School Bus Gets "Ants in its Pants"* (video). New York: KidVision, 1997.

Stewart, Gail. *Gangs.* Farmington Hills, MI: Greenhaven, 2001.

———. *The Homeless.* The Other America. Farmington Hills, MI :Lucent, 1996.

Stewart, Georgianna Liccione. *Cool Aerobics for Kids* (sound recording). Long Branch, NJ: Kimbo, 1999.

Stille, Darlene R. *Snakes.* Minneapolis, MN: Compass Point Books, 2001.

Strom, Yale. *Quilted Landscape: Conversations with Young Immigrants.* New York: Simon & Schuster, 1996.

Suen, Anastasia. *Habitat for Humanity.* New York: PowerKids Press, 2002.

Suid, Murray. *Made in America: Eight Great All-American Creations.* Reading, MA: Addison-Wesley, 1978.

Sumner, Ray, ed. *World Geography.* Pasadena, CA: Salem, 2001.

Sun, Ming-ju. *Traditional Fashions from India Paper Dolls.* Mineola, NY: Dover, 2001.

Susan B. Anthony Story. In Search of the Heroes video series. Richardson, TX: Grace Products Corporation, 1994.

Sweeney, Joan. *Me and My Family Tree.* New York: Crown, 1999.

Tall Tales: Davy Crockett (video). Allen, TX: Lyons, 1998.

Taylor, Helen. *You'd Never Believe It But . . . A Lightning Bolt Is Hotter Than the Sun and Other Facts About Electricity.* Brookfield, CT: Copper Beech Books, 1998.

Taylor, Maureen Alice. *Through the Eyes of Your Ancestors.* Boston: Houghton Mifflin, 1999.

Telecommunications. The Way Things Work video series. Wynnewood, PA: Schlessinger Media, 2002.

Thaler, Mike. *The Librarian from the Black Lagoon.* Scranton, PA: Scholastic, 1997.

Townsend, John Rowe. *John Newbery and His Books: Trade and Plumb-Cake Forever, Huzza!* New York: Scarecrow, 1994.

Travers, Bridget, and Fran Locher Freidman, ed. *Medical Discoveries: Medical Breakthroughs and the People Who Developed Them.* Detroit: UXL, 1997.

Turck, Mary. *Healthy Eating for Weight Management.* Nutrition and Fitness for Teens. Mankato, MN: Lifematters, 2001.

Vanderbilt, Tom. *The Sneaker Book: Anatomy of an Industry and an Icon.* New York: New Press, 1998.

Vaughan, William H. T. *Encyclopedia of Artists.* New York: Oxford University Press, 2000.

Venn, Cecilia. *Ants and Other Social Insects.* Chicago: World Book, 2000.

Veron, Geraldine. *On the Trail of Big Cats.* Hauppage, NY: Barrons, 1998.

Vogel, Elizabeth. *Meet the Librarian.* New York: PowerKids Press, 2002.

Walker, Sally M. *Seahorse Reef: A Story of the South Pacific.* Norwalk, CT: Soundprints, 2001.

Walking on Air (video). WonderWorks Family Movie. Los Angeles: Public Media Video, 1986.

Wallace, Carol M. *Elbows Off the Table, Napkin in the Lap, No Video Games During Dinner: The Modern Guide to Teaching Children Good Manners.* New York: St. Martin's Griffin, 1996.

Wallis, Jeremy. *Cubists.* Crystal Lake, IL: Heinemann, 2002.

Watters, Pat. *Coca Cola: An Illustrated History.* Garden City, NY: Doubleday, 1978.

Weiner, Ellen, and Moss Freedman. *Taking Food Allergies to School.* Plainview, NY: Jayjo Books, 1999.

Weiner, Lori, Aprille Best, and Philip A. Pizzo. *Be a Friend: Children Who Live with HIV Speak.* Morton Grove, IL: Albert Whitman, 1994.

What Is Hinduism? Understanding World Religions video series. Wynnewood, PA: Schlessinger Media, 2003.

Whitman, Sylvia. *Immigrant Children.* Minneapolis, MN: Carolrhoda, 2000.

Why Mosquitoes Buzz in People's Ears (sound recording). New York: Caedmon Audio, 1984.

Willis, Paul. *Dinosaurs.* Pleasantville, NY: Reader's Digest, 1999.

Wilson, Forrest. *Bridges Go from Here to There.* Washington, DC: Preservation Press, 1993.

Wilson, Jacqueline. *Elsa, Star of the Shelter.* Morton Grove, IL: Whitman, 1995.

Winter, Jeanette, and Emily Dickinson. *Emily Dickinson's Letters to the World.* New York: Frances Foster, 2002.

Witherick, Michael E. *Japan.* Crystal Lake, IL: Heinemann, 2000.

Witman, Kathleen L. *CDs, Super Glue & Salsa: How Everyday Products Are Made: Series II.* Farmington Hills, MI: UXL, 1996.

Witteman, Barbara. *Sacagawea: A Photo-Illustrated Biography.* Mankato, MN: Bridgestone, 2002.

Wolinsky, Art. *Communicating on the Internet.* Berkeley Heights, NJ: Enslow, 1999.

Woods, Mae. *Marc Brown.* Children's Authors Set II. Edina, MN: Abdo, 2001.

———. *Stan & Jan Berenstain.* Children's Authors Set 1. Edina, MN: Abdo, 2001.

Woods, Samuel G. *Sneakers: From Start to Finish.* Woodbridge, CT: Blackbirch, 1999.

World Almanac and Book of Facts. New York: Newspaper Enterprise Association, 1868– .

World Book Encyclopedia. Chicago: World Book, 2002.

World Book Encyclopedia of People and Places. Chicago: World Book, 2000.

World Book Encyclopedia of Science. Chicago: World Book, 2001.

World Book of America's Presidents. Chicago: World Book, 2002.

World Book Student Discovery Encyclopedia. Chicago: World Book, 2000.

World Books' Animals of the World (Set 2). Chicago: World Book, 2001.

Worldmark Encyclopedia of Cultures and Daily Life. Detroit: Gale, 1998.

Wright Brothers. Inventors of the World video series. Wynnewood, PA: Schlessinger Media, 2001.

Wyborny, Sheila. *Henry Ford.* San Diego: Kidhaven, 2002.

Yeoman, R. S. *Handbook of United States Coins.* Racine, WI: Whitman, 1942– .

Young, Robert. *Sneakers: The Shoes We Choose* . Minneapolis, MN: Dillon Press, 1991.

Zannos, Susan *Fitness Stars of the Martial Arts: Featuring Profiles of Bruce Lee, Chuck Norris, Cynthia Rothrock, and Carlos Machado.* Bear, DE: Mitchell Lane, 2000.

Zimmerman, Howard, and George Olshevsky. *Dinosaurs: The Biggest, Baddest, Strangest, Fastest.* New York: Antheneum Books for Young Readers, 2000.

Zipes, David. *Oxford Companion to Fairy Tales.* New York: Oxford, 2000.

Zochura-Walske, Christine. *Giant Octopuses.* Minneapolis, MN: Lerner, 2000.

Zoehfeld, Kathleen Weidner. *Terrible Tyrannosaurs.* New York: HarperCollins, 2001.

Zollman, Pam. *Don't Bug Me!* New York: Holiday House, 2001

Zumerchik, John, ed. *MacMillan Encyclopedia of Energy.* New York: Macmillan Reference, 2001.

Subject Directory

Index

About the Authors

PEGGY J. WHITLEY is Director of Teaching, Learning, and Distance Education at Kingwood College, Kingwood, Texas

SUSAN WILLIAMS GOODWIN is Reference Librarian, Kingwood College.